STOLEN HERITAGE

THE GRAND THEFT OF THE *HAMILTON* AND *SCOURGE*

BY GARY GENTILE

GARY GENTILE PRODUCTIONS
P.O. Box 57137
PHILADELPHIA, PA 19111
2008

Copyright 2004 by Gary Gentile

All rights reserved. Except for the use of brief quotations embodied in critical articles and reviews, this book may not be reproduced in part or in whole, in any manner (including mechanical, electronic, photographic, and photocopy means), transmitted in any form, or recorded by any data storage and/or retrieval device, without express written permission from the author. Address all queries to:

Gary Gentile Productions
P.O. Box 57137
Philadelphia, PA 19111

Additional copies of this book may be purchased from the same address by sending a check or money order in the amount of $20 U.S. for each copy (plus $4 shipping per order, not per book). For information about consulting services, workshops, presentations, and a list of available titles that can be purchased by credit card, visit the GGP website:

http://www.ggentile.com

Pictureless Credits

The lack of photographs is courtesy of the City of Hamilton and the Ontario Archaeological Licence Bureau.

International Standard Book Numbers (ISBN)
1-883056-38-1
978-1-883056-38-4

Softcover Edition 2008

Printed in U.S.A.

"The price of freedom is eternal vigilance."
— Thomas Jefferson

"The state should be our servent, and not we its slaves."
— Albert Einstein

"Every right that is not corrected is a wrong that is encouraged. Every injustice that is not challenged is a resignation to slavery."
— Gary Gentile

"A man who wished to make a profession of goodness in everything would come to grief among so many who were not good."
— Nicolo Machiavelli

"He who goes first into the fray, triumphs not; he only fights and fails."
— Roland Huntford

"On one extreme we have the ideology that the governing body (state or international conglomerate) is supreme and the individual is its absolute vassal. At the other we have the spirit of '76, where the governing body is the servant of the people and the rights of the individual are paramount."
— Eric Burgess

"A man may be born, live out a long and eventful career, die and be forgotten, while the machinery of the courts is getting ready to be put into motion."
— Dillon Wallace

"Satisfaction comes not from doing, but from having done."
— Gary Gentile

"Truth is often a brighter lamp than the world cares to see."
— Neal Barrett

"It is not the thing done, but the doing that the gods weigh, and that many have failed to reach their goal who none the less accomplished more than he who, coming to a journey's end, thought that the mere end should justify him."
— Talbot Mundy

"To be neutral between right and wrong is to serve wrong."
— Theodore Roosevelt

"Victory has a thousand fathers, but defeat is an orphan."
— John F. Kennedy

"Challenge and the acceptance of risk are tests of a person's spirit, will power, and physical endurance. To some people, life is about striving and overcoming human frailties."
— Gary Gentile

"In the country of the mad, the sane man is crazy."
— Edmund Cooper

Contents

Foreword	6
Chapter 1 - Tragedy of War	9
Chapter 2 - Controversial Issues	17
Chapter 3 - Legal Preliminaries	30
Chapter 4 - Courting the Law	57
Chapter 5 - Deposition Days	77
Chapter 6 - The Master of Deceit	93
Chapter 7 - The Trials of Postponement	108
Chapter 8 - The Bill 13 Caper	123
Chapter 9 - Money, Money, Money	141
Afterword	164
Author's Biography	166

Foreword

In order to establish a background for my lawsuit against the Canadian government, the reader should know that I have a sordid history of hostile confrontations with malicious bureaucratic officialdom which sought to deny access to shipwrecks so that the minions of the government who were chosen to administer those sites could exercise control that exceeded their authority.

The purpose of this book is to enlighten future generations about rampant political malfeasances that occurred in the latter part of the twentieth century - a time when the prerogative of eminent domain was abused in order to promote the personal agendas of select individuals who occupied positions of responsibility in the governmental hierarchy.

By definition, eminent domain is "the right of a government to appropriate private property for public use, usually with compensation to the owner." I purport to demonstrate that in the case of the *Hamilton* and *Scourge* (both of which will be considered as a single unit), the appropriation was committed without engaging any public benefit; or worse, that there was an intentional political conspiracy to thwart public benefit so that a few individuals could exercise personal power by means of unchecked administrative fiat.

Control freaks (to use a phrase that is more common and less pedantic than the description in the previous paragraph) rise to the fore in all forms of government, much like grease or slag rise to the top of heated pots of soup or lead. Rather than striving in their capacity as "public servants" to serve the public, and rather than executing properly the duties that they were hired to perform, they violate the public trust by furthering their own ambitions in the exercise of control. They are motivated not by greed for monetary gain, but by the usurpation of power. This perversion of authority, this wrongful prosecution of managerial position, is a pathological imperative that assumes theocratic proportions. These malignant cancerous growths in the administrative body are blatantly self-serving: egocentric when they are supposed to be egalitarian. They run rampant beyond the pale of all that is righteous, exercising control that is out of control.

I call this administrative mindset the "junkyard dog complex." A junkyard dog is one whose job is to protect a junkyard from intruders. It generally barks voraciously at trespassers. The perimeter fence is the boundary of its guard duty. After a while, however, the dog comes to believe that it *owns* the junkyard: that the junkyard is its own personal property. It dashes to the fence and barks at anyone who approaches - whether or not that person has business beyond the fence or in the junkyard. The dog continues this aggressive behavior even when told to quit barking by its owner. The dog, in effect, has taken charge of the junkyard.

This impulsive characteristic is apparent in many forms of life, from secretaries who play high and mighty with clients on the phone or at the desk, to clerks who abuse customers because they can get away with it, to people who dominate their spouses, to scientists who lord over their technicians, to corporate executives who ridicule their employees, to government officials and administrators who use their position of authority to derive some personal benefit, whether it be money, power, or prestige. These people are no longer simply doing their jobs, they have become consumed by an unholy thirst for authoritative control. They treat subordinates as annoying bugs to be squashed, or they utilize their position of authority for personal gain.

Shipwrecks have attained a collective position as a target for government exploitation. I first became aware of this persecution effort in the 1980's, when a handful of aggrandizing bureaucrats and self-styled marine archaeologists pooled their resources in order to heist abandoned treasure wrecks from commercial salvors under the guise of "historic preservation."

More injustice has been perpetrated in the name of historic preservation than was ever committed in the suppression of heresy during the Spanish inquisition. Bona fide treasure salvors and recreational divers have become the modern day heretics (enemies of the state), simply because their goals differ from those who are empowered to enforce legislation that seeks to feather their own beds. So-called preservationists branded treasure salvors as "looters." (My definition of looter is "one who takes something that the name-caller would have taken if he had gotten there first.")

Be that as it may, "bocrats" and "archs" banded together in their efforts to have restrictive legislation enacted that would remove from the public every shipwreck that lay in America's jurisdictional waters, and to give "management" (read "control") of those shipwrecks to themselves: a devious mechanism to enhance their own power and income. The proposed Abandoned Shipwreck Act was a clear violation of a public trust, and a clear-cut move away from egalitarianism and toward a form of government ruled by the dictatorship of the bureaucrats.

As a teenager I read George Orwell's prophetic anti-Utopian novel, *1984*. The book terrified me, and ever since then I have been haunted by visions of Big Brother. The book lies within reach of me now as I sit at my desk. As I grew older, I observed the erosion of freedom in nearly every facet of life in which the government exercised authority. The erosion was so gradual - like the withering of grass - that most people could not see it happening. At an early age I realized that freedom was a tenuous commodity, held together by threads of gossamer. Individual freedom became so important to me that I would rather lose my life than lose my freedom. When the opportunity presented itself, I became a crusader - not for a mythical Holy Grail, but for the freedoms that government sought to confiscate.

The Atlantic Alliance for Maritime Heritage Conservation was formed to repel piratical shipwreck boarders: the "bocrats" and the "archs." I joined and supported the Alliance. I have discussed the role of the Alliance at length in Book Two of *The Lusitania Controversies: Dangerous Descents into Shipwrecks and Law*. There is no need to repeat that discussion here. After six years of fierce battle, and rejection by majority vote of the peoples' representatives, the Abandoned

Shipwreck Act was passed into law in 1987, by means of legerdemain and prestidigitation. Authoritarianism reigned supreme. How this gross misconduct of legislative reform was enacted is also discussed at length in *The Lusitania Controversies*.

The Abandoned Shipwreck Act became the Big Brother of shipwrecks, the rats of Winston Smith, the psychological torture chamber of Room 101, the next step in the path toward a totalitarian society. It has often been said, "Eternal vigilance is the price of freedom." But it has not been said often enough for people to accept it as a truism and to inspire them to try to preserve their freedom.

At the same time that the Alliance was conducting a grand scale war, I was engaged in a skirmish of my own against an agency of the federal government: the National Oceanic and Atmospheric Association. NOAA had claimed as its own preserve the wreck of the Civil War ironclad *Monitor*, which lay in 230 feet of water off the Diamond Shoals of North Carolina. Under the Marine Protection, Research, and Sanctuaries Act, the wreck had been proclaimed a National Marine Sanctuary. Two of the primary goals of the MPRSA were "to enhance public awareness, understanding, appreciation and wise use of the marine environment," and "to facilitate to the extent compatible with the primary objective of resource protection, all public and private uses of the resources of such areas."

Despite these mandated obligations, NOAA steadfastly refused to permit me or any other American citizen to look at the wreck of the *Monitor*. I took exception to this "junkyard dog" attitude, and filed suit against NOAA. It took six years and cost many thousands of dollars to win my battle against NOAA. I told the full story of my travails in *Ironclad Legacy: Battles of the USS Monitor*.

I was exuberant over my hard-won victory. Like a crusader seeking a new crusade, I strove to find another cause to champion: a shipwreck case involving government exploitation at the expense of human freedom. My research led me to believe that the grip that the Canadian government held on the *Hamilton/Scourge* violated the individual's right of access. It appeared that minions in the City of Hamilton and the Archaeological Licence Bureau were conspiring to deny its citizens and the citizens of the world the right to look at the wrecks. The case was precisely equivalent to the *Monitor* case.

Having won my cause against the American government, I decided to tackle the Canadian government.

Every wrong that is not corrected is a wrong that is encouraged. Every injustice that is not challenged is a resignation to slavery. Those are my philosophies, and the inspiration for the events that follow.

Justice is a lot like air. People do not think much about it unless they are not getting any.

Chapter 1
Tragedy of War

Caveat

It is not my purpose to repeat the day-to-day events that preceded the loss of the *Hamilton* and *Scourge*. Emily Cain has already done this in tedious detail in *Ghost Ships*. The British occupation and settling of the area, the circumstances that fomented the War of 1812, the construction and subsequent movements of vessels, all are irrelevant to the present volume. I have a grander story to tell.

Stolen Heritage is primarily a book about the very near past, not the long-ago past. Still, in order to place the setting for the reader who is unfamiliar with the history of the wrecks, I offer a brief overview of the catastrophe that precipitated the present day travesty of justice.

The *Diana* and *Lord Nelson*

The *Diana* was an insignificant schooner that approximated seventy-five feet in length, and grossed about 76 tons. She was a merchant vessel whose full-busted wooden figurehead represented the Roman goddess for whom the vessel was named: the virgin goddess of hunting and childhood who was associated with the Moon. A virgin goddess of childhood seems like a contradiction in terms, but the Romans - like the Greeks before them - believed in a pantheon that had nothing to do with logic.

The *Lord Nelson* was even more insignificant. Between fifty and sixty feet in length and grossing some forty-five tons, the schooner hardly seemed like the kind of vessel to be named after one of England's greatest naval heroes. In 1798, Horatio Nelson defeated the French fleet in the Battle of the Nile, thus preventing Napoleon's forces from conquering Egypt. In 1805, Nelson destroyed the combined French and Spanish naval forces at Trafalgar; he died from wounds that he received during the battle. One would have thought that an admiral of his stature would command a larger and more prestigious vessel than a two-masted schooner.

The *Lord Nelson* was captured by the U.S. brig *Oneida*, on June 4, 1812, on the St. Lawrence River. She was transporting a general cargo which she was suspected of smuggling either into or out of United State territory. Hostilities had commenced between England and the United States, but war had not yet been declared - and was not declared for another fortnight. Nonetheless, the vessel was taken as a prize of war, and was purchased by the fledgling United States Navy. The prize money was distributed among the officers and crew of the *Oneida*. Lord Nelson's full-body figurehead now led the charge against British naval forces.

The *Lord Nelson* was renamed *Scourge*, perhaps in denigration of the person for whom the vessel was named, or the nationality represented by the name. The bulwarks of the unarmed vessel were then pierced for eight cannons, and she was outfitted with assorted implements of war: swords, pikes, axes, and so on. Later, two small brass cannons were added to the armament.

The United States Navy purchased the *Diana* outright on November 12, 1812. The *Diana* was renamed *Hamilton* in honor of the first Secretary of the Treasury (whose given name was Alexander). The bust of Diana was not removed from beneath the bowsprit. The schooner was armed with nine cannons and, as the *Scourge*, an assortment of hand weapons to repel and fight boarders.

The weight of the cannons on the upper deck made both vessels top heavy. Her seamen considered the vessels to be "tender," meaning that they were inherently unstable. They maneuvered poorly in high winds and big seas, and exhibited a tendency to lose control in heavy weather.

The Chauncey Report

The *Hamilton* and *Scourge* were components of a fleet of "thirteen sail" under the command of Commodore Isaac Chauncey. Chauncey's plan of campaign in 1813 was to harass British shipping, to convoy supply vessels, and to support American troops during engagements with the enemy. The fighting was hot and bloody throughout the summer. Neither side obtained any clear victories.

On August 7, the number of men estimated to have been onboard the two vessels was eighty-six: fifty-three on the *Hamilton*, thirty-three on the *Scourge*. Chauncey's fleet departed at dawn in an attempt to engage the enemy fleet consisting of six armed vessels. All day long the two fleets maneuvered, but they never engaged. The enemy managed to keep out of range of the guns of the American vessels. Sunset found both fleets becalmed so close to each other that the men could practically count the gun ports of their opponents.

Night settled upon Lake Ontario. Chauncey remained alert, hoping to sneak up on the enemy during the hours of darkness. The fleet was struck by a squall at about 2 o'clock in the morning of August 8. Chauncey's report to the Secretary of the Navy about the incidents of that night was all too brief:

"Wind during the night from the westward and after midnight squally. Kept all hands at quarters and beat to windward in hopes to gain the wind of the enemy. At 2 a.m. missed two of our schooners. At daylight discovered the missing schooners to be the *Hamilton* and *Scourge*. Soon after spoke to *Governor Tompkins* who informed me that the *Hamilton* and *Scourge* both overset and sunk in a heavy squall about two o'clock, and, distressing to relate, every soul perished except sixteen. This fatal accident deprived me at once of the services of two valuable officers, Lieutenant Winter and Sailing-Master Osgood, and two of my best schooners, mounting together nineteen guns."

The Cooper Transcription

Chauncey made the only official report of the loss of the *Hamilton* and *Scourge*. The two schooners were not the first vessels lost in the prosecution of the war, nor were they the last. Chauncey spent little time in bemoaning his losses. He had a war to fight. As any military commander does in the exigencies of war, he put the past behind him and looked toward the future conduct of engagement.

By a fortuitous combination of circumstances, another and more detailed account of the disaster was published thirty years after the event. The author was that prolific teller of tales of frontier America, James Fenimore Cooper. Today, Cooper is best remembered for his enduring Leatherstocking saga, of which the most famous of the five volumes is *The Last of the Mohicans*. His quill produced a large number of lesser known works, both fiction and nonfiction, which have seldom been reprinted in either the present century or the last.

One of Cooper's more obscure and nearly forgotten books was entitled *Ned Myers: or a Life before the Mast*. Myers, who sailed with Cooper before the War of 1812, was a seaman who survived the sinking of the *Scourge* when she was blown over in that fatal squall. After a long and successful career as a novelist and chronicler, Cooper transcribed Myers' story of his vocation as a sailor. The biography was published in 1843: a virtual goldmine of information to modern historians.

The Myers Report

Myers went to sleep on the deck, "as sound as if lying in the bed of a king. How long my nap lasted, or what took place in the interval, I cannot say. I awoke, however, in consequence of large drops of rain falling on my fact. Tom Goldsmith awoke at the same moment. When I opened my eyes, it was so dark I could not see the length of the deck. I arose and spoke to Tom, telling him it was about to rain, and that I meant to go down and get a nip, out of a little stuff we kept in our mess-chest, and I would bring up the bottle if he wanted a taste. Tom answered, 'This is nothing; we're neither pepper nor salt.' One of the black men spoke, and asked me to bring up the bottle, and give him a nip too. All this took half a minute perhaps. I now remember to have heard a strange rushing noise to windward as I went towards the forward hatch, though it made no impression on me at the time. We had been lying between the starboard guns, which was the weather side of the vessel, if there were any weather side to it, there not being a breath of air, and no motion to the water, and I passed round to the larboard side in order to find the ladder which led up in that direction. The hatch was so small that two men could not pass at a time, and I felt my way to it, in no haste. One hand was on the bitts, and a foot was on the ladder, when a flash of lightning almost blinded me. The thunder came at the next instant, and with it a rushing of winds that fairly smothered the clap.

"But the instant I was aware there was a squall, I sprang for the jib-sheet. Being captain of the forecastle, I knew where to find it, and threw it loose at a jerk. In doing this, I jumped on a man named Leonard Lewis, and called on him to lend me a hand. I next let fly the larboard, or lee top-sail-sheet, got hold of the clew-line, and assisted by Lewis, got the clew half up. All this time I kept shouting to the man at the wheel to put his helm 'hard down.' The water was now up to my breast, and I knew the schooner must go over. Lewis had not said a word, but I called out to him to shift for himself, and belaying the clew-line, in hauling myself forward of the foremast, I received a blow from the jib-sheet that came near to breaking my arm.

"All this occupied less than a minute. The flashes of lightning were incessant, and nearly blinded me. Our decks seemed on fire, and yet I could see nothing. I heard no hail, no order, no call; but the schooner was filled with the shrieks and cries of the men to leeward, who were lying jammed under the guns, shot-boxes, shot, and other heavy things that had gone down as the vessel fell over. The starboard second gun, from forward, had capsized, and come down directly over the hatch, and I caught a glimpse of a man struggling to get past it. Apprehension of this gun had induced me to drag myself forward of the mast where I received the blow mentioned.

"I succeeded in hauling myself up to windward, and in getting into the schooner's fore-channels. Here I met with William Deer, the boatswain, and a black boy of the name of Philips, who was the powder-boy of our gun. 'Deer, she's gone!' I said. The boatswain made no answer, but walked out on the forerigging, towards the head-mast. He probably had some vague notion that the schooner's masts would be out of the water if she went down, and took this course as the safest. The boy was in the chains the last I saw of him.

"I now crawled aft, on the upper side of the bulwarks, amid a most awful and infernal din of thunder, and shrieks, and dazzling flashes of lightning; the wind blowing all the while like a tornado. When I reached the port of my own gun, I put a foot in, thinking to step on the muzzle of the piece; but it had gone to leeward with all the rest, and I fell through the port, until I brought up with my arms. I struggled up again, and continued working my way aft. As I got abreast of the main-mast, I saw someone had let run the halyards. I soon reached the beckets of the sweeps, and found four in them. I could not swim a stroke, and it crossed my mind to get one of the sweeps to keep me afloat. In striving to jerk the becket clear, it parted, and the forward ends of the four sweeps got away from me. I then crawled quite aft, as far as the fashion-piece. The water was pouring down the cabin companion-way like a sluice, and as I stood for an instant on the fashion-piece, I saw Mr. Osgood, with his head and part of his shoulders through one of the cabin windows, struggling to get out. He must have been within six feet of me. I saw him but a moment, by means of a flash of lightning, and I think he must have seen me. At the same time, there was a man visible at the end of the main-boom, holding on to the clew of the sail. I do not know who it was. The man probably saw me, and that I was about to spring, for he called out, 'Don't jump overboard! - don't jump overboard! The schooner is righting.'

"I was not in a state of mind to reflect much on anything. I do not think more than three or four minutes, if as many, had passed since the squall struck us, and there I was standing on the vessel's quarter, led by Providence more than by any discretion of my own. It now came across me that if the schooner should right she was filled, and must go down, and that she might carry me with her in the suction. I made a spring, therefore, and fell into the water several feet from the place where I had stood. It is my opinion the schooner sank as I left her.

"I went down some distance myself, and when I came up to the surface, I began to swim vigorously for the first time in my life. I think I swam several yards, but of course will not pretend to be certain of such a thing, at such a moment, until I felt my hand hit something hard. I made another stroke and felt my hand pass down the side of an object that I knew at once to be a clincher-built boat. I belonged to this boat, and now I recollected that she had been towing astern. Until that instant I had not thought of her, but thus was I led in the dark to the best possible means of saving my life. I made a grab at the gunwale, and caught in the stern-sheets. Had I swum another yard, I should have passed the boat, and missed her altogether! I got in without any difficulty, being all alive and much excited.

"My first look was for the schooner. She had disappeared, and I supposed she was just settling under water. It rained as if the floodgates of heaven were opened, and it lighteninged awfully. It did not seem to me that there was a breath of air, and the water was unruffled, the effects of the rain excepted. All this I saw, as it might be, at a glance. But my chief concern was to preserve my own life. I was coxswain of this very boat, and had made it fast to the taffrail that same afternoon, with a round turn and two half-hitches, by its best painter. Of course I expected the vessel would drag the boat down with her, for I had no knife to cut the painter. There was a gang-board in the boat, however, which lay fore and aft, and I thought this might keep me afloat until some of the fleet should pick me up. To clear this gang-board, then, and get into the water, was my first object. I ran forward to throw off the lazy-painter that was coiled on its end, and in doing this, I caught the boat's painter in my hand by accident. A pull satisfied me that it was all clear! Someone on board must have cast off this painter, and then lost the chance of getting into the boat by accident. At all events I was safe, and I now dared to look about me.

"My only chance of seeing was during the flashes, and these left me almost blind. I had thrown the gang-board into the water, and I now called out to encourage the men, telling them I was in the boat. I could hear many around me, and occasionally I saw the heads of men struggling in the lake. There being no proper place to scull in, I got an oar in the after rowlock and made out to scull a little in that fashion. I now saw a man quite near the boat, and, hauling in the oar, made a spring amidships, catching this poor fellow by the collar. He was very near gone, and I had a great deal of difficulty in getting him in over the gunwale. Our joint weight brought the boat down, so low that she shipped a good deal of water. This turned out to be Leonard Lewis, the young man who had helped me to clew up the fore-topsail. He could not stand, and spoke with difficulty. I asked him to crawl aft, out of the water, which he did, lying down in the stern-sheets.

"I now looked about me and heard another; leaning over the gunwale, I got a glimpse of a man, struggling, quite near the boat, I caught him by the collar too, and had to drag him in very much in the way I had done with Lewis. This proved to be Lemuel Bryant, the man who had been wounded by a hot shot, at York, while the commodore was on board us. His wound had not yet healed, but he was less exhausted than Lewis. He could not help me, however, lying down in the bottom of the boat, the instant he was able.

"For a few moments I now heard no more in the water, and I began to scull again. By my calculation I moved a few yards, and must have got over the spot where the schooner went down. Here, in the flashes, I saw many heads, the men swimming in confusion and at random. By this time little was said, the whole scene being one of fearful struggle and frightful silence. It still rained, but the flashes were less frequent and less fierce. They told me, afterwards, in the squadron, that it thundered awfully, but I cannot say I heard a clap after I struck the water. The next man caught the boat himself. It was a mulatto, from Martinique, who was Mr. Osgood's steward, and I helped him in. He was much exhausted, though an excellent swimmer, but alarm nearly deprived him of his strength. He kept saying, 'Oh! Masser Ned - Oh! Masser Ned!" and lay down in the bottom of the boat like the two others, I taking care to shove him over to the larboard side, so as to trim our small craft.

"I kept calling out to encourage the swimmers, and presently I heard a voice saying, 'Ned, I'm here, close by you.' This was Tom Goldsmith, a messmate, and the very man under whose rug I had been sleeping at quarters. He did not want much help, getting in, pretty much, by himself. I asked him if he were able to help me. 'Yes, Ned,' he answered. 'I'll stand by you to the last; what shall I do?' I told him to take his tarpaulin and to bail the boat, which, by this time, was a third full of water. This he did, while I sculled a little ahead. 'Ned,' says Tom, 'she's gone down with her colours flying, for her pennant came near getting a round turn around my body, and carrying me down with her. Davy has made a good haul, and he gave us a close shave, but he didn't get you and me.' In this manner did this thoughtless sailor express himself, as soon as rescued from the grasp of death! Seeing something on the water, I asked Tom to take my oar, while I sprang to the gunwale and caught Mr. Bogardus, the master's mate, who was clinging to one of the sweeps. I hauled him in, and he told me he thought someone had hold of the other end of the sweep. It was so dark, however, we could not see even that distance. I hauled the sweep along until I found Ebenezer Duffy, a mulatto, and the ship's cook. He could not swim a stroke, and was nearly gone. I got him in alone, Tom bailing, lest the boat, which was quite small, should swamp with us.

"As the boat drifted along, she reached another man, whom I caught also by the collar. I was afraid to haul this person in amidships, the boat being now so deep, and so small, and so I dragged him ahead, and hauled him in over the bows. This man was the pilot, whose name I never knew. He was a lake-man and had been aboard with us the whole summer. The poor fellow was almost gone, and like all the rest, with the exception of Tom, he lay down and said not a word.

"We had now as many in the boat as it would carry, and Tom and myself thought it would not do to take in any more. It is true we saw no more, everything around us appearing still as death, the pattering of the rain excepted. Tom began to bail again, and I commenced halloing. I sculled about several minutes thinking of giving others a tow, or of even hauling in one or two more, after we got the water out of the boat; but we found no one else. I think it probable I sculled away from the spot, as there was nothing to guide me. I suppose, however, that by this time all the Scourges had gone down, for no more were ever heard from.

"Tom Goldsmith and myself now put our heads together as to what best be done. We were both afraid of falling into the enemy's hands, for they might have bore up in the squall and run down near us. On the whole, however, we thought the distance between the two squadrons was too great for this; at all events, something must be done at once. So we began to row, in what direction even we did not know. It still rained as hard as it could pour, though there was not a breath of wind. The lightning came now at considerable intervals, and the gust was evidently passing away towards the broader parts of the lake. While we were rowing and talking about our chance of falling in with the enemy, Tom cried out to me to 'avast pulling.' He had seen a vessel by a flash, and he thought she was English, from her size. As he said she was a schooner, however, I thought it must be one of our own craft, and got her direction from him. At the next flash, I saw her, and felt satisfied she belonged to us. Before we began to pull, however, we were hailed. 'Boat ahoy!' I answered. 'If you pull another stroke, I'll fire into you.' It was clear we were mistaken ourselves for an enemy, and I called out to know what schooner it was. No answer was given, though the threat to fire was repeated, if we pulled another stroke. I now turned to Tom and said, 'I know that voice - that is old Trant.' Tom thought we were 'in the wrong shop.' I now sang out, 'This is the *Scourge's* boat; our schooner is gone down, and we want to come alongside.' A voice now called from the schooner - 'Is that you, Ned?' This I knew was my old shipmate and schoolfellow, Jack Mallet, who was acting as boatswain on the *Julia*, the schooner commanded by Sailing-Master James Trant, one of the oddities of the service, and a man with whom the blow often came as soon as the word. I had known Mr. Trant's voice, and felt more afraid he would fire into us than I had done of anything which had occurred that fearful night. Mr. Trant himself now called out, 'Oh-ho; give way, boys, and come alongside.' This we did, and a very few strokes took us up to the *Julia*, where we were received with the utmost kindness. The men were passed out of the boat, while I gave Mr. Trant an account of all that had happened. This took but a minute or two.

"Mr. Trant now enquired in what direction the *Scourge* had gone down, and as soon as I told him, in the best manner I could, he called out to Jack Mallet: 'Oh-ho, Mallet - take four hands, and go in the boat and see what you can do - take a lantern, and I will show a light on the water's edge, so you may know me.' Mallet did as ordered, and was off in less than three minutes after we got alongside.

"Mr. Trant now called the Scourges aft, and asked more of the particulars. He then gave us a glass of grog all round, and made his own crew splice the mainbrace. The Julias now offered us dry clothes. I got a change from Jack Reilly, who had been an old messmate, and with whom I had always been on good terms. It knocked off raining, but we shifted ourselves at the galley fire below. I then went on deck and presently we heard the boat pulling back. It soon came alongside, bringing in it four more men that had been found floating about on sweeps and gratings. On inquiry, it turned out that these men belonged to the *Hamilton*, Lieutenant Winter - a schooner that had gone down in the same squall that carried us over. These men were very much exhausted, too, and we all went below and were told to turn in.

"I had been so much excited during the scenes through which I had just passed, and had been so much stimulated by grog that, as yet, I had not felt much of the depression natural to such events. I even slept soundly that night, nor did I turn out until six the next morning.

"When I got on deck, there was a fine breeze; it was a lovely day, and the lake was perfectly smooth. Our fleet was in good line, in pretty close order, with the exception of the *Governor Tompkins*, Lieutenant Tom Brown, which was a little to leeward, but carrying a press of sail to close with the commodore. Mr. Trant, perceiving that the *Tompkins* wished to speak to us in passing, brailed his foresail and let her luff up close under our lee. 'Two of the schooners, the *Hamilton* and the *Scourge*, have gone down in the night,' called out Mr. Brown, 'for I have picked up four of the *Hamilton's*.' 'Oh-ho!' answered Mr. Trant, 'that's no news at all, for I have picked up twelve; eight of the *Scourge's* and four of the *Hamilton's* - aft fore-sheet.

"These were all that were ever saved from the two schooners, which must have had near a hundred souls on board them. The two commanders, Lieutenant Winter and Mr. Osgood, were both lost, and with Mr. Winter went down, I believe, one or two young gentlemen. The squadron could not have moved much between the time when the accidents happened and that when I came on deck, or we must have come round and gone over the same ground again, for we now passed many relics of the scene, floating about in the water. I saw sponges, gratings, sweeps, hats, etc., scattered about, and in passing ahead we saw one of the last that we tried to catch; Mr. Trant ordering it done, as he said it must have been Lieutenant Winter's. We did not succeed, however, nor was any article taken on board. A good look-out was kept for men from aloft, but none were seen from any of the vessels. The lake had swallowed up the rest of the two crews, and the *Scourge*, as had been often predicted, had literally become a coffin to a large portion of her people."

Aftermath

Notwithstanding his losses, and his fear that the enemy now possessed a numerical superiority of vessels, Chauncey attempted to engage the enemy fleet that day. Contrary winds conspired to keep the two fleets out of each other's way. That evening, Chauncey retired his vessels to Niagara.

Naval engagements continued throughout the remainder of August and well into September. But the ensuing battles are not relevant to the topic of the present volume.

Chapter 2
Controversial Issues

A Case in Point

At the time of her capture, the *Lord Nelson* was owned by James Crooks and William Crooks, brothers in commerce as well as brothers by blood. James Crooks was an industrialist who entered politics after the war. For the rest of his life he held important elected positions in the Canadian government. William Crooks was a merchant who stayed out of politics altogether. Both men maintained that the seizure of their vessel was illegal because, at the time the seizure occurred, war between England and the United States of America had not yet been declared. After the war ended, the Crooks pressed their claim for reparations against the United States government.

An entire book could be written about the legal debacle which resulted, and which dragged through the courts for more than a century. I will describe only the highlights of the litigation and political manipulations which spanned one hundred seventeen years of unceasing effort. Injustice has been the very centerpiece of the vessel's long existence.

In 1817, the Court of the Northern District of New York found that the seizure was indeed illegal. The court decreed that the Crooks brothers should be reimbursed for the value of the vessel and her cargo - one thousand pounds in Halifax currency. Despite the decree, the Crooks brothers did not receive their settlement because the clerk of the New York court, Theron Rudd, embezzled all the court's money.

James Crooks was not without political connections. The settlement claim was pushed through a succession of assemblies and legislative bodies, including the Senate and the House of Representatives. In addition to Congressional acceptance, the Crooks brothers claim was backed by the President of the United States, James Monroe, in 1819. Despite this awesome amount of political pressure and unanimous approval, payment was still not forthcoming - for reasons that were never adequately explained.

After the Crooks brothers died, their descendants and heirs kept the case alive. In 1886 - sixty-seven years after President Monroe lobbied to settle the claim - another President took up the cause. Grover Cleveland was no more successful than his predecessor.

Forty-one years later - in 1927 - a settlement agreement was finally reached. By this time the number of claimants had grown to more than one hundred. Of these descendants and heirs, twenty-five were selected to receive payment. The case was finally settled when disbursements were made in 1930.

Search and Discovery

Daniel Nelson, a dentist and amateur archaeologist who lived and practiced in St. Catherines, Ontario, was the person most responsible for the initiative to locate the wrecks of the *Hamilton* and *Scourge*. From historical records he ascertained that the schooners sank off Port Dalhousie, near St. Catherines. Nelson was a member of the Royal Ontario Museum, which was based in Toronto. He urged the formation of a project to locate the wrecks - a project for which the Museum would provide the funding and technical expertise.

Search operations commenced in 1972 and continued sporadically until 1975, when both wrecks were located by means of side-scan sonar. In November 1975, a television camera secured to a remotely operated vehicle (ROV) captured footage of one of the wrecks. Clearly shown were spars, cannon balls, and skeletal remains. The presence of cannon balls dated the wreck to an era when cannons were in use during time of war. No vessels were known to have gone down in the area during the Revolutionary War, which commenced in 1776, so it was concluded that the wreck was of the vintage of the War of 1812.

While proof of the identities was not firmly established, there seemed little doubt that the wrecks could be none other than the *Hamilton* and *Scourge*.

Location, Location, Location

The precise locations of the wrecks have been withheld from "unauthorized" personnel. Notwithstanding this condition, evidence indicates that the wrecks lie approximately 11 kilometers (7 miles) north of Port Dalhousie at a depth of 85 meters (279 feet), separated from each other by a distance of either 500 feet or 500 yards. Reference numbers triangulated by satellites that maintain the Global Positioning System have been leaked to me. These GPS numbers are:

North 43-18.423
West 79-16.005

Alternative sources contend that the wrecks lie 17 kilometers (10.5 miles) off Port Dalhousie at a depth of 100 meters (328 feet). This appears to be a blatant attempt to mask the true location, and to make the wrecks appear to lie deeper than they actually do.

Another source places the wrecks at depths of 94 and 95 meters (308 and 312 feet), with original loran positions converted to Universal Transverse Mercator: N.4796131 and E.637302.

United States Navy

The U.S. Navy wasted no time in asserting its ownership of the wrecks. This action brings to light some curious naval anomalies.

The USN is alone among U.S. military departments in maintaining a policy of never abandoning lost or sunken property. The Army, Air Force, and Marine Corps make no such claim unless the property possesses components of advanced technology. For example, the Air Force has not abandoned aircraft that crashed after 1962. Otherwise, lost or sunken military property has been officially abandoned by means of government fiat. Anyone may salvage or recover property that

CONTROVERSIAL ISSUES 19

has been legally abandoned.

Aircraft enthusiasts have recovered World War Two Army bombers from under the ice in Greenland. They have recovered Marine fighters that were shot down in the jungles of islands that were occupied by the Japanese in World War Two. And they have recovered Air Force training planes that crashed in American lakes and rivers. All these aircraft have been lovingly restored - some have even been flown - by ardent collectors with a penchant for preserving the glories of the past. And all these recovery operations have been conducted without government intervention.

But the Navy is presently suing a man who recovered a Navy plane from the swamps of North Carolina ten years ago, and who spent a decade in restoring it to its original condition. Not only is the Navy seeking fines, punitive damages, imprisonment, and the return of the plane, but it wants the plane delivered to a chosen Navy facility at the expense of the possessor! In another case - this one from the 1990's - the salvage of a Navy plane from an American lake was highly publicized. The Navy took no action until the plane was successfully recovered. Then it had the FBI conduct a midnight raid on the salvor's house on the night before his wife was due to deliver a baby. At gunpoint, an FBI SWAT team dragged the salvor to jail in handcuffs!

The Navy extends its paranoid claims of ownership to all sunken Navy vessels anywhere in the world, including obsolete vessels that were scuttled as an expedient means of disposal.

Hard to believe - but true.

The indicative word in all the examples given above is "Navy."

To enable the reader to understand the truth of the situation, let me digress for a couple of paragraphs.

I once wrote to one of the departments of the USN to request historical documentation of past activities that had been conducted by that department. In his reply, the commander of the department explained why he could not provide the records that I sought: "The function of the Navy is national defense." He went on to explain that his department neither kept nor maintained files for historical purposes.

The only department in the USN which stores historical Navy documents and records is the Naval Historical Center. The NHC maintains offices and a warehouse in the Washington Navy Yard, in Washington, DC. Despite its Navy locale and affiliation, the NHC is staffed by civilians. A handful of these civilians - the managers of the NHC - has wrested certain autonomous controls from the Navy at large. While the overwhelming majority of the Navy is dedicated to its primary goal of national defense, and has no time leftover to be concerned about lost or sunken property of past generations, this handful of fanatical civilians has taken it upon themselves to be the custodians and watchdogs of discarded Navy property.

In what may seem to some as an abuse of their authority, they - the NHC managers - have gradually increased their power to the point at which they can now direct Navy investigators and FBI agents to harass civilians whom they believe may possess recovered aircraft and salvaged shipwreck materials. And their power is growing unchecked like cancer. In early 2004, the NHC was responsible for dispatching a Navy investigator to the home of a recreational diver who was accused of recovering a cage light from a sunken Navy vessel. Later, to continue the harassment, the NHC dispatched an FBI agent to the same diver's house.

The reader should understand that the Navy in general is not devoted to the witch hunt against commercial and recreational rescuers of old and unwanted property, but that the civilian managers of the Navy Hysterical Center are solely responsible for this questionable activity.

Be that as it may, the "Navy" asserted its claim of ownership after the *Hamilton* and *Scourge* were discovered in Canadian territorial waters.

Wrongful Ownership

The justification for ownership that was given by the "Navy" was the wartime service of the vessels in question. Since the "Navy" claims that lost or sunken Navy vessels are never abandoned (unless they are sold), the *Hamilton* and *Scourge* supposedly belonged to the Navy's sunken fleet. In order to arrive at this conclusion, however, the "Navy" had to overlook a flaw in the legal ointment.

The U.S. federal court ruled, and the U.S. Congress confirmed, that the *Lord Nelson* (which became the *Scourge*) was seized illegally. The vessel and her cargo should have been returned to the rightful owners. Because the *Scourge* sank in a gale, making her return impossible, the rightful owners (in the guise of their heirs and descendants) were awarded instead a settlement in cash. But that did not alter the fact that the U.S. Navy never possessed clear title to the vessel.

If the U.S. Navy did not have the lawful right to own the *Scourge* in 1812, it follows that it did not have the right to assert ownership after the wreck was discovered in 1975. But power-hungry bureaucrats are seldom bothered by mere technicalities.

Royal Ontario Museum

On April 27, 1979, Secretary of the Navy W. Graham Claytor, Jr. submitted the official transfer of title of the wrecks to the Royal Ontario Museum:

"In response to your request of January 5, 1977, I am happy to inform you that by the authority vested in me by the act of August 10, 1956 (P.L. 1028, 84th Congress), 10 U.S.C. 7308 and pursuant to the acquiescence of the United States Congress as required by that statute, I now transfer title and custody to the obsolete vessels (wrecks) *Hamilton* and *Scourge* on an 'as is, where is' basis at their present site on the bottom of Lake Ontario on the following conditions:

"1) The Royal Ontario Museum (hereinafter referred to as the 'DONEE') or its duly constituted assigns shall carry out scientific studies to ascertain the condition of the said wrecks and develop feasibility studies on the basis of which the DONEE or its assigns may raise one or both of the Vessels for use as a static display.

"2) The DONEE or its assigns shall be responsible for delivering to the United States Navy any and all bodily remains that may be recovered during the course of salvage operations and for instituting appropriate measures for the protection and storage of said remains from the time they are located and recovered until they are delivered. Upon locating any bodily remains, the DONEE or its assigns shall promptly notify the Armed Forces Institute of Pathology, Forensic Pathology Division, Washington, D. C. 20306, by either telephone or letter. Upon such notification, a representative of the Armed Forces Institute of Pathology will advise the DONEE, or its assigns, as to how the recovered remains shall be transported to the Armed Forces Institute of Pathology, the means of transportation to be governed by the condition of the remains at the time of recovery. The DONEE or its assigns shall also be responsible for obtaining the appropriate permits and transportation documents as may be required for shipping the remains from the point of recovery to the Armed Forces Institute of Pathology.

"3) The DONEE or its assigns shall, if one or both of the Vessels is raised, establish it or them as a public memorial or museum only, exhibit it or them as historic ships at a suitable site and maintain it or them in a condition such that the Vessel(s) shall not cast discredit upon the U.S. Navy or upon the proud tradition of the aforementioned Vessel(s) and that it or they shall not become a menace to navigation, public health or safety.

"4) The DONEE or its assigns shall report the decision to raise or not to raise the Vessel(s) to the Commander, Naval Sea Systems Command, ATTN: OODG, Washington, D. C. 20362 and shall invite the said Navy representative to view the Vessel(s) in the exhibited state if raised.

"5) The DONEE may, at its discretion, transfer and assign its rights and responsibilities for the Vessel(s) or any part thereof to another responsible government agency in Canada and will, if it does so, inform the Secretary of the Navy or his duly authorized representative of the transfer and assignment. . . . "

As noted above, the U.S. Navy did not own the *Scourge*, and therefore had no right to transfer title of the wreck to the Royal Ontario Museum.

Passing the Buck

On May 1, 1980, the Royal Ontario Museum conveyed title of the wrecks to the City of Hamilton, with certain provisos and stipulations:

"The City hereby assumes, and covenants and agrees to observe and perform, all of the terms, conditions, obligations, liabilities, indemnities, and stipulations in the said contract which are to be observed and performed by the Museum. . . .

"In connection with its obligations under paragraph 1 of the said contract, the City further agrees:

"(a) to first complete the survey of the Vessels referred to therein, and in connection with such survey and such further studies as may be required leading to a decision whether or not such Vessels can and should be raised to consult, and if necessary employ, trained personnel to be responsible in such areas of specialized knowledge as may be required including underwater research, conservation, historic archaeology and display, and

"(b) to be responsible for a publication programme in order to acquaint experts in Canada, the United States of America and abroad with the historic and scientific results of this unique project."

Special Legislation

The City of Hamilton was an incorporated municipality which possessed no legal mechanism that empowered it to embark upon the kind of venture that was mandated by the assumption of ownership of the wrecks. Therefore, the federal government passed The City of Hamilton Act.

This Act read: "The council of the Corporation may pass by-laws for investigating, planning, engaging in salvage operations and in archaeological explorations of historical or cultural artifacts of interest to the municipality, including surveys, field work, research, scientific and feasibility studies, preparation and publication of scientific and historical papers, documentation and reports and recovering, raising, restoring and displaying of artifacts, and entering into agreements, in the municipality or, specifically with respect to the historical vessels known as the *Hamilton* and the *Scourge*, outside the municipality."

First Examination - the Cousteau Society

In the summer of 1980, Jacques Cousteau led an expedition aboard the *Calypso* to film and photograph shipwrecks in the Great Lakes for a television special. On board the *Calypso* was the diving saucer *Soucoupe*, which was piloted by Cousteau's longtime colleague, Albert Falco. The *Soucoupe* was deployed over the *Hamilton*. Falco was so awed by the bust of Diana that he lost control of the *Soucoupe* and crashed into the figurehead, nicking the face in the process.

Daniel Nelson went for a ride in the *Soucoupe* during one of the saucer's submergences. He reported that the two wrecks lay 1,500 feet apart.

Unfortunately, one of Cousteau's divers suffered a fatal accident under water (not on the *Hamilton* or *Scourge*). The accident was hushed up, the proposed television special was never produced, and the Cousteau Society withheld the release of information about the expedition, including photodocumentation.

National Geographic Society

In May 1982, the NGS mounted a major expedition to photograph the sites of the *Hamilton* and *Scourge*, in order to feature the wrecks in the Society's monthly magazine. During the course of the film shoot, NGS obtained approximately 23 hours of videotape and about 1,500 slides by means of a remotely operated vehicle (ROV). The person in overall charge of photography was Emory Kristof.

NGS published a feature article in March 1983. The figurehead of Diana was depicted on the cover. Daniel Nelson wrote the text. He recapitulated his search efforts, presented the historical context, and commented on the importance of the wrecks. Visibility averaged ten feet.

As with most NGS articles, the highlight was the spread of underwater photographs. Dramatically shown were both figureheads, standing masts, fallen spars, a cathead, an anchor hanging by a fluke, deadeyes, cannons, boarding axes, swords, bilge pumps, femurs, and a skull. An artist's impression - drawn from the video footage - showed both wrecks sitting perfectly upright, and a virtually non-existent field of debris. Such perfect containment is typical of a ship which sinks quickly in a stationary position.

The City of Hamilton found, "This material is extremely valuable for both scientific and publicity purposes."

Although it was not mentioned in the article, it was later reported that a mast of one of the wrecks was either damaged or knocked down "by a barge anchor," presumably during the deployment of the anchors for the four-point moor that stabilized the work barge. The ROV that the NGS employed measured 37 inches in length, 38 inches in diameter, and weighed 360 pounds. Operators noted that minor cable snags were encountered.

Woods Hole Enters the Picture

In 1990, Woods Hole Oceanographic Institute organized an expedition to photograph the wrecks and to conduct an archaeological survey of the sites. Additional funding was provided by the Marquest Group ($775,000 in case, $200,000 in services), the National Geographic Society, and the EDS Corporation ("which provides satellite transmission services in connection with the Jason Museum network programs," and which "has made substantial case contributions in support of the project, and has provided additional substantial in-kind services.")

(According to an article printed in a contemporary Hamilton newspaper, the cost of the expedition was estimated at $9.5 million. This figure seems like a gross exaggeration, and probably includes the capital investment for the equipment. For instance, *Jason* cost $3.2 million to build. The construction was funded by WHOI under a grant from the U.S. Navy.)

The spokesperson and titular leader was Robert Ballard (known to some as Mr. Limelight), but the person in charge was Margaret Rule, the British archaeologist who oversaw the excavation and recovery of the *Mary Rose*. The license to conduct archaeology was issued in her name. She held veto power to stop the expedition if she considered that the ROV was "likely to cause damage to either vessel or the surrounding artifacts on the lake-bed."

The actual work was done by the technicians and operators of the ROV's known as *Medea* and *Jason*. *Medea* was a towed sled from which *Jason* was operated by means of a fiber-optic tether. This sophisticated system was state of the art, bar none. *Jason* measured seven feet in length and three and a half feet in diameter (although squarish): roughly the size of a fat phone booth. *Jason* weighed 2,900 pounds (the weight of a small car). *Jason* was propelled by seven thrusters, each driven by its own motor: three mounted vertically, two mounted horizontally fore and aft, and two mounted horizontally athwartships. The thrusters could be used individually or concurrently. Two manipulators could be articulated by means of fiber-optic telemetry.

Despite its massive weight, *Jason's* buoyancy was such that it was only ten pounds negative in the water. However, *Jason's* momentum and braking distance were derivative of its mass, not of its slight negative buoyancy. The connecting cable was negatively buoyant in fresh water. This meant that the farther that *Jason* moved away from *Medea*, the more the catenary of the cable sagged.

The barge from which *Medea* and *Jason* were deployed, and on which the entire crew was housed in trailer-like modules, measured 290 feet in length and 50 feet abeam. During a two-week period, the WHOI expedition shot nearly 100 hours of videotape and exposed some 4,000 frames of photographic stills. All these images could be scanned and digitized later in WHOI's laboratory.

Ballard touted that the primary research objective of the expedition was "to create a photomosaic of both *Hamilton* and *Scourge* and conduct extensive archaeological surveys using highly advanced inobstrusive and nondestructive sonar and video imaging, and electronic still camera techniques." The Marquest Group was developing a wireless acoustic positioning system known as the Sonic High Accuracy Ranging and Positioning System, or SHARPS. This device incorporated a transceiver tip which could be triggered at desired locations to initiate a position fix. When all these "fixes" were plotted on a computer, the result was a graphic interpretation of the trigger points - similar in appearance to a child's connect-the-dots outline, or the dots in a newspaper picture: essentially, a three-dimensional image of the wreck.

Peter Storck, chairman of the Technical Study Team, contended, "Dr. Ballard is really not capable [of fulfilling the feasibility needs] and his organization is not orientated to marine archaeology." He added, "They're not primarily focused on underwater archaeology."

Storck may have been correct in his assessment of the WHOI expedition. It appeared to other critics as well that Margaret Rule was hired because of her reputation as an experienced and bona fide archaeologist, in order to add credibility to the project and to appease the City of Hamilton. It seemed to some that Ballard's primary goal was not archaeology, but commercial exploitation in the guise of public education. He hoped to beam "live television broadcasts using a remotely operated vehicle equipped with cameras and lights to children and youths between 10 and 16 years old in museums and education centres across the United States and Canada."

This high-tech interaction was known as "telepresence."

Closed circuit television signals were transmitted to a satellite, then downlinked to receiving stations with multiple monitors. The hype lent the appearance of a lofty educational goal, until one read a little farther. The Turner Broadcasting System in Atlanta handled the live television feeds. "Participating network museums [must] also pay a programming fee to the Jason Foundation for Education toward program costs." The charge for the service was unspecified.

There was nothing wrong with making money. Profit is the foundation of a capitalistic society. But critics were quick to note that if the operation was a commercial enterprise, it was deceptive to promote it as a public service.

I submit that the so-called "primary" goal was irrelevant. The expedition produced the greatest amount of documentation to date - not only to date in 1990, but to the publication date of the present volume, in 2004. That the City chose not to take advantage of the work will be shown in subsequent chapters.

Contention and Conflicting Viewpoints

There was other dissention among the ranks of the *Hamilton/Scourge* Committee. According to Storck, "Hamilton wishes ultimately to raise the wrecks ... and to do that certain things must be done ahead of time. How stable the wood is and can it be lifted. This involves conservation work, a map of the site so you don't step on things when you do go down to look at things, getting samples of artifacts and the hull to determine the integrity of the wood and how it can be preserved in perpetuity."

Storck later resigned his position, stating, "The project has become more political than scientific. Others have quit in disgust. And others still on the committee feel betrayed and insulted by the City of Hamilton, the Ontario Heritage Foundation and the Ontario Ministry of Culture and Communications. Also, that man who located the War of 1812 ships, Dr. Daniel A. Nelson, a St. Catherines dentist and research associate of the Royal Ontario Museum, has been ignored by the foundation and the ministry."

Nelson was outspoken in his views about the WHOI expedition. "The city politicians involved with this project seem more interested in hurling invective at those who express serious concerns about the Ballard venture than in objectively examining the substance of those concerns." Like the City of Hamilton's "bocrats," he was afraid of the potential for damage to the wrecks by means of collision with an ROV that weighed a ton and a half. But if the City minions objected to what was arguably the most sophisticated underwater surveillance platform in the world, how could they ever expect to conduct any safer or better reconnaissance? And by whom?

Perhaps Ballard was guilty of practicing more showmanship than science. But the same could be said of Jacque Cousteau. And certainly the National Geographic Society made no pretension of conducting science; its primary purpose was to sell magazines and increase circulation. The most disrespectful critics complained childishly that WHOI and the others had not done the City's work. So be it. It was the City's responsibility to conduct the feasibility study, not Cousteau's nor NGS's nor WHOI's. The City forced WHOI to jump through so many hoops before it would condescend to grant its official sanction that WHOI was forced to write into its proposal such untried and untested concepts as SHARPS. The City had no right to make such demands.

Ballard joined the fracas in his own defense: "I've discovered as I've entered this world of archaeology there is a tremendous degree of possessiveness. It is sort of pervasive through the profession and clearly we've bumped into that."

He may have hit the nail on the head when he said, "When you have people of the quality that we have and someone with much, much inferior qualifications questions it, then they rise. . . . We're going to respond with the most quality act that you could humanely deliver, because we're capable of it."

This may sound egotistic, but it was truth and not blown smoke.

Nelson lamented the lack of affirmative action: "Since 1982, in excess of $100,000 per year of the city taxpayers' money, over and above the $500,000 to support the current work, has been allocated to the project, so far with little tangible results."

I would go as far as to say that there were *no* tangible results. It appeared that the money went only to pay the salaries of those with a sinecure on the Steering Committee, and who certainly had not done any useful work in that regard.

Discarded Rule

Margaret Rule noted: "Experience shows that it is not sufficient to simply leave a wreck unexplored to guarantee its preservation. Changes to the environment, whether microbiological, chemical or physical can occur, and unless a wreck is monitored using non-destructive remote sensing equipment, it may be too late to remedy the situation by the time it is observed and understood.

"A 'domino effect' can occur when dormant or previously absent wood degrading micro-organisms are encouraged to colonise a wreck as a result of chemical changes in the environment. Experience elsewhere indicated that physical breakdown of waterlogged timber accelerates after microbiological colonisation. Previously 'intact' timbers on the site of the *Mary Rose* (Solent, U.K.), and on the site of a third century Gallo-Roman wreck (Guernsey 1984/5) rapidly lost surface detail after colonization firstly by wood degrading fungi and then by marine borers such as limnoria (sp). Unless these sites had been monitored by diver inspection and by remote sensing we would have been unable to retrieve and record vital evidence of ship construction methods.

"It would seem wise to establish an ongoing programme of work to record and evaluate the integrity of these important wreck sites [*Hamilton* and *Scourge*]. It is only by carrying out a carefully considered programme of surveillance over a period of years that an assessment of how best to preserve these ships for future generations to enjoy can be made."

No more prescient prophecy was ever made, either by the Oracle at Delphi or by Nostradamus. Yet Rule's golden rule was pooh-poohed by the inferior minions of the City of Hamilton.

Rule: "Our maritime heritage . . . is something that belongs to *everyone* for *everyone* to enjoy and learn from." (Her emphasis.) This was strong professional advice which the City of Hamilton chose to ignore.

The Merchants of Death

What did the City of Hamilton truly want from the *Hamilton* and *Scourge*? Not archaeology, but gross exploitation. The City intended to capitalize on the death of American sailors.

"According to a city plan, the two preserved ships would be placed in a lakeside museum attracting hundreds of thousands of visitors each year."

One *Hamilton/Scourge* Committee member stated: "It'll be the single biggest tourism boost in the history of the city."

According to a previous study (conducted in 1988), "A museum at Confederation Park would attract between 400,000 and 1.1 million visitors each year depending on the size and scope of the facility."

By comparison, each year some 750,000 tourists visited the *Mayflower* replica and Pilgrim museum in Plymouth, Massachusetts. Annually, 500,000 tourists visited the restored *Vasa* in Stockholm, Sweden.

The City of Hamilton dedicated two hectares (five acres) at Confederation Park for the eventual exhibit.

According to one reporter, "The capsizing of the U.S. warships, killing 53 sailors was the single largest casualty count on the lakes during the War of 1812." Joe Fardell, the convention manager for Hamilton-Wentworth's tourism, commented on this grim statistic: "We could market something like that quite well."

Fancy Words, No Action

In 1993, the City Council created a pedantic and longwinded Development Plan that outlined the lofty if imaginary goals of the City for the study of the *Hamilton* and *Scourge* . . . and let the Plan die a lingering death.

The Plan was the vanity of academic delight that never got farther than the "what if" stage: nearly fifty pages of doubletalk (or perhaps Orwell's "newspeak" is a more accurate description). The highfalutin lingo in which the Plan was framed made it appear as a conceit to academia - and academic the issue certainly was. The pie-in-the-sky Plan pinned its hopes for delivery on divine intervention instead of human implementation.

It was estimated that the feasibility study alone would cost $5.5 million.

No portion of the Plan was ever executed, not even the so-called feasibility study, much less "raising the ships and their associated artifacts," which the Plan claimed was the ultimate achievement.

City Obstructs Free Research

In 1994, a great opportunity was offered to the City of Hamilton by Undersea Research Ltd. and Harbor Branch Research Oceanographic Institute. These two organizations offered to conduct a scientific and photographic study of the *Hamilton* and *Scourge*, at no expense to the City. Canadian explorer Joe MacInnis was the owner of Undersea Research, and coordinator of a six-week expedition to investigate shipwrecks in the Great Lakes through the viewing port and camera lenses of a Harbor Branch mini-sub named *Clelia*, operating from the mother ship *Edwin Link*.

The *Edwin Link* was a converted offshore supply vessel that measured 168 feet in length. She was specially fitted to support marine science research, ocean engineering research, and submersible operations. An 18-ton A-frame handling system located on the after deck allowed safe submersible launch and recovery operations in seas up to Force 5 (a fresh breeze between 19 and 24 miles per hour; moderate waves, taking longer form; many whitecaps; some spray).

The *Clelia* could accommodate two scientist/observers and a pilot. It was outfitted with active sonar, still and video cameras, and a hydraulic manipulator with various sampling devices.

The "bocrats" chose to squander this opportunity to obtain follow-up imagery to the Woods Hole expedition.

MacInnis commenced the organization of this complex expedition in February. He established a tight schedule to take advantage of every minute that the *Edwin Link* and her highly trained personnel could be available during the upcoming summer. The dates slated for the *Hamilton/Scourge* segment were June 9 through June 12.

My FOIA request for relevant documents was denied. Even under a court order, the City and the Bureau refused to release to my attorney the most damaging documents relevant to MacInnis's trials and tribulations. I can offer at best only a sketchy exposé of the shenanigans.

MacInnis described a number of scientific objectives in his proposal: he wanted to investigate the sediments surrounding the wreck sites, take core samples of the lake bed, conduct "side-scan and sub-bottom profile lines to confirm site, debris field locations and buried artifact locations," and shoot video that could potentially result in the production of an IMAX film that would vastly increase public awareness of the wrecks.

The most incriminating documents were withheld from public scrutiny, so that I am unable to describe the roadblocks that the City placed between MacInnis and the *Hamilton/Scourge*. One document that slipped through the political strainer proposed that MacInnis pay $10,000 to Phil Wright as the City's archaeological consultant. Wright preceded Englebert as the head of the Archaeological Licence Bureau, and was a current member of the Technical Study Team which advised the City of Hamilton on how to proceed.

Elsewhere it was stated, "Any moorings or anchor placed to secure the research vessel or any other surface floats or markers must be done in such a manner as to not impact or disturb the wrecks or the wreckage field surrounding them." No specifics were given with regard to the distance or direction from the wrecks.

According to MacInnis, "These ships are in 290 feet of green water, but you have to travel through 290 miles of red tape to get to them. . . . We offered three days of free diving that was worth $100,000, but they just made everything so extremely difficult." A spokesperson for Undersea Research bewailed the fact that the wrecks were "scuttled because of the incredible shroud of bureaucracy that covers the ships."

MacInnis eventually received last-minute approvals from both the City and the Bureau, but not with sufficiently advance notice for him to take advantage of the window of opportunity that was open between other phases of the project. The *Edwin Link* maintained a tight cruise schedule in order to visit a large number of sites.

The real losers, of course, were not MacInnis and the City, but the *Hamilton* and *Scourge* and the general public. Had it not been for the political quagmire in which the wrecks were embedded, increased public awareness could have considerably alleviated their plight.

The Royal Carpet

In 1995, the HMCS *Cormorant* was scheduled to visit the City of Hamilton. In conjunction with this visit, Frederick Eaton proposed to conduct a submersible dive to the wreck sites on July 19, when he was "Captain for a Day," using the *Cormorant* as a deployment vessel. Objections ranged from the sublime to the absurd.

Sublime: the submersible weighed 15 tons.

Absurd: the data from the 1990 WHOI expedition had not yet been analyzed (after five years). "Any additional dives on the wrecks would be of more value if the results of the previous dives were available."

The City must have thought that it had the *Cormorant* over such a barrel that the City could dip its sticky hands into the *Cormorant's* deep pockets. As a condition for granting permission, the City requested a "contribution" of $200,000.

Shakespeare wrote, "A rose by any other name would smell as sweet." In the United States, this kind of "contribution" is called a "bribe."

After intense negotiations, the *Cormorant* refused to pay the ransom for the privilege of endowing the City's coffers, and of enriching the "bocrats" whose salaries could be augmented by a windfall perquisite.

The City Obstructs More Free Research

The National Geographic Society proposed to conduct a photographic reconnaissance of the wrecks in 1996 - again at no cost to the City.

I tried unsuccessfully to obtain additional information about the NGS proposal. The FOIA clerk refused to release the relevant documents to me. Under court order, the City refused to release the relevant documents to my attorney. I requested the information direct from NGS, of which I had been a paying member and stockholder for more than a quarter of a century. NGS denied my request. I promptly canceled my membership.

From collateral sources I have been able to ascertain that the NGS also proposed to take wood core samples of the wrecks. Hamilton's alderman William McCulloch stated, "All this will eventually lead to the possibility of the raising of the ships." He also stated that it was "crucial the ships be raised because the longer they sit at the bottom of Lake Ontario, the greater the risk of deterioration. There are concerns the historic treasures are being damaged by currents, pollution and waterborne silt."

I suspect that the City tried to make the NGS leap through a large number of hoops. Perhaps the City put the bite on the Society for "contributions."

The Society had so many irons in the fire that it merely shrugged its corporate shoulders at the City's lengthy list of restrictions, and moved on to other ventures that were not manipulated by politics.

Chapter 3
Legal Preliminaries

Partnership

I would never have considered initiating the case without the promise of free legal support. I discussed this issue with Peter Hess. We had worked together on the *Monitor* case. I furnished the funding, did the background research, submitted the permit applications, conducted lengthy correspondence with NOAA, and helped to research and write the legal briefs. We met at the office of the firm for which he worked for long writing sessions, and went to the law library together to research case law. He submitted the briefs in my name, handled the legal issues and correspondence with the courts, and represented me at the four separate hearings that resulted.

The *Hamilton/Scourge* case would be more complicated because we had to file the suit in another country. Since Hess was not licensed to practice law in Canada, and did not know rules of the Canadian legal system, we had to obtain local representation. Hess thought that he could find a Canadian attorney willing to handle the case pro bono (that is, without compensation). In law, pro bono is short for the Latin phrase *pro bono publico*, which translates literally as "for the good of the public."

I paid all the expenses of the *Monitor* case: filing fees, court costs, mailing and shipping expenses, long distance telephone charges, the costs for photocopying the multitudinous documents (of which thousands were generated), travel expenses, meals, lodging, expert witness fees, and so on. Hess furnished his time.

The division of labor would be the same for the *Hamilton/Scourge* case. I would write the letters, submit the permit applications, make the phone calls, and do everything necessary to obtain a valid permit to view the wrecks - until I exhausted all the possibilities short of filing a suit. If the "bocrats" and "archs" acted with honesty and integrity, permission would be duly granted. But we had no illusions in this regard.

If it became necessary to force the issue through the court system, Hess would take over as my attorney. He would then do all the legal work that was required. The local attorney would simply submit Hess's materials under his own name, as if he had originated the documents and legal briefs himself. The local attorney would also have to advise Hess on local procedure, and on the format for the submission of documents to the court. Format is important. For example, in the *Monitor* case, a Washington, DC court would not accept our first petition because the vertical space that separated the names of the litigants from the Civil Action number was denoted by a row of asterisks; the court demanded that this space be separated by a row of close parentheses. Such anal-retentive "procedure" was part and parcel of the legal system.

We expected the *Hamilton/Scourge* case to cost more than the *Monitor* case because we had to exchange documents between countries, travel outside the country, and incur the expense of working through another attorney. In our preliminary discussions, we anticipated that even without the fees of a local attorney, a strong opposition could cause the cost to skyrocket. In fact, it is a common practice in suits against a government for government attorneys to adopt the tactic of escalating the cost of the suit for the plaintiff. In this manner the case may never get tried on its merits.

In theory, a just democratic government should welcome lawsuits from the citizenry, because they present opportunities to test the validity of the laws. In practice, however, dishonest government officials tend to obstruct the legal process as much as possible, in order to promote their own personal agendas - which may not coincide with the spirit of the law for the benefit of the public. The most effective way in which a government can oppose litigation is to wear down the plaintiff by making the case too costly to pursue. The government has unlimited financial and legal resources.

Hess shared my exhilaration over prevailing in the *Monitor* case. He often said that the case was his most rewarding legal experience. The successful conclusion elevated his professional standing. Another such success could firmly establish his reputation in admiralty law, and help to increase business. Because of these potential benefits, he agreed to share the cost of litigation 50/50. In this case we would be not just client and attorney, but partners.

In the following narrative, multiple threads of action were woven into a tapestry of deceit. I will follow each of these threads separately, but the reader should know that these threads occurred contemporaneously.

Round One

My initial strategy was to test the honesty of the government officials whose job was to manage the sites. I lost my naivety with controllers in the *Monitor* case. Nonetheless, I did not want to prejudge the Canadian controllers without giving them fair opportunity to establish their willingness to cooperate with the public by providing important information about the present condition of the wrecks. I started by giving them the benefit of the doubt. They could then prove their lack of bias, or hang themselves by their perfidy.

On October 10, 1994, I kicked the first ball in the game by posting identical letters to the relevant controllers: Corley Secore (Manager of Cultural Services, of the Department of Culture and Recreation, of the City of Hamilton), and Peter Englebert (Marine Archaeologist for the Ontario Marine Heritage Conservation Program, of the Ministry of Culture, Tourism, and Recreation).

"I am given to understand that the wrecks of the *Hamilton* and *Scourge* are categorized as tourist attractions, and will eventually be placed on display to the public in order to benefit tourism. In this spirit I would like to see and photograph the wrecks in 1995, prior to their recovery. I have contacted Canadian and American personnel who are likewise interested; plus, I have made charter arrangements with a Canadian vessel to carry personnel to the sites and to support them while they are there.... Would you please forward to me any forms that need to be filled out and filed with respect to visiting the *Hamilton* and *Scourge*? I appreciate your prompt reply."

Note that I did not use the word "dive." In the eyes of the public, diving is a leisure time activity that involves such innocuous pursuits as observing coral reefs, taking photographs of marine life and shipwrecks, catching lobsters, spearing fish, collecting mussels, clams, and abalone, and so on. But in the eyes of "bocrats" and "archs," diving is perceived as a hostile and destructive activity akin to demolition. They use the word as a pejorative. A diver is perceived as an enemy of the state.

The Archaeological Licence Bureau (of the Ministry of Culture, Tourism, and Recreation) replied with a formal multi-page Application for an Archaeological Licence. Such a license was inappropriate under the circumstances because I did not intend to conduct archaeology, or to recover samples for study. For example, one question asked for the "proposed methods of recovery of archaeological objects, including excavation techniques." In the provided space, and in the spaces for similar questions, I typed "not applicable."

I completed the form in order to comply with formal procedure. Under Purpose I typed, "To see for myself and to photograph the American shipwrecks *Hamilton* and *Scourge*." Under Research Objectives I typed, "To obtain clear, artistic, and esthetically pleasing photographs of the sites and objects on the sites before their archaeological provenance is disturbed by future salvage rumored to be planned by the City of Hamilton." By way of explanation I added, "The purpose of this project is to view and photograph an archaeological site, using the resultant photographs to contribute to the knowledge base of the two sites, and to add to the baseline photographic data laid down by National Geographic photographs and thereby demonstrate the change or continued degradation of the sites, if any." I appended my resume and a list of my published books.

This language echoed the language in my applications to dive on the *Monitor*. NOAA minions scoffed in reply, claiming that recreational divers could not produce photographs of useful quality. Yet, after I prevailed in court and dived on the wreck, subsequent NOAA representatives pleaded for use of my photographs to illustrate a *Monitor* brochure. I granted permission not only for the brochure, but for the *Monitor* website. NOAA went so far as to issue a huge poster of one of my underwater images.

Bernice Field, Engelbert's subordinate, acknowledged receipt of my application. She wrote, "Since the city of Hamilton own these wreck would you please provide this office with a letter from the city giving you permission to dive the site."

Round Two

My letter to Corley Secore went unanswered. I submitted it twice again before receiving a reply from Marilyn Havelka, Secore's successor, two and a half months after its first submission. She wrote, "Currently we are in the process of investigating a sedimentology study for the next phase of the project. In the meantime, it is important that no intrusive activity takes place." Photography, of course, was not intrusive. Furthermore, as revealed by documents later retrieved under court order, no such study was being either contemplated or conducted, and never was. Her comment was a cover-up for the City's consistent lack of affirmative action. But since I did not know that at the time, I continued in blissful ignorance - or so Havelka must have thought.

It is important for the reader to understand the magnitude of intentional obfuscation that is produced by bureaucratic language (as in George Orwell's "newspeak.") "In the process of investigating" could mean that she contemplated sedimentology only for the moment at which she wrote the word while conferring with a collaborator who was sitting at an adjacent desk. What did she mean by "next phase," or "project?" Already I felt as if I were getting the runaround. She promised to "take your request to the *Hamilton Scourge* Committee meeting scheduled early in the new year."

She also asked several questions: "names of the personnel," "objectives of the visit, "the archaeologist who would supervise the expedition," and "the names of the prospective vessel owners." ("Visit" and "expedition" are not equivalent terms.) I furnished the names of the supervising archaeologist (Thomas Evans, a Canadian) and the support vessel (*M R Duck*, owned and operated by George Wheeler and Susan Yankoo, both Canadians), as well as prospective participants - American and Canadian divers who had accompanied me on other mixed-gas dive trips.

I asked two additional questions in my reply. In order to estimate travel times to and from the sites, I needed precise coordinates. In order to calculate the most efficient mixture of helium and oxygen for breathing, and to generate decompression schedules, I needed the precise depths. *I have never, to this day, been able to obtain this important information from the Canadian controllers.* Both defendants refused to divulge this information pursuant to Freedom of Information requests and, worse, pursuant to court orders.

Delaying tactics commenced with a stream of requests for additional information from both parties, and with protracted replies. Field wanted to know "what you feel needs to be added to the photographic data," and "why you feel 'change or continued degradation' is occurring at the sites and how your photography will demonstrate this deterioration." She wanted me to "indicate the specifics of your current knowledge of sailing vessels during the War of 1812 in general and of ships such as the *Hamilton* and *Scourge* in particular. Identify the cultural groups involved with these ships." She wanted me to furnish "amongst other things, physical characteristics of both sites including depth, orientation, extent of artifact field and bottom characteristics."

She (as Engelbert's mouthpiece) wanted resumes of every prospective participant, "including any training in underwater activities with dates and institution/instructors' names." She posed a host of other self-defeating questions dealing with every aspect of boating and diving activity, such as "how many dives per day, how many persons on each dive and the duration of each dive. Provide an example of a typical dive profile for the breathing mixture being used."

The breathing mixture and dive profile could not be ascertained until I knew the depth of the wrecks. But of course, she (and Engelbert) knew that I could not furnish answers to questions when they withheld the very information on which the answers to those questions depended.

Sequestered among a dearth of irrelevant questions was this request: "Give precise latitude and longitude."

Thus, in only three months I reached the conclusion that the Archaeological Licence Bureau was a sham, and that the licensing process was designed not to facilitate the issuance of archaeological licenses but to frustrate the performance of bona fide archaeological work. And all I wanted to do was to take pictures.

The Do-Ce-Do Dance Intensifies

The tactic adopted by the Archaeological Licence Bureau was typical for situations in which there was little or no merit for denial: paper the plaintiff to death, create extraordinary work, and cause delay - and perhaps the applicant will quit in frustration at having to jump through so many hoops.

Although I suspected that Engelbert and Havelka had formed a conspiracy, I continued to play the part of the innocent and unknowing victim. I copied to Havelka every document that I submitted to the Archaeological Licence Bureau, and vice versa. I had two reasons for doing this: to give the perception that I was not suspicious of their collusion, and to lay a trap to spring when we went to court by establishing their conspiracy. I was playing a game of cat and mouse, and they didn't have a clue that they were the mice.

I wrote to Havelka, "There is great interest among American divers to see the wrecks of the War of 1812 because the wrecks are so much a part of American history." My purpose was to impress upon her and the Archaeological Licence Bureau that, although the wrecks were presently under the management of the Canadian government, they were very much American in origin, and therefore of great historic significance to American citizens as part of their national heritage in their second bid for freedom. My plea fell upon deaf ears.

I was still fighting a barrage of correspondence six months after my opening gambit. On April 4, 1995, Field wrote, "You are correct, looking at a site does not constitute archaeology." This observation begs the question: then why do I need an archaeological license?

Field's irrationality did not stop there. She also wrote, "It is your responsibility to provide us with the precise location of the site(s) you wish to work at." This preemptive strike employed a Catch-22: in order to receive a license, I first had to provide information which she was intentionally withholding from me. With tongue in cheek, I replied, "I am surprised that your office does not already have that information on file from previous visits to the sites. Perhaps, because the *Hamilton* and *Scourge* are property belonging to and administered by the City of Hamilton, no archaeological licence was applied for by previous visitors, and perhaps none is necessary." My comment also served to bring notice to the absurdity of her question, and the lack of validity for requiring a license.

(Perhaps precision was not necessary. The WHOI proposal stated, "The vessels lie in Canadian waters 10 kilometers off Port Dalhousie, 90 meters deep. The *Scourge* lies on a heading of 185° and approximately 1500 feet to the East Southeast; the *Hamilton* lies on a heading of 243°.")

I sent a copy (of my reply to Field's questionnaire) to Havelka, adding (with deliberate satire): "The Ministry of Culture, Tourism and Recreation . . . appears not to know about the sites of the *Hamilton* and *Scourge*. You will notice that I am asked to provide the precise locations which, as explained in my return letter, is information I do not have. Apparently, the Ministry has no record of previous visits to the sites despite publication in newspapers and popular magazines, or else that information would already be in its files. Perhaps the Ministry and the City of Hamilton should initiate a dialogue for a better understanding of the administration of these sites?"

Field invoked yet another ploy. "Your application suggests that the material you gather from such a dive project would be used for commercial gain. . . . you must contact the Canadian Ministry of Labour to ensure you have their authorization to proceed." My reply: "I reiterate that all participants are volunteers, including myself, and that none will be paid for his services. Quite the contrary, we are all paying our own way and all our own expenses; we are not visiting these sites for commercial gain, but because the wrecks of the *Hamilton* and *Scourge* are, to Americans, important sites of American history. The opportunity to see these sites is justification for the expense."

The reader can see where this was going as clearly as I saw it at the time. The Archaeological Licence Bureau and the City of Hamilton were doing everything in their power to erect roadblocks before the administrative process. By this time I knew that a lawsuit was inevitable, yet I continued to play the game as an ingénue and country bumpkin. My purpose was to gather conclusive evidence of complicity that I could later divulge in court.

Havelka added to the absurdity of the situation on April 21, 1995: "We are not encouraging any activity at the site until we have investigated the project more thoroughly, especially the condition of the 2 ships." Her stance completely ignores that fact that my photographs and observations would provide precisely the information which she claimed that the City needed.

I called her bluff with this: "I was not aware that the City of Hamilton had an ongoing project to investigate the condition of the *Hamilton* and *Scourge* . . . since such an investigation can only be done under water, and it was my understanding that the City of Hamilton had no plans to conduct any such investigation. Now that you have apprised me of the facts, I am very interested to see the reports of past investigations which the City of Hamilton has conducted, as well as copies of current progress reports and copies of the future plans to which you allude. I would also like to see reports from previous years."

Since Havelka was prevaricating, she was unable to provide the results of her imaginary investigative study.

Instead, she danced around the issue by writing, "In 1988, a Technical Study Team made up of experts in the field of underwater archaeology and government officials had recommended . . . that all non-essential research activities be excluded from the site until the site has been fully documented and protected. This information will not be available until the data from the Jason project has been archivally recorded and documented. The extensive photo documentation that exists from the Jason project precludes any benefit of new footage that the recreational divers could potentially produce. To date we are anticipating purchasing the raw data to proceed to the next phase of the project."

In other words, this hypothetical Technical Study team did not want the sites documented until after the sites had already been documented. This was worse than a Catch-22 - it was a virtual impossibility. Yet Havelka portrayed this self-contradictory scenario as if it made perfect sense. In the same breath, she wrote about "the fragile nature of the site and the unknown condition of the two vessels." If their condition was unknown, how could the Team arrive at the conclusion that the sites were fragile? The only work so far conducted on the sites was photographic. Fragility cannot be ascertained from photographs.

More telling was the fact that, *five years after the event*, the City of Hamilton had not yet bothered to obtain to raw data from the Jason project!

I wrote: "By analogy, these statements imply that if you were to take photographs of your three year old child and, seven years later, had not yet bothered to process and print the film, you have no need to take further photographs of the child at the age of ten because no comparisons could yet be made, so there is no need to take more pictures of the child until such time as you have looked at the older photographs. Shipwrecks are like children: they age continuously, and to ignore that the process of aging exists is to deny that change will occur, whether or not you look at the photographs."

My reasoning fell upon ears that were deafened by a conspiratorial agenda. The City of Hamilton refused to grant permission to dive on the wrecks. Nonetheless, I remitted $10 to the City in order to join the *Hamilton-Scourge* Society. My check was cashed, but the Society did not acknowledge receipt of my payment, nor did it send the newsletters for which my money was supposed to have paid. In retrospect, I believe that the Society was an illusory organization whose purpose was to give the impression to the public that it existed.

The Roadblocks of Absurdity

Not until August 8, 1995 did I receive official denial from Field. "Looking at and photographing underwater sites are not of themselves harmful activities. However, when a site, like this one, is of a very fragile nature, even what seems to be a benign activity, such as swimming by, may stir up silt or cause water movement that can affect the stability of the vessel(s)."

Field was stating essentially that fish swimming past the wrecks might create sufficient disturbance in the water to circulate silt, thus causing the wrecks to collapse - another concept that exceeded absurdity by far. This was like claiming that a mouse walking past an antique desk might create air currents that disturbed the dust, resulting in the demolition of the desk. It is absurd to believe that a wreck is held together by the silt that lies on top of it.

I queried her immediately, asking her to provide written documentation from archaeological literature about studies that substantiated her concerns about the harmful effects of the disturbance of silt. "I have consulted with several archaeologists about the idea which you promulgated in previous correspondence, that a diver's mere finwash could damage a site whose exposed position at the bottom of a lake places it in the path of constant swirling currents and sewage outflow of significantly greater volume and velocity. None would stake his professional reputation upon such a concept, nor were they aware of any studies which promoted such a concept. . . . We would be enlightened if you could forward to me some published documentation in this regard."

No such studies had ever been conducted, and no such literature existed, so she ignored the issue completely.

Dissimilar Treatment

In reply to an earlier question, Field admitted that she could not provide Ballard's permit application because "I am unable to find any reference, in our records, to a Mr. Ballard having received a licence from us."

If Ballard had not been required to have a license, then why was I? He had *proclaimed* his intention to conduct archaeological research. I just wanted to see the wrecks and take some snapshots. Or was she deliberately creating a smokescreen, knowing full well that the license had been issued not to Ballard but to the archaeologist in charge, Margaret Rule? I wrote: "You stated that Robert Ballard conducted his photographic enterprise on the *Hamilton* and *Scourge* without an archaeological license. Why is my endeavor being treated differently? Or, conversely, does precedent not therefore establish that no archaeological license is required if the stated purpose is simply to take pictures?"

Once again I snared Field in a paradox. Once again she utilized typical bureaucratic legerdemain by simply refusing to answer the question. Well, we could ask that question again in court, when she would have to answer by the order of the judge.

Thus far in my correspondence, there was nothing to indicate that Field and Havelka had had any contact between them, or that the Archaeological Licence Bureau knew what the City of Hamilton was doing, and vice versa. I suspected otherwise, and subsequent documents that were released by court order fully substantiated my suspicions. There was collusion at every step of the process.

The Great Denial

My request for a permit was denied. The only reason stated for the denial was "that the City will not grant you permission . . . Therefore, until that authorization is forthcoming we will put your 1995 licence application, to dive these wreck, on hold."

I put Field on the defensive with this: "From the language in your letter it appears to me that the Ministry of Culture, Tourism, and Recreation has found no grounds for objecting to looking at and photographing the *Hamilton* and *Scourge*, and that when the City of Hamilton grants permission to do so, an archaeological licence will be issued forthwith. However, I do not believe your letter actually states that position. Rather, it appears to be alluded to.

"In order to clarify this point, and in order to prevent unnecessary delay when the City of Hamilton finds it appropriate for the sites to be visited, would you please put in writing words to that effect? This way, too, if I must wait until 1996 to visit the sites and must reapply for the archaeological licence, all the ground work will have already been laid and there will be no chance for misunderstanding. I write this because there seems no doubt that the visits will occur, the only question is when."

Field did not condescend to send a reply.

I reiterated my point on September 15: "Since, after you asked for elaborations on responses made in my original permit applications, and I responded in kind, you did not ask for further elaboration. I am left to presume that you are satisfied with my answers and that no other questions or procedural obstacles will be forthcoming. This implies in effect that you are prepared to issue a license to me to visit and photograph the sites of the *Hamilton* and *Scourge* as soon as the City of Hamilton grants permission to do so, and that the City of Hamilton's temporary moratorium on visiting these sites is the sole reason that you put my permit application on hold. In this light, it would seem appropriate for you to issue a statement to that effect; or, better yet, to issue a conditional permit which can be activated immediately the City of Hamilton lifts its temporary moratorium; by this means you will need only to rubber-stamp the application and issue the license. I want to avoid (as I am sure you do, too) a situation in which unspecified objections are held in reserve and must be dealt with later and in an untimely and prejudicial fashion, and which would cause unnecessary delay in the performance of an undertaking which will ultimately be beneficial to all. The prolonged history of my attempt to gain permission to visit the sites of the *Hamilton* and *Scourge* predicates that we resolve any potential confusion or possible misconceptions now."

In essence, I made a reasoned and logical request for cooperation - which I did not receive.

The Plot Thickens

The Archaeological Licence Bureau demanded that I obtain approval from the Ministry of Labour. Although I knew that this was just a wild goose chase, I played my part straight so I could later prove in court that I had been intentionally stonewalled by conspiratorial partners. Before I filed the suit, my job was to lay the groundwork that would establish hidden complicity between government obstructionists.

I tackled this task with a carefully worded request which was designed as a trap to establish interagency collusion. I submitted my letter to the appropriate authority in Toronto, on May 9. "I have been visiting Canada for more than twenty years, for a variety of reasons including skiing, hiking, canoeing, diving, and touring various cities. In all that time I have spent more than one year in Canada. This year I am planning to visit Canada on at least three occasions, possibly four.

"On one of my visits in 1995 I would like to see an archaeological site in

LEGAL PRELIMINARIES 39

Ontario. In order not to incur any difficulties with local regulations, I have prepared to see this site by applying for an archaeological license to do so. However, the archaeological license officer, Bernice Field, is withholding the issuance of such a license partly because of my occupation: I am an author and photographer. This has never caused a problem before, in any of my many visits to Canada over the previous two decades. Nevertheless, Ms. Field is afraid that I might take a photograph while in Canada which, years down the line, I might use in a slide presentation or publication, and that such use would violate Canada law. I profess that I do not know Canadian law well enough to understand how taking pictures might constitute a violation. But she wrote, 'you *must* contact the Canadian Ministry of Labour to ensure you have their authorization to proceed.'

"Could you please forward to me a letter to the effect that I have authorization from the Canadian Ministry of Labour to look at archaeological sites, and that taking pictures of such sites does not violate local law? Also, can you please send photocopies of the laws to which Ms. Fields refers, so that I can know how to proceed in future visits to Canada?"

The reply that I received to this letter originated not in Toronto but in Ottawa, and from a totally different agency than the one to which it was addressed. The reply was signed by John Mitchell, Diving Safety Specialist: "For your information, the Ontario Ministry of Labour's mandate with respect to Occupational Health and Safety is to promote a safe environment for workers. To this end, the Occupational and Safety Act of Ontario requires that Owners, Employers, Supervisors and Workers comply with the safety regulations made under the Act. I believe that you may be interested in the regulation concerning Diving Operations (O.Reg 629/94) and I have enclosed a copy for your review with a few Notification of Diving Forms."

Nowhere did I suggest in my letter that my archaeological observation involved diving. Nor did I suggest that I might be engaged in commercial diving activities. So why did I receive a reply that had nothing to do with my request, and from a department of government that was not in the *Hamilton/Scourge* loop? Since Mitchell could not have gained such impressions from my letter, he must have been in cahoots with the minions who were trying to derail my dives. Mitchell's jump to a biased conclusion established proof of bureaucratic duplicity. Mitchell's letter was important ammunition that I could later use in court against both him and his co-conspirators.

Ironically, the 95-page document which Mitchell sent to me, concerning Occupational Health and Safety Act regulations for commercial diving operations, became effective on December 19, 1994: only two months *after* I submitted my first intention to dive on the *Hamilton* and *Scourge*. If I were paranoid, I might have construed the document either as a fake that was created specifically in response to my permit application, or as one containing hastily revised regulations that were passed *because* of my permit application - regulations that were intended to forestall my legitimate right to dive on the wrecks as a recreational diver.

By now I had no doubt that the cabal was multi-departmental: a malignant cancer that was consuming the entire administrative body. Nonetheless, I pursued this new thread as if I were completely ingenuous with regard to conspiracy, and played it straight.

Baiting the Red Herring

None of Mitchell's regulations applied to my recreational dives on the *Hamilton* and *Scourge*. Topic headings included "Duties of Employers, Constructors and Owners," "Duties of Submersible Compression Chamber attendants," "Duties of Diver's Tenders," "Cranes and Hoisting Devices," "Fall Arrest Systems," "Compressor Requirements," "Surface Supplied Diving," "Helmets, Masks and Hookah," "Submersible Compression Chambers, Saturation Chambers and Atmospheric Diving Systems," "Lock-out Submersible Construction and Equipment," "Contaminated Environments," "Code for Cables, Slings and Rigging used in Diving Operations," "Cable Inspection," and similar commercial diving esoterica that had absolutely nothing to do with scuba diving on shipwrecks. In fact, the word "shipwreck" did not even appear in the operations manual.

It was time to stir the pot and see what bugs came out of the brew. I wrote to Field: "Nowhere in my letter to the Ministry of Labour did I mention diving (commercial or any other kind) because that was not the point at issue. The question this begs is how did Mitchell infer that my application for an archaeological licence involved diving? He could not have drawn any such conclusion from my letter; he must have been told by someone. I also wonder how my letter addressed to Toronto reached him in Ottawa. Ironically, although he ended his letter with 'Please do not hesitate to contact me should you require any further information,' and although he initially responded to a letter which was not addressed to him, he has so far refused to respond to a letter *specifically* addressed to him. It appears to me that background bureaucratic events are occurring of which I am unaware. Since I cannot get an answer from Mitchell, and it seems to me that it is within your purview and official capacity to have knowledge of these affairs, my question to you is: did you or anyone you know or suspect, contact Mitchell or in any way see to it that he was contacted with respect to me or to diving or to the *Hamilton* and *Scourge*?"

This letter was intended to send a message directly to Field's puppeteer, Englebert. I wanted him to know that I could not be frightened or dissuaded by ridiculous stratagems, and that I could ask hardcore questions when it was necessary to do so.

Englebert (through Field) refused to rise to the bait, and political machinations continued to operate in the background. All the better, I thought, because it will later come to light in the legal process. In the event, it was later brought out during depositions that Englebert was the architect of these gimmicks.

Not to be occluded by Englebert's trickery, I contacted the Ministry of Labour direct, and expressed my concerns about the concealed ambiguities of the situation. I also presented my history of visits to Canada. If the Ministry of Citizenship, Culture, and Recreation categorized everything I did as work, then I could be "arrested while skiing, canoeing, or diving, because I have a camera in hand."

In response to my letter I received a call from Pina Pelosi. She assured me that my taking photographs within the borders of Canada would not violate local labor laws, my occupation notwithstanding.

I passed this information along to Field and Mitchell, ending each letter with, "Thanks again for your continued help and cooperation." I did not feel the sentiments that I asserted. I was simply maintaining my cover as a beleaguered citizen who was being bamboozled by maleficent bureaucrats. Every letter I wrote was carefully crafted as a course of cinderblock in the foundation of anticipated legal action.

Once again Englebert (through Field) ignored the issue. But Mitchell must have gotten intimidated by the pressure or by the pollution in the water. He replied after five months of follow-up letters, and informed me that he had been advised by Field that I was planning to "survey the *Hamilton* and *Scourge*," and that I intended to make a financial profit from the resulting photographs. He was not able to state categorically how this constituted work-for-hire, but he very definitely wanted to pass the ball to where it belonged.

I informed Mitchell of Pelosi's determination of my status as a tourist. "Should you persist in your opinion . . . with respect to categorizing my diving in Canadian waters as 'work,' . . . I am quite willing to turn over the *Hamilton/Scourge* project to someone who is unpublished, thus relieving you of the responsibility of classifying the project as one of commercial enterprise." My final milquetoast sentence read, "Thanks for your cooperation in facilitating these endeavors."

Mitchell opted out of the whole sordid mess: backpedaling, I suspected, in order to divorce himself from illegal shenanigans. "If indeed all participants, including yourself, involved with your proposed visit to the *Hamilton* and *Scourge* sites are there completely voluntarily, and neither you nor anyone associated with this proposed undertaking will provide or receive monetary compensation for, or commercial gain from, these activities, then Ontario Regulation 629/94 ("Diving Operations") would not apply to your proposed diving activity on the above-noted ship-wrecks."

Pelosi, who apparently was not privy to the real reason for having my dive trips categorized as commercial operations, acted in her official and unbiased capacity by confirming Mitchell's begrudging pronouncement, and informed Field directly.

I won that round without taking it to court.

Entrapment

I wrote a satirical letter to Field, the purpose of which was to inform her of the illegitimate manner in which she was handling what should have been a straightforward permit application (or of the illicit manner in which Englebert was instructing her to proceed, as the case may have been). I reminded her of my letter in which I stated in no uncertain terms that my visits to the *Hamilton* and

Scourge were recreational in nature, and of her evident failure to submit the truth of the situation to Mitchell.

"I am sure this was an oversight on your part. Without this additional information, which clearly explains the non-commercial nature of the project, Mitchell was operating under the mistaken impression that the project is a commercial enterprise. In retrospect, I think that in the future it would be helpful if you would first discuss with me matters which might have an adverse effect upon the successful completion of the project. Not only do mistaken impressions and partial or false information work against the facilitation of the project, but they may prove counterproductive and difficult to counteract. As your function and desire is to facilitate archaeological study, I am sure that you appreciate both my efforts in this regard and my feedback so that you can better serve this function of the archaeological licence bureau.

"I assume that this licencing procedure is not conducted in a vacuum and that relevant documentation has been generated in the process. It would be helpful to me, with respect to understanding the hierarchical infrastructure of the archaeological licencing office as well as the behind-the-scenes process of the licencing procedure, to review the documents which my request for a licence has generated. Therefore, would you please forward to me copies of the letters, memoranda, telephone logs and the like, which pertain to my request for a permit - excluding our own correspondence, but including correspondence to and from John Mitchell. My comprehension of the bureaucratic procedure will allow me to help you facilitate the issuance of the permit."

Field did not favor me with a reply. It took a court order to have the relevant and embarrassing documents released.

Neither Field nor Englebert could have been so stupid as to fail to recognize my awareness of the chicanery in which they were engaging. I put them on the spot for several reasons. I wanted them to continue their underhanded mishandling of my permit application, but to be more circumspect about it, so when we asked the court to demand the release of documents for the trial, their conspiring methods would prove to be more insidious than they were already.

I also wanted them to know that I had stolen the fort with a flanking maneuver. Knowing Englebert's character as I did, I hoped that my figurative and victorious slap in the face would arouse his ire, and incite him to greater efforts to act in bad faith. More important, however, this letter was intended as a message to the court. Every letter represented an intentional strategic maneuver that would be revealed to the court when the time was ripe.

I was not perpetrating a sting. I gave Englebert fair opportunity to behave forthrightly and indiscriminately. It was solely his conscious decision not to do so. The unctuousness of my writing style was intended to underscore the way in which he subverted the legal process that was due to an ordinary citizen.

I cast a baited hook in Englebert's direction. He could have ignored it. Instead, he chose to swallow the entire rig.

LEGAL PRELIMINARIES 43

The Devious Device

By this time the reader might be wondering why Englebert was contriving so much hokum in order to classify my proposed photographic trip as a commercial venture. His purpose was twofold. To work in Canada, a citizen from another country was required to obtain a work visa. This requirement could be employed as another roadblock that would help to frustrate the eventual success of my mission. Worse, if Englebert could pull some other political strings, he might be able to prevent the issuance of such a visa.

Second, and more important, a commercial diving operation was obligated to conform to OHSA employment standards. This meant at the very least that I would be required to have a recompression chamber on the boat. Chambers were expensive to buy or rent. Furthermore, chambers were large and were attended with bottles of compressed oxygen, all of which would require the use of a large support vessel. Along with a chamber was the necessity for an operator, and perhaps a hyperbaric physician.

Additionally, deep commercial diving operations were not permitted to be conducted on scuba. A commercial diver had to be linked to the surface by means of an umbilical hose, through which the breathing medium was supplied. An underwater communication system was also required: a special helmet fitted with transmitting and receiving devices, waterproof wires, and so on. All this paraphernalia was costly - in the hundreds of thousands of dollars - and required an even larger support vessel, as well as topside tenders and additional crew members.

Englebert's purpose was apparent: to make the proposed trip so costly that the participants could not afford to pay the price should I prevail in court.

Zebra Mussels

While Englebert was busy erecting obstacles to prevent any proper study of the wrecks, I was establishing bona fide reasons for encouraging investigation. In the late 1980's, an environmental disaster of cataclysmic proportions struck the Great Lakes: the infestation of a European bivalve mollusk known as the zebra mussel. Scientists theorized that zebra mussel larvae (each larva being the size of a grain of sand) were pumped into the ballast tanks of ocean-going vessels overseas, then were released into the clean fresh water of the Lakes, where they proliferated.

In an incredibly short time, zebra mussels spread at such a prodigious rate that shipwrecks in the lower Lakes were almost completely encrusted with their distinctive black-and-white striped shells. Municipal water intake pipes became severely clogged, restricting the flow of fresh water to millions of inhabitants. The cost of scraping these shells off the walls of conduits was an economical nightmare. Water clarity increased dramatically as the filter feeding organisms consumed particulates that were their nutrient, but this benefit to divers was far outweighed by the expenditure of millions of dollars that was spent to keep the fresh water flowing out of the faucets of households and businesses.

Zebra mussels required a solid substrate on which to attach their shells. Once the first generation died off, the next generation attached their shells to the shells of the first generation - and so on ad infinitum. As a result, shipwrecks were sprouting massive conglomerations of shells. The weight of untold thousands shells dragged navigation buoys to the bottom, and caused parts of shipwrecks to collapse. Cities hired divers to clean the intake pipes, but no effort was made by the government to remove the creatures from the wrecks: an impossible task even if the funding was available. In the grand scheme of things, and despite the outcries of preservationists, taxpayers and their representatives gave not a moment's thought to the damage being done to their underwater heritage. To the public at large, a sunken shipwreck was as worthless as a train wreck or crashed automobile - merely a useless vehicle or vessel to be towed to the junk yard and forgotten or dismantled for usable parts.

The notion that neither the City of Hamilton nor the Archaeological Licence Bureau ever considered was: how much damage was being done to the *Hamilton* and *Scourge* as a result of the agglutination of zebra mussels?

I shared my concerns with Field and Havelka. I also shared them with William McCulloch and Kevin Christenson: board members of the so-called *Hamilton Scourge* Steering Committee (neither of whom ever responded, giving me cause to wonder if the committee actually existed, and if the names were purely fictitious).

On September 15, 1995, I wrote: "All information available to me indicates that no one has seen or recorded observations on the sites of the *Hamilton* and *Scourge* since 1988. This implies that no one has the least idea of what changes may have occurred during the intervening seven years to sites which you referred to in previous correspondence as 'fragile,' and whose environment has undergone drastic and harmful transformation during that time. I refer, or course, to the zebra mussel infestation so largely in the news. Zebra mussels now cover every observed wreck in the lower Great Lakes, without exception. What is being done to protect the sites of the *Hamilton* and *Scourge* from the damage inflicted by zebra mussel encrustation, or what studies are being conducted to observe and check zebra mussel growth on these two historic sites? Or are these sites to continue to go unobserved and disregarded?"

None of my recipients deemed to reply. I wrote again: "You should be excited to know that I have enlisted the voluntary cooperation of zebra mussel expert Arthur Bogan, Ph.D., of the Freshwater Molluscan Research team, who has agreed to interpret our photographic evidence of zebra mussel population density and potential long-term damage to the wood of which the two wrecks are constructed. The glue extruded by zebra mussels in order to attach themselves to the substrate exerts a potentially harmful effect which may cause infected shipwrecks to deteriorate faster than normal. Any information we obtain in this regard will increase our overall knowledge of the condition of the wrecks, as well as add to the database of information needed to make informed decisions about how best to protect these historically significant wrecks from ecological hazards or whether to salvage the hulls before eventual dissolution."

Alas, although the powers that be adopted an implacably harsh stance about the imaginary effects of a slight movement of silt, they failed to accept or chose to ignore the empirical scientific evidence of the deleterious consequences of zebra mussel masses and their acidic glue reaction on wood. It appeared to me that they would rather let the wrecks rot away than to give someone the opportunity to look at them.

The Runaround Continues

The reader might be wondering by now why I have quoted so extensively from my correspondence and not from official replies. I can address this issue best by quoting once again from one of my numerous letters, this one dated March 9, 1996, and submitted to both Field and Havelka: "Although I have not received a response to my letter of February 26 (nor to my letter of September 15, 1995, my letter of November 16, 1995, my two letters of December 17, 1995, my two letters of January 30, 1996, and my two other letters of February 26 - nine letters in all) I feel compelled to write again about the current situation with regard to the *Hamilton* and *Scourge* and my licence to photograph the sites."

Every non-response was evidence of lack of cooperation. So I kept writing, building a case for the lawsuit that was the ultimate course of action. After a month passed without the receipt of a reply, I resubmitted my letter - and submitted it again one month later, and again, and again . . .

In the *Monitor* case, I went over the head of the obstructive Sanctuary manager, directly to the Chief of NOAA. This action resulted in a response to my queries which had not been forthcoming from the manager. I had hoped that by informing the chief about his subordinate's dereliction of duty, the chief would correct the situation. Instead, it established that the intra-agency conspiracy went all the way to the top of the hierarchy.

Taking a similar tack, I wrote to Anne Swarbrick, the Minister of the Ministry of Citizenship, Culture and Recreation (to which the Archaeological Licence Bureau was subordinate). I complained of the bureau's continual procrastination, the lack of cooperation, and the steadfast refusal to reply to specific questions. This complaint eventually forced Field to reply to my many letters, but her replies were uninformative rubber stamps that produced no useful information.

Consider this bit of absurdity from Field: "The location of archaeological sites is not considered public information. It is the responsibility of this Ministry to keep site location information confidential for the protection of the resource and is only released to authorized persons for specific purposes." The reader must keep in mind the fact that Field had previously made it a requirement of my permit application to furnish the location of the wrecks.

At my insistence Field grudgingly admitted, "Since the last dive on the *Hamilton-Scourge* in 1990 there may indeed have been an effect of these wrecks by zebra mussels. At this time I have no further information on this matter."

In laying the ground for comparisons, I wrote to Field: "The Ontario archaeology bureau, and you personally, approved photography of the *Gunilda* site despite its having a chain of title leading to a current owner. You noted specifically to the permittees of that photographic project that photography does not constitute trespass, any more than it is trespass to walk around a building in order to photograph it. Surely you must agree that the situation with respect to the *Hamilton* and *Scourge* is identical. Unless you would treat me unequally, you should have issued the permit.... Why did you not do this, when under your own guidelines you knew all along that permission from the City of Hamilton was not required? And why did you keep from me the relevant facts? I am getting the feeling that you have not been working in my best interests, that perhaps you have been trying to frustrate my project rather than to facilitate its achievement. Please reassure me that all this is a misunderstanding due to a lack of proper communication."

I reached this point of accusation after two years of thwarted negotiations. My persistent requests for cooperation were part of a carefully conceived plan of campaign. I was leading the City and the Bureau by the nose to the butcher shop. I did not write this letter to Field in anticipation that she would have a sudden attack of reason or impartiality. I wrote this letter as evidence to be submitted in court.

The reader should also understand that the letters I quoted above represent only the tip of the iceberg of my prolific output. I knew that I could not win by the application of logic. My game plan was to have on record the *reductio ad absurdum* of the City's and the Bureau's arguments.

Field's forced reply was: "Looking at and photographing underwater sites are not of themselves archaeological activities. However, the intent of the use of photographs may indeed make this activity the purview of this Ministry."

A self-serving response was also forced from William McCulloch, who truly existed: as chairperson of the council for the City of Hamilton. With respect to my insistence on the presence of zebra mussels throughout Lake Ontario, he wrote, "They do not survive in waters of that depth."

Contradicting Havelka's statement, McCulloch wrote, "We are just as anxious as you are that the ships be recovered." He must have confused his own feelings with mine, for I felt no anxiety in that regard. He also wrote that it was not the City's intention to procure information about the wrecks unless it would "further the recovery of our two ships."

McCulloch expressed concern about the increase of water pollution contributing to degradation of the wrecks, and "the possible danger of a merchant ship dropping a heavy object near or on the site." Apparently, his concern was not great enough to mark the sites with buoys in order to warn passing merchant ships to avoid the area.

As in the *Monitor* case, the minister took the unjust side of her subordinates, and refused to implement official intervention.

Voodoo Photography

In order to have grounds for contesting photography of the wrecks, Havelka's superior Ross Fair claimed, "The risk is too high." He also wrote, "I regret that you do not like the pace with which we are proceeding."

My reply: "I have been taking pictures for twenty-five years and have never harmed a subject by exposing film in a subject's direction or by capturing a subject's image on film. Such harm is believed to occur only among the most backward peoples and cultures in the world. Please submit documentation which establishes your position that photography constitutes damage or destruction."

Rationale from the Bureau: "We take the view that for sport divers on many wrecks which involve no contact, and where photography is the objective, a licence is not required. Where the purpose of the dive is to conduct research or to assess the condition/deterioration of a ship, a licence is required. The proposed use of systematic photography to document the condition of a wreck is often an indicator that a licence is required. In your case, you say that you do not wish to undertake an archaeological dive, yet you do want to document the deterioration of the wrecks and evaluate the potential impact of zebra mussels. We consider this type of action to be licensable underwater archaeology."

I overcame this tautology by submitting another permit application from which photography was deleted. I stipulated that there would be no evaluation of the impact of zebra mussels. In this latest application - which was submitted with all the supporting documentation that accompanied my previous applications - I stated categorically that we (the participants) would take no pictures and would ignore zebra mussel encrustation: we would merely *look* at the sites.

Although this application overcame all the previous objections, the Archaeological Licence Bureau still refused to issue a permit - this time without offering any absurd justification - and the City deigned not to respond.

The Deceit of Delay

Consider this bureaucratic means of deceit. I learned that the National Geographic Society had submitted an application for a license to photograph the *Hamilton* and *Scourge*. I wanted to ascertain if the Society was receiving preferential treatment, so I asked Field "about other potential permittees." Field postponed favoring me with a reply for four months, then claimed that no other licenses were in the works. The Society subsequently withdrew its application between the time of my request and the time of Field's reply.

I wrote to Field: "Your timing and semantics create a deception not in keeping with the truth. . . . By your waiting four months to answer my question, by which time National Geographic's proposal was withdrawn, your statement that 'the City of Hamilton is not considering any proposals to dive at this time' may be technically correct, but it cleverly and maliciously attempts to deceive me of intervening events which a more timely response would have divulged. Why do you feel it necessary to keep public information secret and to maintain a charade of ignorance about the Steering Committee's lack of affirmative action?"

Once again, although I addressed my letter to Field (and by proxy, to Englebert), I actually wrote the letter for the judge who would eventually handle the case. It was well that I did, for Field did not favor me with a reply.

By now there was no doubt in my mind that the Archaeological Licence Bureau was a façade, that the City of Hamilton's Steering Committee was a fiction, and that the so-called *Hamilton/Scourge* "project" was Machiavellian in scope. I had handed them an unknotted rope. They could have dealt with the situation honestly. Instead, they tied the rope in knots and proceeded to hang themselves with it.

It was time to raise the stakes and call the bureaucratic bluff.

Freedom of Information

When "bocrats" deliberately withhold information, one recourse that a citizen possesses is to file a request pursuant to the Freedom of Information Act (FOIA). By now I had been working on this case for two years, with almost nothing to show for my efforts. The *Hamilton/Scourge* debacle was a can of worms, but one on which the City of Hamilton and the Archaeological Licence Bureau were keeping a very tight lid. As they would not release requested information voluntarily, and as they filled their meager correspondence with misdirection, it became necessary for me to appeal to authority that exceeded their own.

FOIA is not a panacea. According to common misconception, FOIA is an inviolable mechanism for retrieving documents when ordinary approaches have been stonewalled by unwilling "bocrats." The reality is quite different. In many cases, the FOIA clerk - the person who is charged with the responsibility of responding to FOIA requests - works in the same office and for the same manager of the agency that withheld the information in the first place. Thus a FOIA clerk may perform in allegiance to political pressures from co-workers and superior officers.

FOIA is replete with exclusions, many of which are arbitrary in nature. These exclusions may be invoked according to the whim of the FOIA officer, or to the political machinations of the managing agency. Thus the rights of the requester as intended by the law may be violated for the good of the agency or for the good of the "bocrats" who have conflicting personal agendas. The first job of such a "bocrat" is to convince the FOIA clerk why certain information should be withheld, and which exclusions can be applied in order to support the denial to produce.

These arguments are never put in writing. They are strictly oral in nature. Only physical and pre-existing documents can be requested by means of FOIA. A FOIA request cannot demand the *creation* of documents. The best way for a "bocrat" to hide damning information is to avoid putting it on paper. Alternatively, a "bocrat" with something to hide may either destroy damning documents, or hide them from the investigating clerk by misfiling them until a later date. All these situations occur on a regular basis. Transgressors who get caught committing "indiscretions" are neither apprehended nor punished, because an agency will always stand by its own lest its reputation get besmeared.

The wording of a FOIA request must be precise and all-encompassing. Any lack of precision, or implied limitation of scope, can and will be used to hedge the release of documents with the standard bureaucratic phrase, "No such documents were found relevant to your request." For example, if you ask for correspondence, you will not receive photocopies of interoffice memos or of transcripts of telephone calls. Requests must be made broad and inclusive: "all documents, letters, correspondence, instructions, orders, inter- and intra-office memoranda, conversation notes, telephone transcripts, preliminary drafts, jottings, recordings, and any other forms of written or oral expression."

Even then, copies of documents may be heavily redacted. The Canadian word for "redacted" is "severed"; in any language, the process means "edited" or "censored." If the FOIA clerk can be persuaded by affected "bocrats" not to release pertinent information, the officer may photocopy the documents for release, but black out damaging disclosures with indelible ink. The requester receives a sanitized version of the document with only the innocuous sentences still legible.

An additional counterincentive for the release of public documents is the exorbitant charge that must be paid in advance. There is an application fee, an appeal fee, an hourly rate for the time spent in searching through records and preparing (redacting) the documents for release, and a photocopy fee (per page). The requester pays for the search even though no relevant documents are found. The requester also pays for the time taken by the FOIA officer to redact and sanitize the documents.

Since I had exhausted all the possibilities of obtaining information from the City of Hamilton on a voluntary basis, FOIA was the penultimate step that preceded court action. In acknowledging receipt of my FOIA request, responding FOIA clerk Darryl Lee suggested, "There are reasonable grounds to believe that the request is frivolous or vexatious."

I appealed. The City FOIA clerk was uncooperative, but eventually relented grudgingly to my request.

The search fee was charged at the rate of $30 per hour. This was equivalent to $1,200 per week, or two to three times the actual wages that were earned by a salaried FOIA clerk. Thus there was a profit motive for the City to refuse to act on a voluntary basis.

Although I received only a partial release, the $300 that I paid for the least innocuous documents which the FOIA clerk permitted me to see, provided invaluable information that contradicted *all* the City's touted points of view, and disclosed the dark prevarications of the Archaeological Licence Bureau.

FOIA Requests of the City

From the City of Hamilton I requested all documents relating to what the City histrionically called the *Hamilton/Scourge* Project. As it developed, only one such document existed: the Development Plan described in Chapter 2. This implied that the so-called Project was a chimera. Or, if such a Project did in fact exist, it existed only in the imagination of the City's Board of Directors. The "project" was the sole function of the Steering Committee. However, the Steering Committee appeared to be rudderless: the Board of Directors met quarterly, did not record the minutes of the meeting, took no action, then ignored the *Hamilton* and *Scourge* for the next three months. They played this game of nonperformance for two continuous decades.

I requested all documents that led to the conclusion that "diving" was an intrusive activity. Again, none existed. This implied that diving as an intrusive activity was a self-serving subjective perception.

I requested all documents "relating to the denial by the City of Hamilton of my application for permission to photograph the *Hamilton* and *Scourge*," excluding correspondence which I already possessed: that is, documents which I created, or the dearth of replies to my numerous letters. Relevant to this request, the City invoked an exclusion under the guise of protecting the interests of third parties whose comments had been solicited. The FOIA clerk claimed to have contacted the affected third parties, all of whom supposedly desired the "non-release of records in which they have an interest." Access to those records was denied to me.

I requested a copy of Dr. Margaret Rule's final report on the 1988 Photographic Reconnaissance that was conducted by the Woods Hole Oceanographic Institute, and for which Ballard was listed as leader. This was the photographic expedition which, I had been informed by Field, neither applied for nor received a license from the Archaeological Licence Bureau. The City tried to have this request quashed along with the others. But, the FOIA clerk found, "In the absence of written submission from Dr. Ballard, the City does not possess adequate evidence to justify the non-release of these records."

The City filed an appeal to have these records withheld, but was unable to obtain a withholding notice from Ballard within the prescribed thirty day allowance for response. These documents were eventually released to me but not without a fight.

Jason Underwater Archaeological Report

According to Rule, instead of a condition of fragility, "The Ships were found to be sound."

Rule recommended "the removal of all loose masts, booms and spars from the Vessels." This was contrary to the City's newly avowed rationale against salvage.

She wrote: "The lake bed is a smooth layer of fine silts. These are colonized by amphipods and small fish (sculpen) which scurried about stirring up the fine silt. . . . [T]he movement we observed suggested that colonization of the site by small animals was likely to cause small but uncontrolled changes to the silt dust building up on the ship and on the lake bed." In opposition to the City's proclamation with regard to disturbance, the movement of silt was an ongoing and unrestrained process against which the potential slight currents created by a diver's finwash were irrelevant.

Skid marks left by the runners of the ROV filled in within hours due to "surprisingly brisk animal activity. . . . A noticeable current began to erode the sharp outline we had created and 16 hours later it had almost completely disappeared." Rule found that bottom currents increased predictably every afternoon, shrouding the wrecks in obscurity with floating detritus.

She found "abundant fungal or algal growth" on the figurehead of the

LEGAL PRELIMINARIES

Scourge. "This should be sampled and identified; it is unwise to assume it is non-destructive. . . . as its adhesion to the timber may contribute to the breakdown of the surface layers."

Most important of all, she wrote: "Resurvey the hulls of both Ships is necessary."

She concluded with her opinion of the need for "further monitoring and sample taking."

Thus the City was acting in diametrical opposition to Rule's recommendations with regard to the recovery of loose artifacts and continued observation. It was ironic that, although Rule was the only archaeologist to ever see and survey the wrecks, the City of Hamilton chose to ignore her professional recommendations.

To me, that information was worth more than the time, effort, and money that I had expended in obtaining it.

Furthermore, according to Ministry documents that were beyond the reach of underlings to hide or destroy, the Ministry "granted Dr. Rule and archaeological licence and provided a grant of $250,000 to the City of Hamilton to assist in defraying the costs of the project."

Since the expedition was underwritten entirely by Woods Hole, with support from the National Geographic Society, I cannot help but wonder what the Steering Committee did with the Ministry's quarter of a million dollars. Was the money used to pay the Board of Directors for sitting on the quarterly committee meetings?

But the best was yet to come.

Permit Granted!

Louise Hastings and Diane Varga were FOIA clerks for the Ministry of Citizenship, Culture and Recreation, to which the Archaeological Licence Bureau was subordinate. Hastings called to discuss the parameters of my request; Varga submitted an itemized bill. They both took their jobs seriously and compiled a considerable list of documents that were relevant to my request. They also submitted several pages of rules that governed exclusions. I was prepared for another whitewash. Yet the documents that they released contained not a few surprises.

The greatest surprise came when I learned that Jane Marlatt, Assistant Deputy Minister in the Ministry of Culture, Tourism, and Recreation, had not only approved my application for an archaeological licence, but had committed her approval to paper. She wrote:

"Dear Mr. Gentile: It is with pleasure that I issue you a licence for archaeological field work. . . . I would draw attention to the conditions under which your licence has been issued, and I would emphasize the reporting requirements associated with your licence. . . . By way of information, I am also enclosing a sample 'Archaeological Site Record Form'. Additional forms may be secured from the Data Coordinator. I wish you every success in your continuing studies of Ontario's archaeological heritage."

Marlatt was far up the hierarchy of the Ministry, at the opposite end of the Archaeological Licence Bureau. Yet I had never received a copy of her letter, which was addressed specifically to me at my home address. The implication was profound. Someone had taken her letter and, instead of mailing it as instructed, had suppressed it.

It was difficult for me to believe that the Archaeological Licence Bureau had failed to notify the City of Hamilton that it had granted such a permit. That letter should have been in the City's files. Had Darryl Lee, the City's FOIA clerk, overlooked the letter? Had he intentionally ignored the letter? Had he been convinced not to release the letter? Or had the letter been secreted from him?

More important, which individual in the Archaeological Licence Bureau had taken it upon himself (or herself) to disregard a direct order from the Assistant Deputy Minister, and maliciously concealed the document instead of sending it to me? Unless the guilty party makes a deathbed confession, we will probably never know.

The Most Damning Evidence

According to Ministry briefing notes for February 26, 1996, "The City of Hamilton has long been investigating the *Hamilton* and *Scourge* and hopes to raise them."

Several paragraphs later: "The process of issuing a normal archaeological licence takes between 6-8 weeks" (not three years).

Worst of all: "It is the ministry's policy that heritage ships are not recovered due to the cost, liability and the fact that such recovery diminishes the value of these resources as dive attractions. . . . Sport divers are not covered by any legislation and may dive the wrecks at will."

These last two sentences were paramount to an open invitation to dive on the wrecks without applying for permission to do so!

I also learned that Englebert composed a three-page list of obstacles that could be used to post obstructions to my permit application. Field repeated his words almost verbatim. This was proof that Englebert was Field's advisor, and the motive force behind the obstruction process and ultimate denial.

Englebert also initiated the involvement of the Ministry of Labour. He twisted language from my resume in order to proclaim the falsehood that I wrote, "the results [of photography] will be used for speaking engagements and magazine articles." Mitchell's submission of OSHA rules was a direct result of Englebert's statement, "receiving monies for these activities . . . makes it a commercial proposition."

Elsewhere, Englebert harped on the condition of commercial gain by advising Field, "Mr. Gentile . . . stated that the results of his activities on the *Hamilton* and *Scourge* would be used in the writing of magazine articles."

Neither of these statements was true. I neither created such language nor implied such goals with respect to the *Hamilton* and *Scourge*. In fact I did quite the opposite. Although I was a freelance photojournalist, I was very specific in my applications and proposals to separate my occupation from my hobby of diving on shipwrecks. Englebert employed dishonest political license to paraphrase words and concepts which he attributed to me, in order to give the impression that my intended trip was a commercial enterprise.

What did *not* come as a surprise was a letter from Englebert to Havelka, in which he advised her *not* to grant permission for me to visit the sites. Now we knew for certain what we had suspected all along, and what the Bureau did not want me to know: not only was there collusion between the two major parties involved, but Englebert was the prime instigator of the conspiracy.

Lack of Credentials

What did we know about the chief architect of obstructionism and his various and sundry artifices in the name of the Archaeological Licence Bureau?

Hess was tangentially involved in the case of the *Atlantic*, a paddle wheel steamer to which a group of California treasure salvors claimed salvage rights. The basis of their claim was their "discovery" of the wreck, in Lake Ontario. The outfit neglected to mention to the Admiralty Court in California that the wreck had previously been discovered by Mike Fletcher, in 1984, or that Fletcher had conducted a considerable number of survey dives on the wreck. The case was hotly contested by the Canadian government. The wreck lay on the Canadian side of the lake, and the government did not want the wreck to be salvaged (or salvaged again - the wreck had been partially salvaged shortly after its loss, in 1852.)

At one of the hearings in 1996, Englebert was called to testify on behalf of the Canadian government. Under voir dire (a preliminary examination concerning the competence of a prospective witness), Englebert was forced to admit that he had never conducted a full-scale underwater archaeological survey. This was a glaring lack of experience for the head of Ontario's Archaeological Licence Bureau.

One concern of the court was future access to the site. The court wanted assurance that any settlement between parties would not adversely affect the rights of the public to visit the wreck. When, by way of comparison, Englebert was asked how many divers had received licenses to dive on the *Hamilton* and *Scourge*, he was forced to admit that not one license had ever been issued.

Hess sent me a memo about the hearing: "The Judge concluded that the arch'ist is the biggest obstacle to settlement and then kicked him out of the negotiations."

The Intimidation Charade

Many Americans crossed the lakes in their boats in order to dive on shipwrecks on the Canadian side of the border. One weekend, three couples took their boats to Port Dover, on the north shore of Lake Erie: Michael and Georgann Wachter, Dave and Annette Soule, and a third couple whose name Georgann could not remember when she told me this story. (The third couple were friends of the Soules.) They had been in Port Dover for two nights when they visited a nautical antique shop that was located a couple of hundred feet from the marina.

The Wachters purchased a light, the Soules bought a small boat compass.

Englebert must have had spies and informants everywhere. Before long, he and Jim Murphy (a local resident and member of the Port Dover chapter of Save Ontario Shipwrecks), appeared at the marina and confronted the Wachters and Soules about their wreck-diving activities. After some innocuous introductory questions about which wrecks they had dived, Englebert accused them of removing artifacts from Canadian heritage wreck sites. Englebert thought that he had caught them red-handed. He attempted to confiscate the items.

Englebert told them - as he has told countless others throughout the years - that he was empowered with the authority to arrest anyone whom he believed had broken Canadian archaeology laws, that he could call for police backup if anyone protested his authority, that he was authorized to search them, their boat, and their equipment, and that he could have their boat and their personal belongings impounded until further notice - only on suspicion.

These were all boldfaced lies. Englebert had no such powers of arrest, search, or seizure. Nor did he have any working relationship with the police. He relied on intimidation to prevent people from calling his bluff, and it generally worked. He proceeded on the grounds that the Wachters and the Soules were guilty without proof.

The Americans, however, had an ace up their sleeve - or rather a receipt in the bag. Georgann showed Englebert the price tag on the bottom of the lamp. Annette had a store receipt. They pointed to the shop where they had made their purchases, and suggested that Englebert ask the proprietor about the items. Georgann mentioned that she was simply taking photographs of the wrecks, in order to illustrate a book that she and Mike were writing.

A red-faced Englebert was not mollified. He continued his harassment, warning them that he would order the police to maintain surveillance over them for suspicion of conducting illegal diving activities. He enumerated these illegal activities in which he believed they were engaged: searching for shipwrecks without an archaeological license, disturbing the silt that had accumulated on the wrecks, photography for the purpose of book publication. This latter activity was a commercial operation which required strict adherence to OSHA regulations: surface-supplied air, voice communications, and a recompression chamber on the boat.

He left in a huff.

Englebert threatened many people. He never arrested any of them.

For the Wachters and the Soules, innocence had its virtues. But to add injury to insult, Englebert spread the word that he had "caught" them removing artifacts from Canadian shipwrecks. This was a clear attempt to damage their reputations in contradiction to the truth.

The first diver he informed - just days after the incident - was Joyce Hayward. She had the impression that Englebert was trying to bait her into admitting that the Soules and Wachters had a history of recovering artifacts. She knew quite the opposite: that they would never take artifacts off a Great Lakes shipwreck. She told him so.

Know Thine Enemy

All the correspondence from the Archaeological Licence Bureau was signed by Bernice Field. Peter Englebert's name was never mentioned. Hess met Englebert at the above-mentioned *Atlantic* hearing. When Hess introduced himself, Englebert refused to shake his hand, and turned on his heel and stormed away, his face a horrid caricature of anger and hostility.

After the hearing was adjourned, one of the trial participants introduced Englebert to Hess. Englebert did not stalk away this time, but he glared with offensive antipathy. Then he said with evident rage and hatred, "Your client will never dive the *Hamilton* and *Scourge*."

This was an ironic statement for Englebert to make in 1996, at which time I had not yet filed for injunctive relief. Nor was Hess acting as my attorney in that regard. Englebert must have been referring to our previous attorney/client relationship with respect to the *Monitor*. Or, perhaps through some arcane archaeological grapevine, he had learned or begun to suspect that Hess and I were working together on the *Hamilton/Scourge* case. The Wachter situation clearly demonstrated that Englebert had long ears.

We already suspected Englebert's complicity in the matter, but his statement served to confirm his attitude about public access and involvement in what he obviously considered to be his own personal domain. Englebert was the true nemesis and enemy of the people. Ironically, he also appeared to be an enemy of archaeology. Instead of welcoming free public participation in the study of Ontario's underwater history, he put people through a maze of hoops that lasted for several years. Only after years of wrangling would he permit the issuance of a license - and then only if the volunteers promised not to do anything related to archaeology.

A case in point was the *Judge Hart*, which sank in Lake Superior in 1942. A steel-hulled freighter of such recent vintage possessed no archaeological significance. Hundreds of similar vessels litter the bottomlands of the Great Lakes, and other similar vessels remained afloat, and were still in service. After learning that recreational divers had discovered the wreck, and that other divers were eager to explore the site, Englebert posted the wreck off-limits because it supposedly lay within his jurisdiction. He claimed that a license was required for diving on the wreck, and he steadfastly refused to issue any such licenses. He threatened divers with arrest if they were caught diving without his authority to do so. The fantastic irony of the situation was that, although Englebert had heard about the discovery through the rumor mill, he did not know the wreck's location. Thus he refused to grant permission for people to visit a site whose location was unknown to him!

Harry Zych was a commercial diver and salvor who prevailed in a bitter battle over salvage rights to the *Lady Elgin*, which sank in Lake Michigan in 1860. He was elected spokesperson for commercial diving interests at the meetings of the Great Lakes Underwater Cultural Resources. Zych wrote, "Attendance was approx. 175 people. I happened to be seated 3 seats away from Peter Englebert, when he stood up to give his opinion on how to solve the Underwater Cultural Resources (shipwrecks) diving problem, in the Great Lakes. Peter Englebert said,

'We should put a moratorium on diving in the Great Lakes for fifty years.' This man will be in charge of issuing licenses for wreck site access."

Such reports and eyewitness accounts made Englebert appear as a staunch obstructionist to progress with respect to underwater archaeology. Hess and I entertained no illusions or misconceptions about Englebert's misanthropic dedication. It pays to know thine enemy before going into battle.

Passing the Torch

For three years I handled the case entirely alone, and bore my own expenses. My whole purpose was to demonstrate to the court that the City and the Bureau had acted in unconscionably bad faith. That was the reason for the initial milquetoast tenor of my correspondence, and the increasingly accusatory tone of my later letters. I laid the groundwork that exposed to the court how the City and the Bureau had conspired to frustrate my bona fide efforts to either see or document two submerged icons of American history.

My major contribution was done. The rest was up to Hess and the legal process.

Or so I thought.

Chapter 4
Courting the Law

A Canadian Attorney

After spending three years in laying the foundation for the case, the majority of my work was completed (or so I thought). It was time to begin Phase Two: the filing of a suit against the City of Hamilton.

Because Hess and I had agreed to share equally the cost of litigation, we discussed the issue of being co-plaintiffs in the proceedings. He thought that his role as an attorney might be hampered by his status as a litigant. According to an age-old legal dictum, "He who defends himself in court has a fool for a client." But in this case, Hess thought instead that he would have more freedom as an attorney with me for a client. (In retrospect, Englebert's belief in our relationship was prescient if untimely and anachronistic.)

Hess's job was to find a Canadian attorney to accept the case pro bono. According to our plan, Hess would do the actual legal work, while the Canadian attorney would simply file the paperwork and advise him on local law.

Additionally, Hess did not want to be classified as a litigant should we later seek recourse by alternative avenues. One possible future tactic was to seek an alliance with the United States Navy. A provision in the contract that transferred title of the wrecks from the Navy to the Royal Ontario Museum read, "Donee undertakes to comply with all relevant Canadian Civil Rights laws ensuring non-discrimination in all matters pertaining to the study and possible raising and exhibition of said Vessel(s)."

Since the City had approved Cousteau's, the National Geographic Society's, WHOI's, and MacInnis's visits the site, but not mine, we had a good case for discrimination. Another provision read, "In the event that the Donee, or its assigns, shall fail to perform the obligations assumed under this contract, the Secretary of the Navy or his duly authorized representative may terminate this contract . . . in which event the Donee or its assign shall transfer title to the Government [of the United States]."

In other words, the Navy could reassert its title to the wrecks. Hess thought that there was a faction within the Navy that regretted bequeathing the wrecks to an assign which refused to take affirmative action with regard to studying and preserving the wrecks. Denying an American citizen the right to embrace his own heritage might serve as an additional incentive for the Navy to take the action that the City was unwilling to take. Hess felt that he could lobby this cause better as an attorney than as a client with a vested interest in the outcome.

I photocopied my entire case file - which was several inches thick - and gave it to Hess. He submitted the case file to Steve Yormak, a Canadian attorney with whom he had worked on other cases, and who had professed an interest in pursuing the cause of justice - and who, Hess informed me, would take the case pro bono.

Yormak was willing to invest his time but not his money. He wanted a retainer of $4,000 to cover anticipated expenses: filing fees, court costs, preparation charges, appearance expenses, research and photocopy costs, long-distance telephone charges, examination of witnesses by means of deposition, and so on. Hess did not think that this amount was extraordinary, so he agreed.

But although Hess agreed to pay the amount that Yormak requested, and although Hess was my co-equal partner in the case, he pleaded a temporary pecuniary deficit. He wanted me to pay the entire $4,000 up front. He promised to reimburse me when his financial status was more stable. Subsequently, I sent a check to Hess in the full amount, and he forwarded the money to Yormak.

Procrastination

I did not want any delay between my final correspondence with the City and the notification of legal action. After giving the City a last chance to live up to the terms of the Navy contract, I wanted to hit the recalcitrant Board of Directors fast and hard.

Hess and Yormak dragged their feet. Weeks passed, then months. I called Hess periodically to request a progress report. He claimed that he could not proceed because Yormak was still "researching" the case. I also called Yormak, but he never accepted my calls. No matter what time of the day I called, he was always "out" - or so his secretary claimed. She took my messages, but Yormak never once returned any of my calls. From my perspective he was a complete nonentity. I was beginning to wonder if he even existed. Hess claimed that he had spoken with him. This gave me cause to wonder why Hess could catch Yormak in his office but I could not, or why Yormak returned Hess's calls but not mine.

As hard as it is to believe, an entire year passed during which I heard absolutely nothing from Yormak: not a phone call, not a letter, nothing. Hess informed me that Yormak was still "researching." Apparently, he worked on the *Hamilton/Scourge* case only during spare moments between other, more pressing obligations. My frustration was unbounded. I had accused the City of Hamilton and the Archaeology Licence Bureau of inordinate delay, now my own attorney was procrastinating far worse than the "bocrats" ever had. Unfortunately, there was no legal mechanism that I could employ to force Yormak to produce. And he already had my $4,000.

After twelve months the case was still in limbo - nor had Hess reimbursed me for his portion of the advance. Yormak still would not speak with me - he continued to refuse to answer my calls, and he declined to return them. But he would talk with Hess occasionally upon other matters. I failed to understand why an attorney so steadfastly refused to speak with his client. The situation was abominable.

I finally lost my patience. I told Hess to fire Yormak and to have my money returned, then to find a Canadian attorney who would take action on the case. Hess forwarded my sentiments, after which Yormak would not return his calls, either. Hess then sent Yormak a formal letter of intent, requesting the return of the money.

This drastic measure forced a response from Yormak. He claimed that he had already expended the money in my behalf, and that there was none left to return. He was willing to quit the case at this point if I so desired. He was also willing to proceed by filing the suit. He would not require additional funding at this time. Hess and I discussed the matter. The $4,000 that "we" had invested in Yormak would be lost if we switched attorneys. So would a year of so-called legal research.

Hess tried hard to placate me. Finally I acquiesced, but only on the condition that Yormak speak with me directly. I wanted no more of a disembodied attorney. Yormak agreed to a conference call. At last we were ready to go to trial - or so I was led to believe.

A New Beginning

The three-way phone conversation lasted over an hour. At the end of our discussion I was firmly convinced that Yormak had done his research. His grasp of the case was profound. He rattled off case law like a college student reciting the ABC's. He suggested a multitude of offensives which the City might make, and had prepared not only a defense but a counteroffensive for each and every one. He opined on the fluidity of the City's resolve to try the case in court, because of the risk of losing possession of the wrecks; the City might prefer to settle out of court and let me dive. He also expounded upon the political pressures that could be brought to bear, and the possible permutations that the case could take with respect to government intervention.

Yormak instilled me with confidence - not only in him as an attorney, but in the likelihood of a successful outcome in setting another precedent for public access.

What I did not like was Yormak's strategy. He wanted me to submit another request to the City of Hamilton. To me this seemed like going back to the beginning, four years earlier. He wanted to initiate the lawsuit with a clean slate: that is, with a simple request and a simple denial, and not with any of the redundant bantering that characterized the previous requests. He would still utilize my foundation efforts to prove to the Court that my treatment was unwarranted and discriminatory, and that the City had not acted in good faith with respect to its pledged and mandated duties to promote and conduct studies of the wrecks. But he did not want to drag into court such distractions as the archaeological use of photographs or zebra mussel research.

He wanted to stay focused on two fundamental issues: my right to dive on the wrecks and take a few snapshots, and the City's failure to live up to its obligations to the U.S. Navy. These were pure and simple points of law. I argued against the delay, but he assured me that a new application would prove better in the long run. Eventually I acquiesced.

The saving grace was that he did not want me to apply for a license from the Archaeological Licence Bureau. As far as Yormak was concerned, I did not intend to conduct archaeology by any standard or definition of archaeology except for those which it suited Englebert to ordain. I did not have to prove that photography did not constitute archaeology. The Bureau had the onus of proving Englebert's artifice that photography *did* constitute archaeology.

The Fourth Denial

The Archaeological Licence Bureau had an official application form, but the City of Hamilton did not. My application was actually a letter of intent, similar to my previous ones but more simplified and less didactic. Under the heading I typed, "Re: Request to conduct recreational dives on the shipwrecks *Hamilton* and *Scourge*."

The letter was dated January 23, 1998. It was less than one page in length. I stressed the recreational aspect of the dives, noting, "This is strictly a sightseeing endeavor." I wanted to exclude photography altogether, but Yormak wanted me to keep it included. He did not foresee that an impartial judge would categorize photography as archaeology. Indeed, he wanted to clear the record in that regard.

I requested a reply within twenty-one days, so that I would have sufficient lead time to organize the trip. The City chose to keep me in limbo for several months. Havelka refused to take or return my phone calls, and did not reply to my follow-up correspondence.

In the mean time, the Canadian Travel Bureau approved funding to fly me to Newfoundland in order to dive on and photograph shipwrecks. The Bureau wanted to use my name to help advertise and promote diving tourism. I spent the first week of April 1998 diving on shipwrecks in the vicinity of St. John's - at the expense of the Canadian government. The true irony of the situation was that the Archaeological Licence Bureau was under the administration of the Canadian Travel Bureau, and at the bottom of the bureaucratic hierarchy. Thus one hand of the Travel Bureau craved the notoriety that my reputation could bring to wreck-diving, while another hand eschewed it.

The City's denial arrived three months overdue. City solicitor Philip Hooker wrote, "Too bad about the 21 days. Things take time."

The denial was the result of "the FIRST Report of the *Hamilton-Scourge* Steering Committee," and was dated March 31, 1998 (the day on which I departed Philadelphia and arrived in St. John's, in order to promote recreational diving). The capitalization of FIRST is not my emphasis, but the City's. After all these years, it seemed, an ad hoc committee was formed to make its very first report under the guise of the eponymous *Hamilton-Scourge* Steering Committee, which now formally existed (at least on paper) "as adopted by City Council." The so-called Committee declared:

"(a) That any expressions of interest to dive including the use of manned submersibles, remotely operated vehicles or anchoring in the vicinity of the *Hamilton* and *Scourge* sites other than for purposes required and authorized by the City of Hamilton to study and manage the site be declined; and,

"(b) That any requests received by the City by amateur or technical divers to dive or explore the *Hamilton* and *Scourge* Sites be received and applicants be advised of Council's position."

Included with the denial papers was this notification. "The business component will explore a range of viable options available as a result of scientific investigation. This will involve researching cultural tourism opportunities for the City of Hamilton using the ships as a tourism generator."

The City kept contradicting itself, at one time extolling the virtues of the wrecks as tourist attractions (or heritage attractions), then, when pressed upon this point, denying the declaration of such attractions, then later reinstating those attractions. These changing attitudes of convenience made the City seem wishy-washy. I thought that the City demonstrated municipal confusion at the very least, and opportunistic exploitation at the most. It appeared that the City wanted to utilize the wrecks as tourist attractions until a tourist diver professed an interest in seeing the attractions.

Similarly, the City maintained contradictory stances about raising the wrecks, claiming at one time that recovery was the primary protocol, then - when it better suited its purpose - claiming just the opposite.

The denial was delivered to my house while I was diving on shipwrecks in Newfoundland, and discussing the promotion of wreck-diving tourism with representatives of the local government and members of the press.

The situation was totally absurd. Yet the mercurial City minions were oblivious to their own wanton frivolity. There was no end to this silliness in sight.

Formal Complaint

The official denial made it possible for Yormak to file a "Notice of Application for Judicial Review." The action that is called an Application in Canada is called a Complaint in the U.S. Under any name, to me and most of the general populace it means a lawsuit. I was named as the Applicant, the City as the Respondent. In the States, I would be the Plaintiff and the City would be the Defendant. Yormak included an affidavit which he wrote and which I signed.

Hess reviewed the Application before it was filed. This surprised me, because I thought that he was supposed to *write* the Application, not just read what Yormak had written. Hess gave me to understand that the language and format of Canadian lawsuits made it imperative for Yormak to write the Application because of his experience with local procedure.

The City solicitor assigned to the case was Peter Barkwell. His first action in defense of the proceedings was to plead for postponement of the hearing. Barkwell wanted to stall the case because, should we prevail, there was still time to dive on the wrecks in the autumn before the City could file an appeal. In fact, I was prepared to commence diving operations on the day after the decision was rendered. I made charter arrangements and contacted potential participants to be ready to go on a moment's notice. This pre-emptive strike would knock the wind out of the sails of the City's appeal, making it groundless in view of a fait accompli.

Postponement was a typical legal maneuver. The reader should bear in mind that the City had already stymied me for more than three years (after which my own attorney stymied me for another year). Barkwell pleaded that the "rocket docket" that Yormak wanted to pursue would interfere with his vacation. When this excuse failed to find Yormak's favorable ear, he initiated other delaying practices that would serve to offset the hearing until late autumn or winter, when icing conditions on Lake Ontario and frigid water temperatures would preclude any diving until the following spring. He claimed that because of the complexities of the case, he needed time to prepare documents and witnesses.

Barkwell submitted to the Court the affidavit of Phillip Hooker. Hooker stated that he was a City solicitor who had "been involved in responses to requests from the Applicant, Gary Gentile, under the Municipal Freedom of Information and Protection of Privacy Act," and that as a result he had some knowledge of the history of my attempts to obtain permission from the City to dive on the wrecks. Hooker took exception to the fact that in none of my many requests for permission did I submit a precise date on which diving operations would occur.

This was putting the cart before the horse. A precise date was irrelevant until I had obtained the requisite permission. Hooker's stance suggested that the City would have granted permission had I furnished a precise date and time. This was patently absurd.

However, Hooker noted not without validity, "The experts whose evidence will be required by the City of Hamilton are neither City of Hamilton employees nor resident in the immediate vicinity of the City of Hamilton. It will take a considerable period of time to assemble the evidence in a proper manner for presentation to the Court."

Provincial Intervention

My suit was against the City of Hamilton, but Englebert convinced the Ministry to intervene on behalf of the City. The lead attorney for the Ministry of the Attorney General was Anita Lyon. She submitted the affidavit of Elaine Atkinson, a Ministry solicitor. Her bone of contention was that Yormak had not submitted a complete record of the correspondence between me and the City, and that it would take time to compile these documents for review by the Court.

On the face of it this notion was absurd. The City and the Ministry each had a battery of lawyers working on the case, supported by a plethora of clerks, secretaries, and legal aides. The manpower (or personpower) that the City and the Ministry could bring to bear was enormous. They had unlimited legal resources and unrestricted funding. Yormak was a sole practitioner, and so far I was the sole source of funding.

Yormak contended that any history that predated my latest request for permission was irrelevant. The only item at issue was my latest proposal, not any of my previous proposals or associated correspondence. My fourth request was a stand-alone.

Atkinson noted that the Ministry's expert witness was one Peter Englebert, and that the impending trial was likely to interfere with his vacation plans. By these disclosures, vacation seemed to be an important aspect of the defense's strategy.

Atkinson tried to draw a parallel between Cousteau's expedition and mine, noting, "At one point Cousteau's *Soucoupe*, a submersible, touched the wreck. This broke the small hatch cover on the forward deck chain locker." It seemed absurd to me that anyone could contend that a free-floating individual diver could not exercise better control than a multi-ton submersible.

A great deal of correspondence transpired between Yormak and Barkwell, most of which I have never seen. I called Yormak periodically for status reports. He never answered my calls and maintained his policy of refusing to return my calls. I left questions with his secretary, and sometimes she would relay messages to me when I called again. But I never spoke with Yormak. Hess acted distant with respect to the case. He did not appear to have been doing any work on it. We held philosophical discussions by telephone, but these did nothing to promote the cause.

The summer passed in endless and fruitless debate. Yormak and Barkwell did not go to court to argue their points in front of a judge until September 15, in Toronto. Also in attendance at the hearing was Anita Lyon. All parties agreed on dates for depositions to be taken. In addition, the defendants agreed that urgency was no longer an issue, on the understanding that if the court found in my behalf, I could dive on the wrecks the following year without additional legal interference.

Last Minute Affidavit

On September 28, Lyon submitted the affidavit of Peter Waddell in order to bolster the Ministry's case. He stated, "That I am a Marine Archaeologist and Diving Officer employed with the Marine Archaeology Unit of Parks Canada and, further that I am a member of the Technical Study Team for the *Hamilton-Scourge* Project, and as such have knowledge of the matters hereinafter deposed to."

Waddell contended that, although he was not a technical diver himself, "I have knowledge of the requirements of technical diving." I could just as easily state that I know that it takes a rocket to fly to the Moon, but I cannot build or fly one myself.

"Any diver who was intending to photograph or video a wreck would be required to carry with him or herself battery packs, lighting equipment and camera equipment." This was no revelation. I do not know any photographers who are skilled enough to take pictures without a camera.

He contended that scuba gear "would make it cumbersome for a diver to manoeuver [sic] in the water." His belief was not based upon experience. Skilled divers routinely handled their equipment with facility and ease.

"Visibility at these wreck sites is severely limited to zero, and as a result photography of these wrecks or their artifacts would have to be conducted at extremely close range." This statement was stupid. Photography was *impossible* in zero visibility. Margaret Rule found the visibility in 1988 to range between three and ten feet.

"In conditions of total darkness," he believed that "the diver's field of view is limited to the area illuminated by his or her lights, everything outside the beam of light become effectively invisible to the diver." This is nonsense, as anyone can determine by walking in the dark with a flashlight. The perimeter of the cone of light is not a stark line of demarcation, beyond which total blackness and invisibility exist. The flashlight beam diffuses subdued light outside of the perimeter to illuminate nearby areas softly.

Waddell's reason for making this allegation was that "it would be virtually inevitable that divers approaching these wrecks close enough to obtain photographs would come into contact with the wrecks." This statement served only to demonstrate his lack of dark-water experience. Nor did it account for the successful photographs of the *Hamilton* and *Scourge* that had been taken by submersibles and ROV's under identical conditions.

He contended that the proximity of divers would disrupt and dislodge artifacts and human remains from their current position. He neglected to mention how the presence of divers would do this, and how the presence of submersibles and ROV's averted this.

"To date the wrecks of the *Hamilton* and *Scourge* have neither been inventoried nor mapped." Here he was taking words right out of my mouth, for it was *my* contention that in twenty years the City had done nothing with regard to the wrecks. It was a godsend to have someone on the Technical Study Team confirm the City's total lack of action.

He claimed that many objects had "near neutral buoyancy" because "the objects have a density which approximates the density of the water." This nonsense was justification for his contention that these objects would be disturbed by a diver's fin wash. This not only showed his ignorance of anti-silting techniques (the frog kick), but failed to address how these objects were not disturbed or dislodged by the prop wash of submersibles and ROV's. I was prepared to testify that I had photographed human skeletal remains without disturbing them.

Another absurd concept that he tried to assert was that the disruption of silt "by the finning action of divers" would "remove or destroy the record of . . . sediment formation." He contended, "Since we know the moment of their sinking almost to the hour, this silt represents a record of sediment formation in this part of Lake Ontario from 1813 to the present." He must not have read Rule's report, in which she noted the daily appearance of waterborne silt which settled on the wreck and on the bottom, to the extent of filling in the grooves that were made by the ROV's runners. Rule also commented on how the accumulation of silt was blown off the sites by periodic currents which she described as "noticeable." He also ignored the proliferation of fish, whose fins have been washing silt off the wreck for nearly two hundred years. The bottom of Lake Ontario was a dynamic environment, not a laboratory bell jar in which sedimentology experiments could be conducted with even the faintest degree of accuracy.

Finally, "Looting of the site is inevitable." What this allegation had to do with taking photographs was incomprehensible to me.

Yormak and I were not in the least concerned by Waddell's spurious and self-serving statements. Perhaps Lyon, in her ignorance, was convinced of their validity; or perhaps she hoped that she could hoodwink the judge into swallowing Waddell's gaff. But hundreds of expert witnesses could be found to refute Waddell's juvenile remarks and his unsubstantiated opinions.

The City's Legal Response

Barkwell submitted his response to my Application. Yormak sent me a copy and asked for comments. In addition to those items that I have already addressed, in either this or the previous chapter, I found other idiosyncrasies which needed to be addressed in the upcoming depositions. I annotated the City's response and sent them to Yormak.

Havelka openly admitted in Point 62 that the City of Hamilton considered me personally to be a competitor, claiming that if I made my photographs available to the public, it would reduce the City's ability to make money off the wrecks. In a professed democratic society, it is patently illegal for any government agency to use its authority to stifle free enterprise. From Havelka's admission and from the tenor of the City's previously forced replies to my queries, I thought it not unlikely that the City was afraid that my dive trip would steal the City's thunder. Since the proliferation of technical diving, dives to the depths of the *Hamilton* and *Scourge* had become commonplace; they no longer held the awe that was held by prior generations.

Havelka's Point 63 tried to make a big deal out of the fact that I did not include in my affidavit the names of divers or the name of the boat that I planned to charter, as if this had some relevance to the City's denial. As I noted above, this information was like putting the cart before the horse. She neglected to mention that I *had* included that information in one of my previous proposals, which the City wanted included in the court documents when it suited its purpose to do so.

Barkwell noted in several instances that the City considered the *Hamilton* and *Scourge* to be "heritage attractions," again contradicting its avowed goals with respect to raising the wrecks in order to increase tourism. I noted, "This will respond to Englebert's comment about my referring to the wrecks as 'tourist attractions.'" Even Mayor Morrow wrote to a Ms. Copps how "the business component will address cultural tourism." Barkwell's inclusion of this letter as part of the City's court documents implies how little he understood the ramifications of the City's attitude. As if he were contesting his own allegations, on page 7 Barkwell openly discussed the "business component" and "tourism appeal" of the wrecks.

I also noted that I never sought exclusivity. "There is no reason why the CofH cannot conduct archaeological studies on the wrecks concurrently with recreational diving trips - not at the same time of course, but there can be no logical reason for not allowing divers to see the sites when no archaeological work was being done - especially as to date NO such work has been done. Thus there is no reason why rec diving should impede scientific studies (which at this point are only imaginary)."

I suggested that Yormak demand the release of documents that had been withheld from me by FOIA exclusions. In lawsuits, the rule of discovery relies upon the "full disclosure" of documents. This expressly written law meant that the City and the Province were *required* to release *all* documents, even those that were harmful or prejudicial to its case.

Provincial Response

Lyon submitted the Ministry's response. Again, Yormak sent me a copy and asked for comments. Not unexpectedly, most of Lyon's objections were Englebert's reiterations, all of which had already been overcome. Neither she nor Barkwell ever submitted anything having to do with case law.

For example, in point 39 on page 12, Englebert harped about control and maneuverability. In point 42 on page 13, he commented on the movement of silt. In points 75 and 76 on page 22, he raised the issue of commercial diving operations and OSHA regulations. From Lyon's wording, it appeared that Englebert neglected to mention that Pina Pilosi had already defused this issue, and that I had received an exemption from John Mitchell. Englebert may have been feeding his own ego with these overtly false observations and obviously faked protests, but by deluding Lyon about their supposed validity he put her case at a disadvantage. She would go to court with an empty gun - or worse, one in which the cartridges were likely to backfire into her face.

A case may be won by the submission of a single authentic objection, but it cannot be won by the repetitive submission of easily disputable claims.

Excursion to Canada

The depositions were slated to take place in Toronto. Before Yormak would agree to appear, he wanted another $2,000 for expenses. Once again Hess pleaded a temporary shortage of funds. I was already in debt. I had just published another book, and the capital outlay to pay my printer had put my finances in the red. Worse yet, book sales were down due to the suffering economy, so the recuperative power of my financial position was suspect. The one saving grace was that my credit was good. I could borrow my half of the money that was needed to pay for Yormak's expenses. Hess claimed that he was not in a position to borrow, but that he was trying to obtain funding from other sources. He asked me to borrow money on his account. I did.

The time frame for the depositions was so changeable - and so much subject to Canadian vacation schedules - that there was little advance notice of when I was to appear. By the time the lawyers for the defense agreed to a date - the week of October 13 - last minute plane reservations would have cost more than a thousand dollars. As I was already in debt I had to pinch my pennies. I had intended to carpool with Hess, sharing automobile expenses and hotel costs. But several days before the deposition, Hess decided - for reasons that he did not make clear to me - not to attend the depositions. I reminded him that it was his job to conduct the depositions, not Yormak's. But Hess would not accept this important responsibility. He had other things that he would rather do.

Hess's sudden abandonment left me decidedly in the lurch. I did not want to drive all that distance alone. Instead, I chose to travel by train.

Unlike air fares, train tickets could be purchased on the spot without incurring any penalties. The price was always the same. I bought a roundtrip ticket for $164. I took some work to edit on the train, but for the part of the trip I read and had a relaxing all-day ride. The autumn foliage was at its height in northern New York State. The trees were ablaze with color, from fiery reds to striking browns and oranges, interspersed with lingering greens.

Not until I reached the Canadian border did I learn that the train went no farther. By this time night had fallen. I transferred to a bus for the remainder of the trip. I tried to get some rest. The seat that was extraordinarily comfortable for sitting was equally *un*comfortable for sleeping. It was two o'clock in the morning when the bus arrived at the terminal in Toronto. By that time the station was closed and the doors were locked to keep out the homeless. The other passengers had rides waiting for them, or took cabs to an ultimate destination. A light rain was falling.

I had nowhere to go. Yormak lived in London, about an hour and a half to the west. He was spending the night in a fancy hotel in Toronto. I had asked him if I could share his room (for which I was paying), but he spurned my request. When Hess chose not to accompany me, he also chose not to share the expenses of the trip. I could not afford to pay for a room of my own. I intended to sleep in the bus station until daylight.

The bus driver had a key to the door of the station but would not let me enter. He explained that, once the station closed at midnight, it was not open to the public until six o'clock in the morning. I argued softly that I had nowhere else to wait. Eventually, and only because I was a paying passenger, he let me in to use the restroom. I stayed in the restroom an inordinately long time, hoping that he would leave and forget about me. He entered the restroom to check on me. He then told me that I could remain inside the terminal as long as I wanted. The doors opened from the inside but not from the outside. He cautioned me not to let anyone else inside. I agreed.

I lay down on the cold linoleum floor and, using my backpack for a pillow, closed my eyes. I slept fitfully for several hours, curled on my side in order to contain my quickly fading body heat. The lights grew brighter, and the tomblike silence grew louder after early morning travelers arrived and occupied nearby seats. I arose at 6:30 (according to the station clock - I did not wear a watch). In the restroom I splashed water onto my face and combed my hair. I obtained a map of the city from the tourist rack of advertising brochures. The rain was falling hard in the predawn darkness. I donned my rain parka and backpack.

I walked along the deserted streets until I found an open cafe. I bought a large coffee to go. I sipped the hot liquid as I maintained my course for Yormak's hotel. I sat in the lobby and finished drinking my coffee, absorbing the warmth of both internal and external heat. I had never met Yormak and did not know what he looked like. Around eight o'clock I called his room from the front desk. He was about to come down for breakfast.

I stood at a designated location so he could pick me out of the crowd. I was the only person carrying a backpack. Yormak's greeting was warm and heartfelt.

We shook hands, then migrated toward the dining room. He ordered a full breakfast. I glanced at the menu. A six-ounce cup of coffee cost three times as much as the twelve-ounce cup that I had already consumed. Two slices of buttered toast cost as much as a full course meal anywhere else. I was famished, but could not afford to pay such exorbitant prices.

Yormak told me to order anything I wanted; he would put the charges on his room bill. With a perfectly straight face, he said, "I'm on an expense account."

He expressed no sign of irony over the curious circumstance that I was the one who was funding his padded expense account. Any charges that I placed on his expense account he was going to bill me for later. I did not bring this obvious fact to his attention.

Havelka Deposes for the City of Hamilton

Over his breakfast we discussed the results of the previous day's depositions, with Marilyn Havelka and Lorne Murdock. In attendance at the depositions were Yormak, Barkwell (for the City), Lyon (for the Ministry), and court reporter Nancy Lowrey.

Yormak sent me a copy of the transcript several weeks later. Havelka was not as forthright as she could have been. Often, several pages of transcript were required to obtain an answer to a simple yes-or-no question. Yet Yormak's dialogue never showed signs of frustration. He treated Havelka as he would treat a recalcitrant lawn mower, whose motor required multiple pulls of the cord to start.

To be fair, Havelka was placed in the unenviable position of having to substantiate an affidavit to which her signature was appended, but which she clearly had not written. The language indicated that her affidavit had been written by the City's legal staff, and in such a way as to present the City's side of the case in the most favorable light. Thus Havelka had to defend points with which she was unfamiliar, and which for the most part were irrational and indefensible.

Yormak laid the groundwork for each question before he reached the salient point. He embarked upon a sequential line of reasoning whose end was unknowable to Havelka in advance, but whose logical conclusion became inescapable. By his clever use of polemics, he overrode her inclination to make justifications, and led her to make admissions which she and her attorney, Peter Barkwell, tried desperately to wangle out of by means of misdirection.

Havelka stated that, prior to (and subsequent to) the City's acquisition of the *Hamilton* and *Scourge*, the City had never engaged in an historic restoration project that exceeded $100,000 in cost. Although she had worked for the City in various capacities for twenty-seven years, she claimed to have no knowledge of why the City got involved with the wrecks in the first place: she did not know if the Royal Ontario Museum had suggested the transfer of title, or if the City had asked to be the recipient. She did not even know who *would* know. The provenance of the succession of title had either been lost to history through poor record keeping, or - according to Barkwell - might be buried in the tens of thousands of *Hamilton/Scourge* documents that he claimed the City possessed.

In any event, the City enacted special legislation that enabled it to own property that lay outside the jurisdiction of the municipality. Yormak was unable to ascertain if prior knowledge of the forward lateral from the Royal Ontario Museum to the City of Hamilton had been intentionally withheld from the U.S. Navy.

The only connection between the City and the wrecks was the coincidental similarity of names: the wreck of the *Hamilton* and the City of Hamilton. The wrecks were not located in Hamilton Harbor, and were not even physically close to the City. According to Havelka, the wrecks were located 20 to 30 miles from the City of Hamilton, off Port Dalhousie, at a distance of - again, according to Havelka - six miles from shore.

Even without the transfer of title, Havelka believed that the federal government of Canada could exercise a claim to the wrecks because, although they belonged to the U.S. Navy at the time of their loss, they sank in Canadian waters and could therefore be considered as prizes of war. In her opinion, a third potential claimant was the Province of Ontario, because it had jurisdiction over the lakebed. Yormak suggested gratuitously that, by her line of reasoning, if someone dropped a diamond ring on the lakebed, the Province could lay a claim to ownership.

Inactivity and Lack of Authority

When asked about the status of the so-called *Hamilton/Scourge* Project, Havelka admitted that the Feasibility Study - which had been firmly mandated by the U.S. Navy in the transfer assignment nearly twenty years earlier, had yet to be conducted. The Feasibility Study was a necessary prerequisite to determining if the wrecks could be recovered and placed on display, or preserved in situ. "Preserved in situ" was an evasive archaeological term of misdirection, which meant "left to rot."

When asked why the City had failed to obtain the 4,000 images that had been generated by the Jason Project in 1990, she claimed, "it hadn't been determined if we needed that information to proceed with the project."

With respect to diving on the wrecks, Yormak called her attention to the official document which stipulated that if the wrecks were not raised, they should be considered as future recreational dive sites. She acknowledged the existence of the document, but said that before diving on the wrecks could be permitted, guidelines would have to be written in that regard. When pressed about the timeframe for such an occurrence, she not only could not provide a year, she could not provide a *decade*.

When Havelka was not evasive enough, Barkwell helped by interrupting and trying to distract Yormak from the issue. Yormak dealt professionally with Barkwell's interruptions, but was never distracted from the primary question, and kept returning to it indefatigably.

It took twenty pages of questions, evasions, and Barkwell's constant interruptions for Yormak to obtain an answer to his question about the City's authority to regulate the wreck sites. Eventually, however, Havelka was forced to admit that nowhere in the municipal bylaws did the City possess any legal authority to regulate the sites, nor to determine who could visit them. City representatives merely acted on assumption, or self-serving bureaucratic fiat.

Havelka claimed that the *Hamilton* and *Scourge* were archaeological sites. When ask why, she responded, "They're archaeological sites because an archaeological license has been issued." This was a stupidly constructed *a priori* justification.

It took two pages of transcript to record her evasions to Yormak's questions about who she consulted about my proposal. Under Yormak's persistent questioning, she eventually could not avoid admitting that she had spoken with Peter Englebert. She also finally admitted that she had spoken with John Broadwater, the manager of the *Monitor* National Marine Sanctuary, and the person with whom I had dealt the most after prevailing in court in obtaining permission to dive on the *Monitor*. She did not elaborate, but I told Yormak afterward that Broadwater had eventually changed his opinion about permitting recreational divers on the *Monitor*. He had come to learn that they were a free and valuable resource. Havelka did not obtain any commiseration from Broadwater.

Yormak asked Havelka to comment on the letter in which Bernice Field admitted that my proposed recreational diving activity could not be construed as a commercial venture. Lyon made several objections. Yormak reminded Lyon that Barkwell was Havelka's counsel, not Lyon, and that according to procedure she did not have the right to raise objections during the cross-examination of another counsel's witness. Lyon could be present and listen as an interested party, but she could not participate in the proceedings.

Barkwell and Lyon then ganged up on Yormak in order to prevent Havelka from having to answer. But Yormak parried their legal arguments and kept thrusting to the heart of the matter. This particular sparring session occupied ten pages of the transcript. Barkwell absurdly tried to claim that there was no way of knowing that Field was referring to the *Hamilton* and *Scourge* when she wrote her letter. Yormak reminded Barkwell that my correspondence with Field involved *only* the *Hamilton* and *Scourge*, and not any other hypothetical shipwrecks.

In the end, Barkwell advised his client not to answer the question, and there the matter rested.

It took two more pages of evasions, and interruptions by both attorneys, before Havelka was forced to admit that "sightseeing" (as specifically stated in my fourth request) did not imply a commercial enterprise.

The Charge of Discrimination

Havelka admitted that during the time that I was seeking permission from the City, the City received two other private sector proposals which were reviewed and which were given consideration. Negotiations broke down and the prospective participants went on to other projects. These proposals were contained in documents that were withheld pursuant to my FOIA request. Havelka danced around the issue, claiming only that she thought one of the proposals included the possibility of returning one of the wrecks to the United States. She admitted involvement by the National Geographic Society.

Barkwell claimed that these proposals were irrelevant because they had not been granted. Yormak claimed that they *were* relevant because they had been *considered* before they were rejected, whereas my proposal had never even been considered, nor received peer review, but was rejected out of hand. The City's contradictory actions implied discrimination, which was definitely relevant to our case.

That was not the only case of discrimination. Mayor Ross Fair directed Therese Charbonneau and Ania Latoszek to facilitate the dive that was proposed by Frederick Eaton. After four pages of transcript and evasive maneuvers, Havelka was forced to admit that the recommendation was made to permit Eaton's dive in a submersible. That the dive was not conducted was irrelevant.

Another relevant feature of the Eaton recommendation was the conditional $200,000 "donation." Barkwell advised his client not to answer any questions in that regard.

In my opinion, the most important issue about the wreck sites was: what constitutes trespass? In this regard, I had suggested a strategy which Yormak anticipated independently, and which he implemented with fluent perfection that I could never have achieved in oral argument.

The City claimed that the *Hamilton* and *Scourge* were municipal properties to which public access could be denied. These wrecks were equivalent to buildings from which the City could bar public entry. For the sake of argument I will accept the City's position (although that position is disputable). Was it constituted as trespass if I stood a hundred yards from the City-owned, publicly-closed building? Was it constituted as trespass if I stood fifty feet from the building? What about ten feet? Five feet? One foot?

Not until I *entered* the building did the legal concept of trespass become meaningful. Or, I will grant, if I damaged the building's facade. Yormak made a similar comparison to Havelka, using her car as an example. "Is that trespass?"

After four pages of prompting, Havelka grudgingly admitted, "No."

The Grand Confession

Thus the City's prime witness made a number of astonishing admissions: that the City had never conducted the Feasibility Study that was mandated by the transfer of title; that the City was not presently in the process of conducting such a study; that the City possessed no legal authority to regulate the sites or to prevent visitation; that sightseeing did not constitute archaeology; that photography was not a tacit commercial activity; and that close approach to the wrecks did not imply trespass.

Yormak did not elicit these admissions by accident. He knew the answers to his questions before he asked them. He knew because he had researched the relevant case law, had read the City's bylaws, and had studied the available documents that related to the *Hamilton* and *Scourge*. In short, he had done his homework thoroughly. He also had an encyclopedic knowledge of local legislation, and a universal understanding of its applications.

What was almost as astonishing as Havelka's nefarious admissions was her self-avowed ignorance. Again and again she professed that she did not know the answer to Yormak's questions. For example, although she stated that she was a member of the Technical Study Team, she was unable to name all the other members of the Team. Some of the people she mentioned had long since resigned. Furthermore, she admitted that she had no technical expertise. It also became apparent that some of the other members shared her lack of expertise. Thus it comes as no surprise that the Team had never accomplished anything, and was not in the process of accomplishing anything.

The Technical Study Team was an illusion that existed solely on paper: hocus-pocus to confuse the public.

Civil Disobedience

In my initial conceptualization of the *Hamilton/Scourge* case, I considered employing the concept of civil disobedience to achieve my goal of freeing the wrecks from the bonds of bureaucracy. The dictionary meaning of civil disobedience is the "refusal to obey civil laws in an effort to induce change in governmental policy or legislation, characterized by the use of passive resistance or other nonviolent means."

As an expressed philosophy, civil disobedience goes all the way back to Roman orator Marcus Tullius Cicero, in the first century before Christ. He protested the assassination of Julius Caesar, and was executed for his outspoken criticism. Perhaps the most famous historical proponent of civil disobedience was Jesus Christ, who was crucified as a political agitator because of his moral teachings of the coming of the kingdom of God. Other well-known individuals who defied the law by employing nonviolent measures were Thomas Aquinas, Henry David Thoreau, Bertrand Russell, Mahatma Gandhi, and Martin Luther King, Jr. Movements involving collective labor, antiwar, and civil rights are all examples of civil disobedience; they utilized strikes, sit-downs, and organized protests to promote their causes.

Any free democratic society should welcome civil disobedience as a means of testing unjust or unpopular laws. Many unsung heroes have accepted arrest in order to influence lawmakers and to compel government concessions. These people felt obligated by a principle that was greater than the law of the land. The disadvantage of civil disobedience is that it characterizes the protester as a law breaker. The protester has his day in court, but he may be judged by the letter of the law rather than by the spirit of the law. He may go to jail without winning his point; or he may win his point without effecting the desired change. Even with numerous followers and the moral support of the public, a protester may pay severe penalties for his "crimes" against authority. Civil disobedience is not a perfect solution.

Hess advised me not to take such a tack because it would brand me as a law breaker and would put me on the defensive. By challenging the City of Hamilton, he opined that the City would be put on the defensive. His legal advice was sound with respect to what we knew about the situation at the time. In retrospect, however, in light of the information that Yormak ascertained from Havelka, I now believe that civil disobedience would have worked.

If I had ignored the City completely and dived on the wrecks, it would have been beholden upon the City to prove that I had broken some local law. Acting against the "wishes" of City bureaucrats was not the same as breaking the law. However, it was too late for me as an individual to change my strategy. Someone else would have to force the issue by means of civil disobedience, and to place the burden of proof upon the City.

Incomplete Test Case

Enter Scott McWilliam: a father of two children, a former Thunder Bay police officer, a technical diver, and a college graduate with the same degree in archaeology that Peter Englebert possessed. According to McWilliam, Englebert had taken a course in technical diving, but did not display sufficient skill to his instructor to be granted certification. Having failed in his training, Englebert was therefore limited to diving at depths of less than 130 feet. McWilliam, on the other hand, had conducted a successful archaeological survey of the wreck of the *Gunilda*, which lay in 250 feet of water off Rossport, Ontario. McWilliam received his archaeological license from Englebert - but not without having to jump through Englebert's multitudinous hoops.

I had met and spoken with McWilliam at a diving symposium. He was well aware of my ongoing efforts.

In the summer of 1997, McWilliam let it be known that he had made four dives on the wreck of the *Hamilton*. His supposed dives were conducted in 1995, without City knowledge or approval, and without an archaeological license. He was accompanied by four unnamed companions. He brought his dives to the attention of the press in order to alert the media that he planned to dive on the wreck again several weeks later. His bold defiance forced an hysterical response from Marilyn Havelka, who issued a warning to the effect that the City was prepared to prosecute anyone caught diving on the *Hamilton* or *Scourge*.

According to one correspondent, if McWilliam "ends up in court and successfully challenges the provincial law, authorities might not be able to prevent others from diving on significant shipwrecks throughout the Great Lakes. He is arguing the city does not have the power to stop him from diving over the shipwreck and he doesn't believe he needs an archaeological licence from the province because he's just going to look at the vessel."

McWilliam was quoted as stating, "We're going to test this. . . . We're going to be the test case. . . . What exactly is the crime here? . . . I have no intention of touching or entering upon the City of Hamilton's property."

Despite Englebert's continual false pronouncements, McWilliam knew the truth, and wrote: "There are no powers of arrest, search or seizure under the Ontario Heritage Act."

The hysteria escalated when the rumor was spread that divers were presently on one of the sites. Havelka called the police and the Canadian Coast Guard, who rushed to the sites but found no one there. Afterward, Hamilton-Wentworth constable Brian Smyth said, "officers who went to the site last week weren't too sure what charge they could have laid if divers had been found. 'If he's doing what he says he's doing, I don't know whether he's breaking the law.' "

Rui Fernandes, a Toronto lawyer who specialized in maritime law, "also questions the powers of the province and the City. He notes shipwrecks have traditionally fallen under jurisdiction of the federal government through the Canadian Shipping Act. 'It's always been easy for the province to say this because of heritage, but it doesn't wash. . . . I don't know of anywhere else where you can't dive and observe. I don't know anyplace that prevents you from diving on a shipwreck unless they can prove you're damaging it.' "

Despite these supporting sentiments, when the day of the proposed dive arrived, McWilliam and his cohorts backed down from a confrontation with police. I have always thought that this was a shame. The *threat* of civil disobedience proves nothing. It must be acknowledged, however, that civil disobedience may prove costly - not only with respect to a possible jail sentence, but in paying an attorney to provide representation in court. An individual may go broke in his own defense. With unlimited prosecutorial funding, the state always has the advantage.

Many cases are lost because of inadequate finances.

In light of his claim to having already dived on the *Hamilton*, Yormak asked Havelka why the City had not filed charges against McWilliam. She said, "I have no proof that he did." Even so, pressed Yormak, did the City not have an obligation to investigate the matter? She said, "I don't believe he did. I don't think he has been to the site."

After all the hoopla that McWilliam generated, Havelka and the City were content to treat his allegation with disdain: an ostrich posture that was seemingly not in keeping with the City's attitude. This lack of follow-up appears remarkable - until one realizes how uncertain are the City's legal grounds, especially in light of Havelka's grand confessions.

In my opinion, the City did not take McWilliam to court because it was afraid of losing the case.

Murdock Deposes for the Ministry

No overt surprises resulted from Murdock's deposition. He was a self-employed consultant who had previously worked as a conservator for Parks Canada. He was a paid member of the so-called Technical Study Team. In 1988, he was one of the Team that wrote the proposal for the feasibility study. To be clear, the Team did not conduct a feasibility study, it merely wrote a proposal that *recommended* a feasibility study. He admitted that the proposed feasibility study had never been conducted.

Murdock was not a technical diver. In his opinion the *Hamilton* and *Scourge* were archaeological sites. His knowledge of the sites was based upon reviewing the images taken from the three photographic expeditions: Jacques Cousteau, National Geographic, and Woods Hole. He believed that the sites were deteriorating due to floral and faunal action, chemical reduction, and abrasion from particulates that were driven by current.

In his view, archaeological sites needed to be surveyed before permitting public access. This was the protocol adopted at Fathom Five Provincial Park in Tobermory. Divers were not given access to the wrecks until after site plans were prepared. Since the Tobermory wrecks had not been raised and preserved, Yormak asked Murdock to explain how Parks Canada handled or treated the wrecks.

Murdock: "Almost uniformly the approach among the professional community today is to manage resources in situ, and only under special circumstances would somebody consider recovering shipwrecks today."

When pressed upon the point of in situ management with respect to public access to the wrecks in Tobermory, Murdock acknowledge that the most effective management tools were fines and education: fines as an after measure, education as a preventative measure. "Divers and dive charter operators are the ones responsible for the most part. Policing the divers and the divers are policing themselves." Then, he added a stupid and self-serving statement: "On a deep water wreck, that would be an extremely difficult objective."

It appeared that Murdock believed - at least for the purpose of this case - that divers could be held on their own recognizance in shallow water, but that they became irresponsible in deep water. I fail to understand how depth can affect a person's moral responsibility.

The Fin Test

Murdock stated that he and a colleague conducted a "finning" test on some 1749 French wrecks that lay in 40 feet of water in Louisburg Harbor. This was not a controlled laboratory test. No formal report was ever written for publication or peer review. They bought some glass bottles at a flea market, placed them loosely on the bottom, and caused them to move by the hydraulic action of fins from a distance of three feet. They also blew the sand out of brass disks. They conducted no tests on embedded artifacts. Lyon refused to try to produce any substantiating materials to which Murdock alluded: field notes, videotapes, and so on.

Murdock either failed to understand or refused to accept that the most novice reef diver could swim past a coral head without disturbing accumulated silt in the slightest, or that cave-divers employed the frog kick to prevent the disturbance of mud on the bottom, or that experienced wreck-divers moved slowly and employed common anti-silting techniques during the exploration of shipwrecks. Underwater photographers are especially sensitive to fin and body movements, because suspended particles can cause backscatter in their photographs. Murdock proved only that, if he tried hard enough, he could create a disturbance in the water.

Yormak read the sentence in the Rule report that noted, "The lake bed is a smooth layer of fine silts. These are colonized by amphipods and small fish sculpin which scurry about stirring up the fine silt."

Yormak: "Wouldn't that scurrying about be akin to the finning you're talking about?"

Murdock: "Having not been there and observed these fish, I can't really comment."

Yormak: "Well, you commented on everything else and you haven't been there, so I'm asking you if you can comment on that."

Murdock: "Well, I have expertise with regards to finning. I don't have any expertise with regards to how much silt an individual fish or fish stir up."

Yormak pointed out Rule's observation of periodic currents which reduced visibility because of particulate matter in the water. Murdock continued to avoid the obvious conclusion, but after fourteen pages of transcript he was forced to concede that fish and current disturbed the silt on the wrecks of the *Hamilton* and *Scourge*, to the point at which the decks were swept nearly clean.

A Seesaw Defense

The position of the defense was considerably weakened by the facts in Rule's report. These facts contradicted the fabricated notions which the City and the Ministry wanted to assert before the court. In attempting to deny and obscure the evidence of a respected scientist's observations, Murdock abnegated his ethical responsibility to provide an unbiased opinion as an expert witness. Either he lacked impartiality, or he was willing to recite the words which the defense lawyers had placed in his mouth.

In his affidavit he claimed that the reduced level of oxygen contributed to a decreased rate of deterioration. The implication was that the oxygen level was reduced as a function of depth. When pressed upon this point, however, he explained that he was referring to objects that were buried in the mud or clay bottom sediment, and which were therefore insulated from oxygen in the water.

Murdock refused to comment on the number of artifacts - if any - that were teeter-tottering, in which position they could be "teetered" or "tottered" by water movement.

After Murdock completed the defense of his affidavit, Lyon tried to introduce a new item of information. From the groundwork that preceded her question, it seemed to me that she wanted him to state that technical divers could not capture images that were as clear as those that could be captured by an ROV, because of differences in resolution quality with respect to the distance between the lens and the subject matter under conditions of low light and limited visibility.

Yormak refused to allow Murdock answer the question because the issue was not addressed in his affidavit. According to the rules of procedure, afterthoughts were not permitted, and an attorney could not cross examine her own witness on points that had not already been established. After some discussion between attorneys, Murdock answered the question for the record, but his answer was to be withheld from the court unless Lyon could establish justification for its inclusion.

In the event, Murdock apparently misunderstood the point to which Lyon was trying to lead him. "I didn't notice any difference of videotape versus the live broadcast on the monitor." If Lyon had coached her witness better, he might have been able to create an appropriate falsehood.

Chapter 5
Deposition Days

D-day

I have given a number of depositions in my life. None lasted more than two hours. This one lasted two *days*. I was hoping to save hotel expenses by returning home that afternoon, and sleeping overnight on the train (sitting up). The opposition had another scheme in mind.

From an emotional standpoint my deposition was easy, because I did not have anything to hide. All I had to do was answer questions truthfully. I did not equivocate, and I did not give evasive, misleading, or ambiguous answers. I had no need, even if it had been in my nature to do so. I answered immediately and comprehensively, without additional prompting - unless I did not understand the question, in which case I asked for clarification. If my forthright reply raised eyebrows of misunderstanding, I added description and explanatory information.

Ranged against me on the opposite side of the table was a solid phalanx of belligerent individuals: Peter Barkwell, Anita Lyon, Peter Englebert, and Marilyn Havelka. Englebert and Havelka were not permitted to speak or intercede. Havelka observed unobtrusively, but Englebert took copious notes and shoved sheets of paper to in front of the attorneys. Barkwell was my first inquisitor.

Barkwell showed surprise when, in response to his preliminary questions about my educational background, I informed him that I had gone to college for a year and a half before being drafted between semesters - my majors were geology, archaeology, and paleontology. After serving in the Army, I did not return to college but pursued a career in construction as a commercial and industrial electrician. Despite the discontinuance of my formal education, I had read more than one hundred books on archaeology, anthropology, geology, paleontology, and related scientific subjects concerning the physical and cultural evolution of mankind. I had written more than a dozen books on nautical history. I had written two tutorials on wreck-diving, one of which included a chapter on artifact preservation methods. And I wrote the first book on technical diving.

I was gratified to learn that, in preparation for the case, the City of Hamilton had purchased a number of my books to use as exhibits. Also, as it developed, opposing counsel, his staff, and Englebert had read my books with a fine-toothed comb - not in the search for knowledge or enlightenment, but to find inconsistencies that could be used against me.

The majority of Barkwell's initial questions dealt with diving techniques and equipment configurations. Only minutes into the cross examination, I realized that I was essentially conducting introductory workshops on wreck-diving and technical diving - as I had done hundreds of times over the previous two decades. Because Barkwell was a non-diver (by his own admission), I treated him differently in that I made no basic assumptions about his prior knowledge or experience. Rather, I treated him as a novice who was thirsting for esoteric information. I was the educator, he was the student.

Barkwell had me identify and describe every item of equipment that I would carry on a dive to the *Hamilton* and *Scourge*, and how that item would be used. I also gave him a detailed description of the conduct of a typical technical dive, including decompression procedures, and what back-up measures would be employed in case of emergency.

Thou Shalt Not Forget the Word

In his entire cross examination, Barkwell managed to find but a single inconsistency. My affidavit stated, "At no time during these recreational dives was any damage caused." In *Wreck Diving Adventures*, I wrote about an incident on a submarine that had been scuttled in the Patuxent River, and which had subsequently been partially torched apart by Navy divers: "On one dive during an incoming tide the wreck literally came apart in my hands. First, as I gripped the top of the bridge coaming, a great sheet of metal tore free. Then as I was swept along the hull, I grabbed a thick stanchion, which broke in half. I tumbled backward, ricocheting and grabbing and ripping off two pieces of steel decking before I found a secure handle. I felt like the Hulk, tearing the wreck apart."

Barkwell: "Seems to me on that dive damage was caused."

I admitted: "Substantial damage."

Barkwell: "How does that jibe with your statement in your affidavit that you've not caused damage to wrecks?"

I meant "meaningful damage, and if it would make any effect, I would insert that word into this sentence and correct my statement."

Barkwell: "How would you define meaningful damage?"

"As I suggested earlier, the wreck is nothing but an old hulk. . . . falling apart, has no meaning. . . . So I would say the difference is in the word 'meaningful.'"

Barkwell was barking up the wrong tree if he thought that a judge could be convinced that I did not know the difference between a scuttled collapsing hulk and an historic site.

Barkwell continued to beat the dead horse: "Well then, as I understand it now, we are to read this that you have not caused meaningful damage to wrecks and that we are to understand that if a wreck is, to use your word, simply an old hulk, damage is not meaningful?"

I was not offended by his accusation: "That would be a fair assessment of what I am implying."

Rescuing Artifacts

Barkwell tried to catch me in another trap. "I think I read somewhere in one of these books at one point you had in your possession thousands of artifacts you had removed from wrecks, is that fair?"

"That's correct."

Barkwell: "I take it that you don't consider the removal of artifacts from wrecks to be damage to the wreck?"

I suspected where he was going with this line of reasoning. He was going to claim that because I had recovered artifacts in the past, I could not be trusted not to recover artifacts from the *Hamilton* and *Scourge*. This was a juvenile juxtaposition and extrapolation that no judge in the world could fail to see. Barkwell emphasized his accusation as if it was a perceptive revelation, like saying, "Ah *ha*! Isn't it true that you have driven your car at speeds of sixty miles per hour?" To which the answer is, "Yes, but I did it on the highway where that was the speed limit, not while passing through a school zone."

Barkwell neglected to mention that I recovered artifacts only from shipwrecks in the ocean, where the process of deterioration was ongoing and catastrophic. "No, it's preservation. Those artifacts would have been either lost or destroyed as the wreck collapsed on top of them. So I consider removal of artifacts at risk to be preservation of those artifacts." There is not an archaeologist in the world who has not removed artifacts for preservation (unless, like Englebert, he had never conducted field work). I explained the difference between protected wrecks in Provincial and National Parks, and abandoned wrecks which held no historic value. Most shipwrecks were equivalent to demolished vehicles in a junk yard: worthless except for salvageable parts.

Blind Man's Bluff

We took a break at noon. I treated Yormak to lunch. (If I had not, he would have charged me for it later as an expense.) Afterward, Barkwell tackled the issue of visibility. I told him that water clarity had increased dramatically in Lake Ontario since the Woods Hole project - as much as fifty feet. (Since then, I have seen ambient light visibility in excess of one hundred feet, at a depth of 170 feet.) I explained about the penumbra that surrounded the cone of a diver's light.

Barkwell: "If visibility on this site is in the range of two to three feet, does bumping into things in the dark become a problem?"

This was the crux of his argument. He wanted to convince the judge that a technical diver was equivalent to a contestant in a demolition derby. He specifically addressed the issue of side-slung bottles, hinting that they were a hazard because they were behind the diver and out of his view. I reminded him that tanks worn on a diver's back were out of view, too. The only way in which a diver could bang his tanks into the hull was to back into the wreck: an absurd notion that he was trying hard to hypothesize.

What Barkwell failed to understand, or refused to accept, or did not want to hear, was that technical divers were proficient with their equipment. Tanks were extensions of a diver's body. Tanks were to a diver what a hard-hat was to a construction worker. A person who has never worn a hard-hat, and who visits a construction site for the first time in his life, is forever banging his hard-hat against steel beams, scaffold struts, and low-slung pipes and conduits, whereas the construction worker ducks instinctively and never gets a scratch on his hard-hat.

Barkwell could easily have confirmed the truth of the matter. If he chose not to accept my word, he could have deposed any other technical diver in the world

- and a number of them lived in Ontario. But Barkwell was not interested in truth. His strategy relied upon the art of deception. He could not use sycophants Waddell or Englebert to support his allegations because neither one was a certified technical diver. Their word against mine was worse than useless, especially as I had written the book on technical diving. Barkwell had a tough row to hoe if he was hoping to dispute the word of a technical diver of my training and experience.

Analogies aside, I nipped his whole argument in the bud. "No, because I would abort the dive. . . . I wouldn't dive under those conditions."

A Picture is Worth a Thousand Words

Barkwell compared my photograph of the *Lusitania's* after telegraph with a National Geographic photograph of the *Lusitania's* bridge telemotor, claiming that the objects were one and the same. I had seen and photographed both. I sincerely tried not to make Barkwell appear foolish because he did not know the difference; any non-diver - and most wreck-divers - would have been as confused as Barkwell. I pointed out the dissimilarities between the objects, and explained their different functions. Then I made it easy for him: "It's not important whether it's the after docking bridge or not. That's not the point you're making."

Barkwell: "No, what I want to talk about here is the difference in the lighting conditions."

I explained the difference between my hand-held strobe and the surface-powered lighting system that National Geographic employed, and which was half the size of the conference table. Barkwell's point was that an ROV with a high-powered lighting system could obtain a better photograph than I could with a strobe the size of a football.

"No, you're going to get better lighting, not necessarily a better photograph. Remember the constraints of this system prevent it from getting close to the site. You have a six foot grid of lights that has to be lowered from the surface. So it can only photograph discrete portions of the wreck. A diver has much greater maneuverability and control, and because of that can get very close to a wreck and take pictures that cannot be taken by an ROV."

That was not the answer that Barkwell wanted to hear, but so be it.

The Inadmissible Past

Barkwell then referred to one of my earlier proposals. Yormak raised his first objection. The whole purpose of submitting the fourth proposal was to avoid the baggage that accompanied the previous three. Barkwell wanted my entire history of proposals and correspondence introduced as evidence, in order to show how my proposal had evolved from one of archaeological assistance to one of simple sightseeing and taking snapshots. Yormak stated that the prior proposals were irrelevant. A heated argument ensued.

Barkwell put his questions on the record. Yormak refused to let me answer any of them. Barkwell lost his temper and threw up his hands.

Barkwell kept trying to bring the *Monitor* into the case. Yormak asked for relevance. I think Barkwell was trying to imply that I had a history of litigation, and that subsequent to prevailing in the case of the *Monitor*, I published photographs of the wreck. But Yormak refused to let any parallels of the *Monitor* be drawn into the *Hamilton/Scourge* case unless Barkwell was willing to submit the entire historical and legal context of the *Monitor* case. He would not permit Barkwell to pick and choose points out of context.

Philosophical Debate

Finally, Barkwell asked a question which Yormak permitted me to answer: "I'm suggesting to you, Mr. Gentile, you are prepared to say whatever you think people want to hear in order to get permission on these wrecks. Would you care to comment on that?"

If Barkwell expected me to avoid issues the way his witness had done, he was sadly mistaken. "Yes, I would care to comment. I don't think that's true. I think what I was establishing was that the City of Hamilton had no desire to have any studies conducted on the *Hamilton* or *Scourge* in any way, shape, or form. Studies which I thought at the time had relevance to the deterioration and continued degradation of the wrecks. When the City of Hamilton demonstrated that it had no interest in conducting archaeological surveys or biological surveys, I assumed that it was futile for me to offer my services at no charge when the City of Hamilton had no interest in learning about the wrecks. And why have I submitted this application? Because I'm a wreck-diver. I'm an historian. All wreck-divers are historians, and this is what we do. We're very interested in shipwrecks and in the history that comes from shipwrecks and the feeling that we get from being close to historic shipwrecks and observing those shipwrecks. It's a primary motivation for my diving. That's why I dive wrecks instead of caves or quarries or coral reefs. And as a member of the public, I feel I have that right. That doesn't mean that I wouldn't like to be productive in that regard, but I'm still interested in wrecks for what they are."

My soliloquy was followed by a long, loud silence. In the deathly hush that pervaded the room, dust motes clashed like reverberating cymbals. Everyone breathed deeply.

This was my day in court. The deposition was my only opportunity to speak directly to the judge. Live testimony was not given in the Canadian legal system. At the hearing, when the case was argued, I would be permitted to sit in the courtroom as a spectator. But I could not interact. I could not take the stand in my own defense. The judge would not even acknowledge my presence. Only the lawyers could present evidence, from case law, from precedent, from affidavits, and from testimony that was taken from depositions. If I did not speak my mind now, I would never have another opportunity to do so.

After a trenchant lull, Barkwell quoted one of my own written philosophies: "I would rather make love than watch it on television." He asked me to comment on it.

Again I responded without equivocation: "To me, being there is essential and important. It's like if you were to ask a mountain climber how he would feel about taking a helicopter ride to the top of Mount Everest. It wouldn't mean anything to him. The challenge and the excitement and the interest are in *getting* there, not in *being* there. And with ROV's, you're not even there at all. I could sit home and watch it on the boob tube. But I'm an explorer."

Barkwell had no rejoinder for my philosophical musing. The crux of his cross examination had passed. He hashed over some trivialities, but the rest of his cross examination was anticlimactic.

A Matter of Trust

After another long pause, he asked about my mention (in *Wreck Diving Adventures*) of sweeping silt off the deck of the *Dunderberg* in order to see the grain in the wood. (The *Dunderberg* lay on the American side of Lake Huron.) "Why did you do it?"

"Because it was appropriate to do so. To get a better photograph."

"This begs the obvious question, if you're permitted to dive on the *Hamilton* and the *Scourge*, would you be fanning silt off their figureheads to enhance your photographs?"

I was offended by Barkwell's attempt to impugn my reputation. "Not if there is a restriction. I believe you're making the assumption that all divers are criminals and therefore violate the law. . . . If that were true, I wouldn't be here in this room today. I would have dived the wreck four years ago and not told anybody. So I think that begs your question. Then I'm somewhat insulted that you would ask me that."

Barkwell: "I take it then, Mr. Gentile, your position is simply trust me. If you tell me not to touch the wreck, I won't?"

"Yes, I'd agree with that. That's what I did with respect to the *Monitor* and I would respect the same guidelines on the *Hamilton* and *Scourge*."

Ad Hominem

He treated my photography with the same disdain and juvenile consideration with which he treated my sweeping of silt off the deck of the *Dunderberg*. From previous usage of my photographs, he tried to extrapolate that my proposed dives on the *Hamilton* and *Scourge* constituted a commercial operation. I disabused him of his allegation by noting what was written in my proposal. In essence, he was alleging that I was either insincere or lying.

I was blunt about my intentions. "I want to dive this wreck. This is a very historic wreck. I know it's difficult for people who are not interested in history or historical artifacts to understand that. But just accept that wreck-divers are a different kind of people. They enjoy and get great satisfaction from diving historic sites. I've gone all over this country and the United States diving historic sites, not so I can publish photographs of them. So I could experience them."

It appeared to me that Barkwell's only defense strategy was character assassination. He was trying to prove that I was an unsavory person of questionable background, who was not to be trusted and who should not be permitted anywhere near an archaeological site. He missed the point completely. This case was not about *me* - it was about public access to the *Hamilton* and *Scourge*. His failure to comprehend the underlying issue, coupled with his deliberate attempt to disparage me and my accomplishments, directed the entire future conduct of his case.

Barkwell had no further questions. The time was 2:30. For the next several hours I was supposed to be grilled by Anita Lyon. She had been alert and attentive during Barkwell's cross examination. Now that the ball had been placed in her court, she suddenly feigned sickness. She did not look or act sick. She merely stated that she was too sick to proceed with her cross examination. The proceedings were adjourned until the following day.

The Cunning of Continuation

Yormak suspected that Lyon's sham illness was a tactical maneuver whose purpose was to avoid disruption of her cross examination. This implied that the time remaining in the afternoon session was insufficient for her needs. She did not want to commence her cross examination, Yormak opined, unless she could complete it without an overnight interruption. She might lose her continuity. Furthermore, the postponement allowed her the rest of the afternoon and that evening to go over the notes she had taken during the day, and give her time to confer with Englebert and review the notes that he had taken. (Havelka took no notes.) Lyon could also review the questions that Barkwell had already asked - and the answers that I had given - in order to create an abusive atmosphere in which to further impugn my character.

But more importantly, Yormak suspected, Lyon did not want to telegraph her plan of attack unless she could complete her assault in a single session for which Yormak had no time to prepare defensive procedures. "Forewarned is forearmed" as much in a court of law as on the battlefield. She did not want him to have the night in which to anticipate her strategy, so he could prepare objections to obvious irrelevancies, or so he could locate contradictory evidence in the record.

In the purest sense, during depositions and courtroom testimony a witness was sworn to tell "the truth, the whole truth, and nothing but the truth (so help you God)." The reality of courtroom practice is much different if the truth is detrimental to the case. An unethical attorney will try to obfuscate the truth with implications and innuendo. He (or she) will seek to provide only partial truths, and will fight to keep damaging or prejudicial evidence from being admitted. When all else fails, they will lie. In my courtroom experience, I have seen lawyers as well as witnesses state blatant prevarications to the judge, in the mistaken belief that neither I nor my counsel was aware of the facts.

Some lawyers are not interested in seeing that points of law are upheld, or that obvious wrongs are corrected, or that justice should prevail. They (and some judges, too) perceive these ideals as immaterial and irrelevant, as abstract meaningless concepts. To them, "legal ethics" is a strategy to be enforced upon their opponents, and to be abused to their own advantage. For them, it is not important how they play the game, it is whether they win or lose.

Trapped in Toronto

My original plan was to depart for home immediately after my deposition was finished, and sleep on the train in order to save money on lodging. Now I had to spend the night in Toronto. Again I broached the subject of sharing Yormak's room, but he would not hear of it. It was wasteful enough that he was staying at the most expensive hotel in Toronto, but he wanted his $200-per-night room all to himself. Cost was no object to him because he was on an expense account. Although I was paying for his expensive suite, I could not afford to spend that much for myself. I scouted around until I found a cheaper room at half the price.

We agreed to meet for dinner. During the course of conversation I realized the extent of Yormak's grasp on the case. From memory he cited law, procedure, precedent, and the possible ramifications of different strategies. Simple truth was not good enough to win, because the opposition was unethically involved in continuing the charade which the City of Hamilton and the Archaeological Licence Bureau had commenced.

I was also impressed by Yormak's involvement during the deposition. At a deposition for another case, Hess sat dumbly like a bump on a log. He never made a single objection no matter how far afield the opposing counsel strayed. Yormak, on the other hand, jumped into the fracas at every opportunity: to object to irrelevant questions and to keep opposing counsel from going on denunciatory fishing expeditions.

Yormak's insights were little less than phenomenal. I was immeasurably impressed by his comprehension of the law, and by which laws could be invoked to the best advantage. He was like a master chess player who could see the permutations of every possible move.

Again and again, Yormak drew attention to inconsistencies in the opposition's case. Each irregularity could be used as ammunition at the trial. Each double standard, each ill treatment, each deception and sleight of hand, was a hammer blow on the stake through the opposition's heart. Yormak was completely confident that we had righteousness on our side. If found his confidence infectious.

But he was quick to point out that righteousness had little to do with prevailing in court. Politics was a big issue, and I was a foreigner attempting to trounce the hometown team. Although by definition he was not supposed to be prejudiced, a local judge was likely to side with his political affiliations. This is a sad but simple truth in jurisprudence. Strictly logical argumentation often leads to an illogical finding on the part of the court. Nonetheless, Yormak assured me that the chance of our succeeding in making the judge see through the opposition's smokescreen was far from impossible.

I was certain that if any lawyer in the world could win this case, that person was Steve Yormak.

After dinner, I picked up the check. It made no difference whether I paid for Yormak's meal now, or later when he submitted his bill for expenses.

D-day Plus One

Anita Lyon asked me to produce "all letters, momorandums, notes, invoices and contracts for proposed sale or sale or distribution of the story or pictures of the proposed dive to the *Hamilton* and *Scourge*." No such documents existed, so I could not produce them.

She wanted all documents et al relating to the recruitment and location of other participants to the proposed dive." Again no such documents existed. I replied, "That would be like putting the cart before the horse." It made no sense to spend the time to organize an expedition until I was certain that the political roadblocks were removed.

Unruffled, she asked me to produce every book that I had ever written. When Yormak asked why, she replied, "I wanted to examine each one to determine if it was relevant to the proceeding." Now was not the time to read my books - in my presence and during my deposition - to make such a determination. She could have purchased all those books in advance, but chose not to do so. I did not go to Toronto to give away free books.

She asked specifically for *Shipwrecks of Delaware and Maryland*. Yormak asked for the relevance. Lyon could not provide any relevance other than the fact that I had mentioned the title in my affidavit by way of establishing my credentials as an author and historian. Yormak countered, "If the man wrote an expert book on pediatrics, you certainly can't introduce it. . . . No court is going to accept that. Has to have relevance."

She asked for all correspondence between me and the Ministry. When Yormak asked her to clarify which Ministry, she said, "Ministry of Labour, by either Ontario or Canada." This was a stupid request because she represented the Ministry of Labour, and had greater access to that Ministry's records than I had.

She also wanted me to produce copies of all correspondence relating in any way to my first three proposals. Again this was stupid, because Barkwell had all those documents on the table the day before. Besides which, it was irrelevant. Yormak reminded her that the present case referred only to my fourth proposal, not to any of my previous three proposals, or to my suit against NOAA over access to the *Monitor* (which Barkwell had tried to introduce), or to any other part of my past actions and achievements.

Lyon wanted to rehash the entire history of my efforts to dive on the *Hamilton* and *Scourge*. Yormak was insistent that the only proposal that was relevant was my 1998 proposal. This confrontation between Lyon and Yormak persisted throughout the day-long proceeding. She not only wanted to introduce old and irrelevant documents that had no bearing on the present case, but she wanted me to furnish it, when - had she done her homework - she could have produced it herself. She complained, "I can't work in a vacuum," but it was a vacuum of her own creation.

It seemed to me that her entire case was built upon my past proposals and activities, instead of on the proposal for which I had filed suit. She, like Barkwell, wanted to bring my entire life's history under the scrutiny of the court. Instead of confronting the issue of public access, she aped Barkwell's blatant attempt at character assassination.

She wanted to know how many divers I expected to invite on the trip, what brand of camera I expected to employ, whether I planned to shoot video, whether other divers might carry cameras of video equipment, and who would own the resulting film and videotape. I informed her, "That will belong to them." She wanted to know the dimensions of my camera, how the strobe was attached, and the dimensions of the camera and strobe together. She wanted to know the brand name of the strobe and the brand name of the camera's waterproof housing. She wanted to know how I would store my slides.

As Barkwell did the day before, Lyon had me describe commonplace dive procedures and the use of equipment. She wanted to know the weight of a wreck reel, and the weight of the string that was wound onto the reel. These and similar questions were largely repetitions of the previous day's explanations.

She wanted to know if I had ever dived on wrecks as old as the *Hamilton* and *Scourge*. I told her that I had dived on wrecks that were older.

Lyon marked a print-out of my website as an exhibit - for what specific purpose Yormak never ascertained. Lyon established no relevance, but Yormak raised no objection as long as the exhibit was not used to establish my proposed dive as a commercial venture. She wanted to know if I used pictures in my lectures. She wanted to know if I lectured on my diving experiences. And so on and so on. It was obvious that she was trying to draw a conclusion of commercial employment, without evidence and despite my testimony to the contrary.

Big Frog in a Little Pond

Lyon: "Is it fair to say a dive [like] this to the *Hamilton* and *Scourge* would advance your reputation?"

In that she was way off base. My reputation was already assured by dives to such high-profile wrecks as the *Andrea Doria*, *Lusitania*, *Monitor*, *Empress of Ireland*, the German battleship *Ostfriesland* (and other Billy Mitchell wrecks, including three U-boats), and numerous others. Another wreck at this stage of my career would have no additional effect on my reputation. What she failed to realize, and what I tried to explain, was that the opposite circumstance was more likely to occur: that awareness of the *Hamilton* and *Scourge* would be enhanced by my diving on the wrecks.

Lyon, Barkwell, Englebert, Havelka, the City of Hamilton, the Archaeological Licence Bureau, and all the people and political organizations associated with the *Hamilton* and *Scourge*, were suffering from a big-frog-in-a-little-pond complex. They all believed that the wrecks held worldwide significance. Blinded by localism, they failed to realize that very few people on the planet - other than provincial Canadians and a handful of marine archaeologists - were aware of the wrecks' existence. Because the *Hamilton* and *Scourge* lay in their own back yard, these people were duped by the presumption that the wrecks possessed significance beyond their small-scale parochial borders.

The primary value of the *Hamilton* and *Scourge* was not in their archaeological context, but in the dramatic imagery that they presented. But I digress.

DEPOSITION DAYS

Prophet Without Profit

Lyon wanted to know if I expected to receive compensation for organizing a dive trip to the *Hamilton* and *Scourge*. I told her no, that the cost of the trip would be shared by the participants. As a participant, "I pay my share just like everybody else. I just do more of the work."

Lyon: "Is the cost of this legal action going to be included in the expenses of that trip?"

My reply: "No. I certainly wish I could add it in."

Lyon: "Are you alone paying for the legal costs?"

As Hess had yet to donate a dime to the cause, I replied honestly, "Yes, I am." (Although I was expecting some reimbursement.)

Lyon, at Englebert's urging and without proof or evidence, was trying to make the point that this was a money-making venture. As I have already explained, that situation could be used to invoke regulations pursuant to the Occupational Safety and Health Act. This had nothing to do with the merits of the case. It was simply a ploy to frustrate eventuation of the dive should I prevail in court.

A Situation of Gravity

Lyon also laid the groundwork for another circumvention that had nothing to do with the merits of the case or the issue of public access. She asked me about debris fields that might surround the wrecks. This was some of the information that had been malicious denied to me. Nonetheless, I was able to explain that - from the circumstances of the sinkings, and from information provided by the National Geographic article - neither wreck was surrounded by a debris field. Each wreck possessed a closely confined debris field on only one side: the side to which the wreck listed. The other side was clear of any debris, and that is where I expected to establish a downline.

When she asked me how I could be certain that no debris field existed on the opposite side of the wreck, I cited the Newtonian law of gravity: apples and objects fall down; they cannot fall up or sideways.

The hours droned by with Lyon's trivial pursuits, none of which touched upon the merits of the case, but dealt only with me as a person of decidedly ill repute. The grilling continued after lunch.

Neither Forget nor Forgive the Sins of the Past

Lyon persisted in dragging my previous proposals into the fracas. She obviously had some point to make, and the only way she could do so was to introduce these proposals. The argument between her and Yormak became heated. I was asked to leave the room while they debated on the record. When I returned, I learned that Yormak agreed to let me answer irrelevant questions to which he objected, but that the questions and answers would be withheld from submission to the court until - and unless - Lyon could convince the judge of their relevance. This permitted Lyon to ask questions to which Yormak could register an objection; then I would give my answer, but my answer would be withheld unless a motion was brought before the judge and he overruled the objection.

This procedure was adopted in order to preclude my return for another deposition. Since Canadian law did not permit me to testify on the witness stand, this deposition served as my only opportunity to answer questions.

Lyon persisted in making comparisons between my first three proposals and the final proposal. She noted specifically how my objectives had changed through the years. She continually asked irrelevant questions, Yormak registered his objection, then I answered her question for the record.

She maintained this litany for a couple of hours.

I continually noted that my objectives had changed, that I no longer wanted to conduct an archaeological assessment, that I no longer wanted to perform scientific studies, that I no longer wanted to annotate the accretion of zebra mussels, that I no longer wanted to add my photographic images to the baseline begun by National Geographic in order to contribute to the knowledge base of the sites, and that all I wanted to do was "to dive the wrecks for the experience and to take photographs for my own personal use."

My goals were clearly spelled out in my 1998 proposal, but for the purpose of her case, Lyon kept challenging my present position and refused to accept my change of heart. I told her that at the time I had submitted my first proposal, "I had no reason to assume that I could not obtain the cooperation of the Ontario staff marine archaeologist." (Who, by the way, was sitting next to her.)

As I maintained my stance, Lyon grew progressively more abusive and accusatory. She wanted me to make admissions that would bolster her case - admissions that contradicted the printed record. I kept reminding her that the objectives that were stated in my latest proposal constituted my present position, and that objectives that were stated in my earlier proposals were no longer relevant. But she did not want to hear that, so she kept harping on the issue.

Lyon: "Is it a fair characterization to say that you were intent on diving on those sites and that you continued to introduce new inducements in order to obtain consent to dive?"

After Yormak's perfunctory objection, I replied, "No, that's not really a fair characterization. I think, as I said earlier, I thought at the time the City of Hamilton had an interest in preserving these wrecks and learning about them. And so I was offering ways in which my expertise as a technical diver and photographer could help promote those researches."

Lyon rephrased her question, and I rephrased my answer: "At the time I thought that I could be of assistance, that I could help . . . the wrecks of the *Hamilton* and *Scourge*. But the City of Hamilton has made it clear to me that they are discouraging voluntary help."

She rephrased her question again, and again I rephrased my answer: "I was being sincere in that I wanted to help produce new information that might bring these various historical sites to public consciousness. And I've done it with respect to other wrecks. . . . I wanted to do something productive. . . . I wanted to help. . . . I wanted to do something that could promote the *Hamilton* and *Scourge*. And I've been so frustrated in my efforts to do so, that I no longer . . . want to help in this regard."

Lyon: "If you have a public-spirited interest, why aren't you interested in continuing to assist public knowledge about those wrecks?"

My reply: "Because the City of Hamilton has taken a consistent policy to frustrate my efforts to help promote those shipwreck sites and they're continuing to do so. So I've finally thrown in the towel. I'm not any longer willing to help promote the sites."

Lyon refused to accept the fact that a person can change his mind, that life can take different directions, that new objectives can replace the old, and that I was not going to buckle under her continual harassment.

Lyon badgered me and belabored her point. She referred to an earlier proposal in which I offered to make copies of my photographs for the Ontario Ministry of Citizenship and Culture. "Why are you no longer proposing to do this?"

My reply: "It's been my understanding that the Ontario Ministry of Citizenship and Culture is not interested in my photographs, and so therefore there's no reason for me to want to supply them."

Lyon iterated her conviction in different language. I replied: "I'm not going to try to give them something that they don't want."

After another reiteration: "At the time I was hoping that those photographs could be interpreted by an Ontario staff marine archaeologist. But my understanding has come to be that Ontario's marine archaeologist has no interest in continuing on-site photographic evidence of the ship's degradation."

After yet another: "Public awareness of these wrecks may be disadvantageous to the public. They may have come to a very negative opinion about it. It's never been my purpose to promote shipwreck awareness in a negative fashion - only to promote it in a positive fashion. And I think that after going through these proceedings, that there is nothing that I could do to offer that would help - in the spirit of the City of Hamilton's lack of cooperation. I think that would be counterproductive to try to promote the City's obstructionistic attitude."

Finally, Lyon let it go. She returned to the commercial aspects of my photography. And round, and round, and round, ad infinitum, ad nauseum . . .

Obstruction of Justice

At last she broached a new subject area. She wanted me to define a variety of terms in the Ontario Heritage Act. As these were all legal questions, Yormak refused to let me answer.

Afterward, she once again referred to certain of my published books (which she had brought with her). She and Englebert had obviously read every word, seeking negative connotations that could be used against me. She also produced my resume. We played round robin while she attempted to find discrepancies that Englebert had earmarked, but all were easily explained to her satisfaction. For example, she noted that I had made 92 dives to depths of 240 feet or deeper, and that I had made more than 150 dives to the A*ndrea Doria* (which lay at a depth of 240 feet), not counting dives to other wrecks that lay deeper. I explained that I logged the maximum depth that I attained on a particular dive, as opposed to the depth of water surrounding the wreck. The *Andrea Doria* rose to a depth of 170 feet. I did not always go to the seabed next to the *Andrea Doria*, but usually explored the wreck at shallower depths.

Lyon tried to explain away the archaeological license that was issued by Jane Marlatt, and which was later voided, by noting Englebert's affidavit in which he proffered the gratuitous explanation that "it is a common practice to prepare a . . . draft license and letter." The justification was ingenious, but absurd. Why do work that would in all likelihood prove unnecessary, especially since Englebert claimed that the Archaeological Licence Bureau had *never* granted an archaeological license for the *Hamilton* and *Scourge*? Governments do not operate that way. Either Lyon was lying, or she did not know that she was being hoodwinked by Englebert. If she wanted to prove her point, she should have had Marlatt testify to that effect, instead of a known prevaricator and obstructionist.

My comment: "It appeared to me that someone at some level of bureaucracy was intending to issue that license and that some obstructionistic activity occurred afterwards to have it withdrawn."

Lyon: "And what obstructionist activity - what is the activity that you mean when you say obstructionist activity?"

My reply: "People within the bureaucracy that did not want me to make this dive." (You will recall that Englebert once told Hess, "Your client will never dive the *Hamilton* and *Scourge*.")

Lyon: "And who would that be?"

My reply: "I make no allegations."

Lyon: "Well, you just have."

My reply: "To individuals. And it may be an entire bureaucratic mindset. I don't know."

Lyon: "What evidence do you rely on for your belief that there was, for lack, a bureaucratic conspiracy?"

My reply: "The same evidence you just pointed out to me, the letter that was written."

Yormak, ever on the alert, caught Lyon trying to put words into my mouth: "He didn't say conspiracy. You used that word. He said bureaucratic mindset."

Collateral Damage

Admonished, Lyon changed subjects. She tried to paint me as an anti-establishment advocate by noting mention in my books of the war that marine archaeologists waged against treasure salvors, and which resulted in the Abandoned Shipwreck Act (in the United States) - an Act with the potential to relieve recreational divers of their rights to dive on shipwrecks.

Referring to wreck-divers, Lyon quoted from my *Primary Wreck Diving Guide*: "They have become the non-combatant casualties shot down by the willed and misplaced fire from the hips of academics who are machine gunning through a sea of shipwrecks so vast, at the present rate of investigation it will take thousands, tens of thousands of years to survey them all, by which time the wrecks will no longer exist. . . . But the machinations of marine archaeologists and their sinister use of political propaganda to further their political ambitions are beyond the scope of this discussion."

I wrote that paragraph, and I stood by it. "This is a philosophical discussion we're having here. It has no relation to law. . . . It is beyond this discussion. It has nothing to do with the *Hamilton* and *Scourge*."

Lyon: "You don't feel there is any relation with the *Hamilton* and *Scourge* and that attitude?"

My reply: "Oh, you mean with respect to control? In my personal opinion, yes. There is a matter of control."

Lyon: "And would it be safe to say that you have an antipathy to archaeologists?"

Yormak, still alert: "Archaeologists, or marine archaeologists?"

My reply: "I'm not one to crush the wasp nest because I got stung by a single wasp. I would characterize that to only those marine archaeologists who are activists in taking away free rights from the public."

Lyon tried to get me to name individuals, Englebert in particular, but I would not do so. In any event, my opinions and philosophies had no bearing on the case. I might condone murder, rape, and pillage, but those condonations were irrelevant. The issue on trial was public access. Lyon kept straying from that point because she had no way to defend it. She kept trying to put my attitudes on trial. In the free democratic society of the country of which I was a citizen, I was entitled to my attitudes. Nor did my attitudes adversely affect my right to due process.

After re-examination by Yormak, to clarify some misconceptions that Lyon tried to have placed on the record, proceedings were adjourned.

Retroflection

The time was not far from 5 o'clock. Lyon had another witness waiting to be deposed, but there was insufficient time to even swear him in, much less conduct his deposition. A vehement argument ensued. Lyon was uproariously angry over the fact that her witness had been flown to Toronto at great expense to the Province, and had to return that evening without testifying. He would not be available again for several weeks. And the Province would have to bear the additional travel expense.

Yormak expressed neither guilt nor concern over her plight. After all, it was not his fault that Lyon had spent the whole day asking redundant questions and making false and gratuitous statements. It was her fault. Furthermore, had she not feigned sickness on the previous afternoon, she would have been several hours along in my deposition when the morning session commenced. She had no one to blame but herself.

I felt no sympathy because Lyon's dilatory tactics were going to cost me another $100 for overnight lodging. The last scheduled bus of the day had already departed, so I would be trapped in Toronto for another night.

Yormak and I met again for dinner. He had been working since six o'clock that morning, when he arose to review his notes from the previous day. He was attentive throughout the proceedings. He stayed focused on the legal issues that were called into play. He retained a comprehensive grasp of the laws on which the case was based. And his ability to recall trifling details was little less than phenomenal. Yet, his mind was still charged and was racing ahead at full speed.

For me the day had been easy. All I had to do was tell the truth. As I noted above, I did not have anything to hide. But that did not imply that I had been able to relax my guard.

Like Barkwell, Lyon phrased her questions with incriminatory language that would have been inadmissible in court. She tried to put me on the defensive, and to make me lose control of my emotions and reply with diatribe. Not for nothing was I known as Nonchalant Lamont. I possessed an even-tempered personality which enabled me to remain calm under duress - and this day had been anything but stressful. The only difficult part of my testimony was ensuring that Lyon's leading questions, gratuitous statements, and unwarranted assumptions, were cauterized.

I answered the question, not the implication. And I disabused the misconceptions that she was trying to put on the record as facts.

Ironically, Lyon never once addressed the issue of public access: the raison d'etre for the case. She did not even attempt to defend the Province's (read Englebert's) position. It seemed to me that she knew that the Provincial stance was indefensible. Instead of wasting her time and energy on a case that could not be won, she was concentrating her efforts on damage control. She was contriving rationales that could be utilized to thwart my expedition should the court render an opinion in my favor.

Castigating my recreational dive trip as a commercial enterprise could be used to invoke OSHA regulations. The argument that photography constituted archaeology could be used by the Archaeological Licence Bureau (Englebert) to deny the issuance of a permit. The lack of adequate knowledge of a surrounding debris field could be used to preclude anchoring procedures.

Yormak was confident that he could argue each of these points successfully. I was confident that if anyone could argue them successfully, that person was Steve Yormak.

Again I paid the dinner check. (I had paid for lunch as well.) Yormak and I parted ways - he to his expensive hotel to prepare for tomorrow's deposition, I to sleep and catch the early morning bus to the train station on the Canadian side of Niagara Falls.

Yormak did not need my help in deposing Englebert. As difficult a person as Englebert was, I knew that Yormak could handle him quite well alone. And considering Englebert's history of abusive-aggressive behavior, my presence would not intimate him any more than his presence intimated me.

Chapter 6
The Master of Deceit

The Test of Patience

According to Englebert, he had been the Provincial archaeologist since the time when Phil Wright resigned from the program in 1990. Within minutes, Yormak got Englebert to admit that his role as a marine archaeologist had nothing to do with enforcement. He also established that Bernice Field's role was only one of administration, "just basically processing paper." Thus the person with whom I had engaged in long correspondence was little more than a glorified secretary. A committee made the final decision on whether to issue a license, but that decision was based solely upon Englebert's desire. In essence, the committee members did what he wanted them to do.

Englebert did not divulge this information quickly or freely. Three pages of transcript were required to follow Englebert's convoluted and evasive replies into the semblance of an answer. His cagey and ambiguous technique was to plague the entire deposition. But Yormak was never satisfied, and would never let go of his question, until he received an unequivocal answer. Getting straight and clear-cut answers out of Englebert was like pulling fully grown pine trees out of the ground by hand. But Yormak was equal to the task.

Six pages of transcript were required to ascertain that, when deciding whether or not to issue a license, neither Englebert nor anyone in the Ministry gave any consideration to the City's mandate, duties, and obligations to "carry out scientific studies to ascertain the condition of the said wrecks and develop feasibility studies."

Englebert defined archaeology as "a series of techniques that are used to extract information from the material remains that people leave behind. The second part is the theoretical aspect. This information is used to extrapolate the life ways of these people - how they lived, how they interacted with each other, in some cases what they might have thought."

I will not make the reader endure what Yormak had to endure. I will cut through the considerable chaff - much of which was provided by Lyon - in order to enumerate Englebert's admissions.

He had approved the issuances of licenses to divers who simply wanted to photograph shipwrecks in cases in which the resultant photographs were for their own personal use - the same use stated in my 1998 proposal. Yormak called attention to three such licenses that were granted to Scott McWilliam for leading expeditions to the *Gunilda* (a private yacht lost in Lake Superior). Englebert recalled that he had authorized the issuance of those licenses. The purpose of one of those expeditions was to produce a film documentary for television.

When asked which section of the Ontario Heritage Act gave him the authority to deny the issuance of a license, he could not recall the section and could not produce the Act.

When asked why he permitted the issuance of licenses in the above-mentioned cases, but denied mine, he said, "I think that the difference would be the intent of what, your intent towards those vessels, what you intend to do there."

Yormak: "Meaning?"

Englebert: "Well, if you intend to do something which would fall under the definition of archaeology."

Reductio ad Absurdum

Yormak then backed Englebert into a corner of absurdity. "If I have a 12 foot boat that sinks in the middle of the lake tomorrow, I don't think I need to apply for you to get a license."

Englebert agreed, with the caveat that Yormak did not "intend to do something which would fall under the definition of archaeology."

Yormak: "Now, in the example I just gave, where I just leave my boat on the bottom, I'm leaving something behind. I'm a human being, so that would fit that definition (of archaeology)?"

Englebert: "Yes, it would." After a full page of discussion, Englebert reluctantly relented: "No, you don't need a license to go to your boat."

Yormak: "Why not?"

Englebert: "Because in all likelihood your reasons for going out there are not to do archaeology."

One cannot do archaeology on a boat that sank on the previous day. Examining such a boat falls under the category of inquest, or police investigation. Archaeology is the study of the long ago past, not the recent past.

Yormak: "Now, let's say someone else wants to go out there. My cousin wants to know something about me. He goes through my material remains, he calls you. Does he need a license?"

Englebert invoked his magic word "intent," which to him was equivalent to "abracadabra" or "open sesame" because it granted him entrance to a fabulous domain in which he proclaimed himself god. "Under the strict definition, probably yes."

After some discussion, Yormak asked, "How do you determine someone's intent?"

Englebert: "Well, the intent, as you mean it, I think, correct me if I'm wrong, means what they ultimately want to do with the material." After five more requests for clarification: "And I would also look at the intensity of the project, the length of time over which it's going to take place."

Yormak: "How would that impact on intent?"

Englebert: "It would show me whether it was something that was casual, or something that was systematic."

Yormak: "Casual would be defined one day, two days, six days, six years?"

Englebert: "A single dive is what I would call casual."

Yormak: "So a two-day dive can be a systematic dive?"

Englebert: "I think so, yes."

According to Englebert's definition, the week-long *Gunilda* trips constituted "something that was systematic." And certainly the documentary film expedition was more than casual. (It was a commercial enterprise.) By extrapolating from Englebert's definition, if I proposed to make a single dive on either the *Hamilton* or the *Scourge*, it would not constitute archaeology and would therefore not require a license. Yormak drew Englebert to this logical conclusion without naming any wreck sites - he could do that later in court.

Instead, he forced Englebert to admit: "If you're doing a single dive and taking one picture, I don't believe you would be able to construct a description of the site based on that. And therefore, I would have to say that it is not archaeology."

Yormak: "So no license in that case?"

Englebert: "Yeah, I wouldn't think a license would be necessary for that."

Yormak: "If you knew that the individual had in the past taken photos and published those photos, would you accept his application on face value that he would not be using it for publication?"

Englebert: "I wouldn't take the application at face value, no." He was engaging in tautology. First, he was arguing that once a person committed his intentions to paper, he was bound by those intentions for the rest of his life, without any hope for reprieve; he was never allowed to change his mind or his intentions. However, if the person planned to make but a single dive without a camera, and did not intend to make notes of the dive, he did not need to apply for a license, thus obviating the need for Englebert to make a determination on intent. In this looping kind of logic, Englebert was a snake who was biting his own tail.

The reason Englebert gave for his permitting the issuance of those licenses to dive on the *Gunilda* was, "They consulted with me."

Arbitrary and Capricious

His decision making process had nothing to do with the Ontario Heritage Act. The irony was that he issued a permit to conduct archaeology on the *Gunilda* when no archaeology was contemplated or even suggested. From this it could be inferred that McWilliam had not needed to kowtow to Englebert for a license.

Yormak: "On what basis . . . did you advise them they needed a license?"

Englebert must have realized that Yormak had sprung a trap. His definition of archaeology did not conform to the definition with which he had been intimidating people for years. He tried to revamp his definition.

Englebert: "I believed the intent of their activities of on the site fell under the activities that are covered by licensing in the Ontario Heritage Act. . . . Survey, exploration."

Although Englebert claimed that he could not cite the section in the Act that defined (or even mentioned) "survey" and "exploration," Yormak had done his homework. He had obtained a copy of the Act and had read it thoroughly. He was leading Englebert by the nose through his own world of deceit. Englebert may have been able to intimidate divers that he possessed powers of arrest, and that he had sole discretionary authority to grant or deny licenses, but he could not intimidate Yormak because Yormak had the facts in hand. Nor could Englebert's ingenuous testimony be used to sway a judge that he was right and the Act was wrong.

Yormak: "Tell me what you mean by survey and exploration."

Englebert: "Survey to me is looking at the site, photographing it, and these are not mutually exclusive, these are any or all. Taking notes, drawing sketch maps, not taking any measurements, anything at all that could be used to construct a description of the site."

Yormak: "Is that a complete definition?"

Englebert left himself an out for the future: "At the moment, that's complete."

Yormak: "Any other exploration?"

Englebert: "Exploration in my, that's as I understand, is a much more general term. And it's used to, it encompasses survey, survey is also exploration, and it could also mean looking for sites."

Yormak opened another trap by asking about side-scan sonar. Englebert bluffed by claiming that searching for shipwrecks by any means would be in violation of the Act, and was therefore illegal without a license. He claimed that even visual searching - by swimming through the water and looking with one's eyes - required a license. (The Act makes no such mention. These interpretations are solely Englebert's.)

Yormak tightened the jaws of the trap: "Are you presuming, when you say illegal, that that individual is looking for shipwrecks?"

Englebert: "We would presume that, yes."

Yormak: "So if that individual said they were using it for a different purpose, you might look askance to it?"

Englebert: "You would certainly want to investigate that statement, yes. Might be askance."

When Yormak pressed him with the supposition that perhaps the diver was just diving for fun and looking around, Englebert commented, "I would have to know what he had on his mind. I would have to know his intent."

Perhaps Canadian law is different, but in the United States a person cannot be indicted for unsubstantiated intent.

Yormak: "What conclusion would you come to that would say yes, it's under the Act, or no, it's not, referring to intent? What are you looking for?"

After six pages of runaround, Englebert said: "I'm looking for why. . . . Who is giving the answer, what's their past behavior been, what do you know of them." In other words, guilty by prior conduct. Again, in U.S. law, a person cannot be found guilty of a crime because he committed such a crime in the past. He must be found guilty of the crime under consideration.

Englebert stated, "Every shipwreck is a unique situation." Such a discretionary and unilateral stand gave him totalitarian authority.

THE MASTER OF DECEIT

A Question of Qualification

With respect to the *Hamilton* and *Scourge*, Englebert stated: "Mr. Gentile is entirely unqualified to be on those two wrecks." His conceit was ironic in that I wrote the book on technical diving, and developed techniques that came to be accepted practice. Although Englebert was not a technical diver, I do not hold his lack of skill against him. Technical diving is not for everyone. But I submit that his ignorance and lack of skill do not grant him the right to claim that I am unqualified. Englebert later admitted that the deepest he had ever descended was 150 feet.

Yormak tried to get Englebert to be specific in my lack of qualification, but he refused to elaborate, and Lyon objected to the whole line of questioning.

A Matter of Intent

When Yormak asked Englebert if he needed a license to dive on a sunken rowboat in 12 feet of water, for the purpose of writing a paper for school, Englebert said, "Yes, you should have a license." If the water was clear and Yormak could see the rowboat from the surface, would he still require a license? Englebert: "I think that would be a licensable activity. You would be surveying the ship from the surface."

After twisting Englebert into knots over hypothetical scenarios, Yormak got down to the nitty-gritty. He referred to a letter written by Michael Johnson, who Englebert stated was his boss and manager, in which Johnson wrote, "We take the view that for sport dives on many wrecks which involve no contact and where photography is the objective a license is not required." Yormak: "If you take at face value what Mr. Gentile has said his stated purpose is in his letter of request, would you agree with me, at least by Mr. Johnson's view, that he does not need a license?"

Both Englebert and Lyon struggled to escape from the strangling noose, Englebert by making justifications, Lyon by making objections. Yet neither could escape the inevitable conclusions that were dictated by simple logic: a sport or recreational diver was not required to obtain an archaeological permit if he did not contemplate doing archaeology; and photography by and of itself did not constitute archaeology.

Englebert wriggled like a fish on a hook. Ignoring the constraint of facts that Yormak had brought to his attention, he remained steadfast: "I disagree." Again he cited "intent."

Yormak: "So it's your opinion you know his intent then better than he knows it. And what do you base that on?"

Englebert: "I base my assumptions on his books, his writings, the license application he submitted, and his previous correspondence to us."

Yormak: "So when Mr. Gentile presents himself to you or anybody else, in writing or in person, and says this is for personal use, it is not for commercial use, is he lying?"

Englebert: "I couldn't say. I don't make those kinds of determinations."

Yormak: "Isn't that exactly what you're doing?

Englebert maintained his facade of chicanery despite the absurdity of his answer. "No." Redundant discussion continued for ten more pages without approaching any semblance of logic.

I do not know if Englebert had Lyon buffaloed, or if she was part of the conspiracy.

A Figurehead with Authority

After a break for lunch, the discussion continued for eight more pages. Englebert had a knack for obfuscation that would try to patience of a saint. Yet Yormak remained cool, calm, and persistent. He quoted from Bernice Field's letter to me: "Looking at and photographing underwater sites are not of themselves archaeological activities."

Yormak: "Do you adopt that?"

Englebert agreed, but with the caveat of "intent."

Yormak tried to pin down Englebert on how many photographs a person would have to take before he considered it a licensable activity. One? No. One hundred? Definitely. Ten? Depends on what he intended to do with them.

Yormak: "One picture of the *Hamilton/Scourge*?"

Englebert: "That's a hard call." Why? Because it might be a picture of a figurehead.

Yormak: "Would it make a difference to you?"

Englebert: "Yes, I'm telling you why. The figurehead on the *Dunderberg*, and he would like to look at the figureheads on the *Hamilton* and *Scourge*. It would make a difference to me because it shows there is something systematic that he's doing in his study or his interest in figureheads, which he has already admitted he has and he wants to do that, it would definitely constitute archaeology."

According to Englebert's twisted illogic, if I photographed any object on the *Hamilton* and *Scourge*, and I already possessed a photograph of a similar object from another wreck, he would consider my activity as archaeology. (Although, I suspect that a great number of bona fide archaeologists might beg to differ.)

Yormak: "Is there a picture of a less significant area of the ship . . . the hull, or the deck or whatever, one picture?"

Englebert: "Every picture of those sites would hold significance." Ironically, the City of Hamilton begged to differ with him. In one of its pre-suit memos, the City found that no useful information could be gleaned from any photographs that I might take on the *Hamilton* and *Scourge*.

The reader should remember that I once suggested making the dive without a camera - a situation which would obviate this discussion. Unless, of course, I entered the dive in my log. Englebert might construe such a notation as the recording of information, and therefore as archaeology. It seemed that Englebert could contrive to make any activity one that was licensable if he chose to do so.

Quack, Quack, Quackery

Yormak caught Englebert in another series of lies. "When I first saw his license application, I wasn't aware of his activity in his publishing."

Yormak read from my initial application: "I prepare a written account of the survey to be published with the photographic results and suitable magazines geared to the lay public in order to increase public awareness of the world's underwater heritage."

Englebert reluctantly conceded the point. "Prior to that I had no knowledge of the man."

What about Peter Hess's initial letter of introduction, the letter which predated my own correspondence?

Englebert: "Yes, we had Mr. Hess's letter."

What about the time that Hess discussed possible dive plans with Englebert at the *Atlantic* trial?

Englebert: "And so I did know of Mr. Gentile."

Successful liars need tremendous memories, so they can recall precisely what lies they told, and to whom.

Face Value

Regarding my authorship and public speaking, Yormak persisted, "You took that at face value at that point, didn't you?"

Englebert: "There is supporting evidence for that, so I guess yes, I would. . . . We had his books in front of us."

Yormak: "So you had no reason to doubt that and you didn't doubt it when you got the application, did you?"

Englebert: "That he publishes?"

Yormak: "That he is being truthful and accurate about everything he said."

Englebert: "I have no information which would contradict anything in this license application, so, yes, I would take it at face value."

Yormak now wrestled with Englebert as a terrier would worry a rat: "You would agree with me you didn't have any reason to doubt his word, right?"

Englebert: "No, he gave me no reason to doubt his word."

The Truth at Last - No Enforcement Authority

Yormak moved on to other subjects. He quoted from Johnson's letter, "We can see no benefit to the resource which would result by exposing these archaeological sites at this time to recreational and commercial exploitation." Yormak zeroed in on the words "no benefit." "It's fair to say that the issue of public access is not part of the mix that you guys are considering right now?" Englebert agreed.

Yormak asked if the four thousand photographs from the Woods Hole expedition had ever been analyzed. "No."

Yormak called his attention to a passage from one of Bernice Field's letters: "Our concern for accidentally disturbance by divers' movement around the wreck is based on earlier studies of these specific wrecks."

Englebert: "The only thing I could imagine she's talking about there would be the previous expeditions that went there from Cousteau, the National Geographic."

Yormak: "Can you show me the studies that show that?"

Englebert tried for two pages to avoid the subject, but when Yormak insisted that he produce a copy of the study, Englebert was forced to admit that no such study existed. Another lie was exposed.

Yormak asked Englebert about the time frame for completion of the so-called Feasibility Study: "A year? A decade? A century?"

Englebert: "I have no idea about that."

Englebert admitted that the Technical Study Team had never produced a single document. All they did at their meetings was talk. Nor had the Team conducted any studies of the *Hamilton* and *Scourge*.

Then Yormak hammered the stake into Englebert's heart: "Do you have the ability to prohibit people, do you have legislative authority to say to people you're not allowed to go on a wreck?"

Englebert equivocated: "I don't know. I don't know." This statement was in direct contradiction to what he had been telling wreck-divers for years. Yormak addressed the question to Lyon, but she claimed that she did not know the answer either.

It seems odd to me that Englebert was so ignorant about the Ontario Heritage Act when it was his full-time occupation to interpret its guidelines; and that Lyon, as full-time counsel for the Province of Ontario, was so ignorant about Provincial laws.

Exposing the Scam

Because it was to his advantage to do so, Englebert vociferated concern over the fact that I had banged into the hull of the *S-49*, and perhaps had had physical contact with other shipwrecks. Yormak argued this point. By analogy, it could just as well be said that I had banged into demolished cars in a junk yard, but I had never banged into a painting or artifact while visiting a museum. Englebert did not want to acknowledge that there was a difference in the amount of care taken when circumstances warranted.

Englebert did not believe that the *Hamilton* and *Scourge* could be raised today, nor that technology to do so would be available within the next fifty years. He did not want anyone diving on the wrecks for the next half century - he wanted the wrecks left strictly alone. He also believed that the wrecks could not be successfully conserved - that the conservation cost was prohibitively high.

Yormak: "If we had a billion dollars, it wouldn't matter? Is that what you're saying?"

Englebert: "No, it wouldn't matter."

If this were true, and not just his justification for permanently denying access, then why was anyone even thinking about spending millions of dollars on a feasibility study? What could possibly be proven or established by conducting such a study - other than to maintain control over the sites while holding the wrecks in stasis? The only benefit that could accrue from such a study would accrue to the members of the Technical Study Team (which included Englebert), who stood to make a tidy and ongoing profit from the sinecure.

It seemed to me that all the "bocrats" involved with the *Hamilton* and *Scourge* were running a money scam.

Unrequited Love

When Yormak asked Englebert about Margaret Rule's report, Englebert prefaced his response by stressing his association with her. "We had many, many conversations over the space of the two weeks. . . . Margaret and I have a very good, very collegial relationship." Nonetheless, Englebert disagreed with Rule's findings in nearly every instance, particularly with regard to structural instability, unchecked rate of deterioration, and the dearth of silt.

Months later, Yormak telephoned Rule in England in order to obtain her archaeological insights on the condition of the wrecks, and how they differed from Englebert's self-serving evaluations. Rule informed Yormak that Englebert had not even been on the expedition. Phil Wright was still the head of the Archaeological Licence bureau at that time, and it was he who worked with Rule on the Woods Hole expedition.

Ergo, Englebert's avowed "conversations" and "relationship" were either figments of his evil imagination, or - more likely - carefully contrived fabrications intended to add authenticity to his statements.

Yormak spoke with Wright and obtained his corroboration. Wright told him that he - not Englebert - worked as Rule's assistant. Rule's final report was "gagged by the Ministry" and was never published because of its recommendations. Wright admitted that he left the Ministry because of bureaucratic "bullshit." (Wright's word).

Databaseless

It was necessary for Englebert to implant these falsehoods in order to convey a sense of validity to his opinions. The reader is reminded that the City of Hamilton never bothered to obtain copies of the photographs that were taken during the Woods Hole expedition. Englebert had confirmed this fact earlier in his testimony. This begs the question: how could Englebert reach conclusions that contradicted those of Margaret Rule, if he had not been party to the expedition and had never seen the photographs of objects on which Rule's assessment was based?

Englebert lacked first-hand experience, and had no access to second-hand data. He glibly claimed that he had watched videotapes of the wrecks - but neglected to mention specifically that these were Woods Hole expedition videotapes. Knowing Englebert's propensity for doubletalk, he may have been referring to National Geographic videotapes. This could have been another one of Englebert's deceptions. Or perhaps it was audacious imposture.

As it developed, the only footage to which Englebert and the City of Hamilton had access was that which was broadcast. As Yormak phrased it: "A very small part of a mountain of material." To which Englebert could do nothing but agree. Thus Englebert's testimony was based at best upon a few scraps of footage, and not the scores of hours of live-feed which Margaret Rule had seen on the monitors and later on videotape.

It is worthwhile to note that before this litigation Englebert had never voiced or documented his disagreements with Rule's professional findings. He disagreed at the time of his deposition, when such disagreement could be utilized to promote his personal interests.

I wondered: Did Lyon support Englebert's falsehoods, or was she ignorant of them?

Noteless

When Yormak asked Englebert if he had taken notes during the expedition, Englebert replied, "I took some notes of daily activities." When Yormak asked him to produce those notes, Englebert was not certain that he kept the notes, and Lyon objected to their production. Englebert countered by claiming that his notes were not archaeological in nature, but "times that the work was done and on what ship we were working on."

Yormak: "So you didn't keep notes at that time and you're telling us now that Ms. Rule is wrong in some cases and just has a different interpretation of observations?"

Englebert: "That's correct."

Yormak established that Margaret Rule drafted her report within six months of the end of the expedition, while her memory was still fresh and after having had time to review *all* of the footage that had been shot.

Raising the Issue of Raising

Segueing from Rule's report, Yormak asked Englebert if was concerned about damage to the wrecks. Englebert stated unequivocally that he had no immediate concerns. If Englebert believed that Yormak's question referred to a concern that I had articulated, he was sadly mistaken.

Yormak read from a letter which William McCulloch had sent to me: "We're just as anxious as you are that the ships be recovered. We have identified three major areas of concern. One, the apparent affect of the increasing water pollution in Lake Ontario; two, the possible danger of a merchant ship dropping a heavy object on or near the site; three, the danger of vandalism." McCulloch was the chairperson of the *Hamilton-Scourge* Steering Committee.

Yormak directed a question to Englebert: "You told us and I have written down you have no immediate concern. What do you say to that person's concern?"

Englebert was caught in the middle. He had to either save professional face by disabusing McCulloch, or to side with his co-conspirator and reverse his stand. "One, there was no evidence that increased water pollution in Lake Ontario is causing any problems for these ships. Or that water pollution period has caused a problem. I'm not aware that it's increasing, either. Two, merchant ships dropping a heavy object. This is not on the merchant shipping lanes. It is far removed from the merchant shipping anchorage for the Welland Canal. . . . "

Before he could proceed, Lyon objected to any reference to vandalism. Lyon

THE MASTER OF DECEIT 103

had a hang-up about the issue of vandalism. She had already objected to any discussion of vandalism on at least three occasions. Lyon: "We'll raise the same objection that due to safety concerns, we don't want to get into that." I have no idea what safety concerns had to do with vandalism, or on what her bias was based.

Yormak totally ignored her obsession. Nor did he bother to suggest at the time that, while merchant vessels might not anchor in the vicinity of the *Hamilton* and *Scourge*, or pass over the area, fishing boats might either drop anchors while anglers fished or might snag fishing nets in the wreckage.

The World Must Be Wrong

He quoted another of McCulloch's statements: "It's crucial that the ships be raised because the longer they sit at the bottom of Lake Ontario, the greater the risk of deterioration. There are concerns that historic treasures are being damaged by currents, pollution and water borne silt." To Englebert: "Can you comment on those three items?"

He had previously stated that the Woods Hole ROV was maneuvered by propellers that were mounted atop the unit, and that therefore the propeller wash was deflected upward, away from the lake bed and the wrecks. This was hogwash rather than properly deflected prop wash. Perhaps he did not know that I had obtained the ROV specifications by means of FOIA, and that I knew that drive and steering propellers were mounted aft and on the sides. Englebert's lie was crucial to his premise that divers would disturb the silt unavoidably while ROV's did not.

Englebert: "I don't agree with that statement. I think it's overstated." He thought that "currents are probably minimal." He thought that "the issue of current born silt or water borne silt isn't a real problem."

Yormak: "Now, you've got Mr. McCulloch apparently in different situations coming up with five or six different concerns. You've got Ms. Rule who you stated has overstated her observations. How do you figure? Is everybody overstating things?"

Englebert: "Yeah, I would say they are."

Yormak: "Why do you figure they're doing that?"

Englebert: "I don't know what's in their minds." Lyon then objected that the question called for Englebert "to speculate on information he doesn't have."

Yormak: "All right. Can you think of any motive they may have that would cause them to overstate an agenda that you're aware of?"

Lyon objected again.

Yormak: "Do you have any reason to believe these are anything other than their own honest opinions, differing as they are from yours?"

Lyon objected once again. Yormak dropped the line of questioning. But he had established the point that both the City of Hamilton and Englebert (as the oppressive moving force behind the Archaeological Licence Bureau) had, with the sleight-of-hand facility of a stage-show prestidigitator, engineered contradictory objections to public access.

Dereliction of Duty

Yormak next referred to a scribbled note that was dated October 27, 1994: "Peter called Marilynn Havelka . . . City don't want divers on wreck. There are no plans at present to raise H and S. It is not a tourist attraction."

Yormak wanted to know why, with the knowledge that an archaeological license was moot until the City granted permission to dive on the wrecks, Englebert continued to make requests for revisions, and pursued alternative means of preventing a dive from occurring (such as attempting to invoke OSHA regulations), and eventually put my license application on hold. "Do you think you owed him some sort of duty . . . to inform him of the development from this memo?"

Argument raged throughout eight pages of transcript. Englebert spent two pages contesting that he was the Peter in the reference. There was one other Peter in the department. Yormak finally got Englebert to admit that the other Peter had nothing to do with either my license application or underwater archaeology. Englebert finally conceded that he was the Peter in the reference.

Both Barkwell and Lyon ganged up on Yormak with a variety of objections and blatant diversions. Barkwell claimed that Havelka was only an employee of the City, that her word did not constitute policy, and that her verbal assurance did not necessarily represent the City's official position. Lyon did not think that Englebert had a "duty to perform." Englebert claimed that an informal telephone conversation did not constitute a formal declaration on the part of the City.

Yormak persisted, despite concerted attempts at obfuscation: "Do you feel any moral obligation, Mr. Englebert?" Lyon objected, and would not permit Englebert to answer. Yormak: "So in other words, you . . . allowed this applicant to continue up and back with a licensing application, fully being aware . . . that the City of Hamilton was not going to allow him to dive, and you feel that you had no reason to tell Mr. Gentile of this development?"

Lyon raised objections, and so did Barkwell. Counsel did not want this question answered. A truthful answer from Englebert would have been an admission of conspiracy.

Yormak: "I'll just leave it at that. If you don't want to answer the question why you wouldn't advise an applicant, a potential licensee, of a development like this, . . . don't . . . answer."

The refusal to answer was a clear indication of guilt. The point that Yormak made for the record, and which he would call to the attention of the judge at the trial, was that Englebert had been intentionally jerking me around.

A Tissue of Lies

Time and again during his deposition, Englebert claimed that he did not know the answer to Yormak's questions, such as those that dealt with administrative hierarchy, the people who were involved in handling my application for a license, the background machinations, and policy. His answers were seldom direct; instead, they were evasive and demonstrably unclear: smokescreens designed to hide an awful truth.

The reader might suppose that Englebert could not be wholly knowledgeable about my case. On the contrary, it was firmly established that he had insinuated himself into every aspect of my proposal, even before I submitted it. He was the chief artificer of the tactics that were designed to protract the licensing process and to frustrate the successful accomplishment of the proposed dive trip. He initiated contacts with the City of Hamilton and the Ministry of Labour, and went out of his way to give advice on how to obstruct me. Englebert's stance - that he was not conversant with every feature of the case - was completely spurious. He was in the thick of it from before it even began.

The reader should know that Yormak had no say in the selection of Ministry witnesses. When the Ministry interceded in the case, it assumed a legal and moral obligation to furnish witnesses who could answer questions fully and truthfully. Lyon *chose* Englebert as her star witness. This choice was supposed to be based upon his background knowledge of the case. To claim during the deposition that Englebert lacked such knowledge was a clear demonstration of bad faith. It appeared that Lyon chose Englebert specifically because of his well-established skill in doublespeak: the capacity to give meaningless or confusing answers that could be easily misinterpreted. In that regard Englebert was a master bar none.

Yormak often engaged in dialogue that occupied several pages of transcript in trying to get Englebert to respond to a simple yes or no question. Even then, after numerous sidetracks and oblique references, Englebert's answer was more likely to be, "I suppose so," or "It could be." Englebert's deposition reads more like a fencing match than an attempt to provide useful information.

In American jurisprudence, a lawyer is an officer of the court. As such, an attorney was bound by a strong code of ethics to be honest and forthright. Before my deposition, Yormak told me that he was not permitted ethically to coach me a witness, so he did not. He gave me only three words of advice: "Tell the truth." I did.

I wonder what kind of advice Lyon gave to Englebert.

Summation

Englebert expended an inordinate amount of time and effort in trying to justify two pet concepts: that every activity could be construed as archaeology, and that the *potential* publication of a story or photograph constituted a commercial enterprise. He wanted to propound these concepts because the conduct of archaeology required a permit which he was empowered to withhold, and because a commercial enterprise had to conform to OSHA diving regulations, which would make the proposed dive prohibitively expensive.

The former notion is absurd. No professional archaeologist or impartial tribunal could possibly accept his self-serving definition of archaeology. Englebert painted himself into a corner with the circular argument that what made a shipwreck an archaeological site was that a license was required in order to dive on it.

The latter notion was unduly presumptuous.

Yormak wanted to know how many archaeological licenses were issued per year, and how many applications were denied. Englebert claimed not to know (although it was his full-time job to handle license applications), and Lyon vigorously refused to furnish the information. What they were trying to hide?

Later, from Scott McWilliam, we learned that only ten licenses were presently active, and most of those had been granted for recreational activities, not archaeological projects. Imagine that - an entire bureau existed to process and maintain less than a dozen licenses!

In order to ascertain the validity of the practice of automatically drafting a license approval, such as the one that Jane Marlatt had written in my name but which was later voided by person or persons unknown, Yormak asked the Ministry to furnish a similarly voided license. Again, the Ministry refused. Thus it could not be verified that this was the common practice. Nor did we ever ascertain which individual or group of individuals decided to void the license which Marlatt had granted.

Rumors cannot be introduced as evidence in court, but they can reveal dark truths and offer lines of investigation, while offering insights about which questions to ask and how to ask them. I was informed anonymously that Phil Wright quit the Archaeological Licence Bureau because he could not stand the infantile bureaucracy, and that subsequent to his resignation he was diametrically opposed to Englebert's thwarted views with respect to the measure of control that he exerted. Unfortunately for the case, I was also told that Wright did not want to make his personal views known publicly. Too bad, or we could have used him as a witness.

Both Havelka and Englebert claimed that they did not know the answers to many of Yormak's questions. Likely they were avoiding the truth by professing ignorance. In both cases, the witnesses were chosen (Havelka by the City, Englebert by the Ministry) because they were supposed to be knowledgeable about their area of expertise. If they were truly as ignorant as they presented themselves, who did know what was going on?

Murdock spoke about education, diver awareness, and self-policing. If these mechanisms worked on other shipwrecks, why would they not work on the *Hamilton* and *Scourge*? Depth of water does not reduce self-awareness or make divers stupid or erratic - at least, not when they are breathing a helium mix.

Murdock described "finning" as a destructive activity, by stressing that the straight-leg kick stirred the silt. Either he was unaware or he refused to accept the anti-silting technique of the frog kick. He testified that artifacts that were gently placed on top of a gravelly bottom could be moved by a powerful, full-legged kick. He failed to realize that original artifacts would have nestled into the lakebed. Yormak forced him to admit that the depth of sediment on the decks of the *Hamilton* and *Scourge* was constantly changing because of dynamic water flow, in which case "finning" was irrelevant.

All three bureaucratic witnesses were reluctant to give direct answers to Yormak's questions. It was only through Yormak's persistence in rewording and asking his questions over and over that he obtained any kind of intelligible information. Englebert was the worst in this regard, often equivocating for three or more pages of transcript before arriving at an answer.

None of them was willing to admit that visibility on the sites must have increased dramatically since the introduction of zebra mussels. I will touch upon that subject later.

Chapter 7
The Trials of Postponement

Disorder in the Court

Once again I was led to believe that my active participation in the case was at an end. Now it was up to Yormak and Hess to proceed with the legal preparations for the trial. After four years of concentrated effort, I expected to quietly retire from the case, and leave the remainder of the proceedings to the attorneys. Little did I know . . .

I expected the history of lies, deceit, and conspiracy to be brought to the attention of the court forthwith. Instead, the case assumed new twists, unpredictable turns, and unpardonable delays - wheelings and dealings in which the opposition excelled. The opposition did not want all the damaging facts disclosed, and they did not want the case to go to trial.

From this point forward it would be confusing to describe events in a strictly chronological sequence. Many events happened concurrently or in overlapping fashion. Instead, in the following sections, I will bring each event to its ultimate conclusion.

Funding Fakery

Barkwell announced to Yormak that the City had obtained $1.3 million in funding for what had been fancily termed the Ghost Ships Millennium Project. "You should treat this information as revising answers given on the examination of Ms. Havelka regarding the availability of Federal funds."

The purpose of Barkwell's announcement was to forestall recreational diving on the notion that the public would be enjoined from access to the wrecks during on-site investigations that could now be commenced. Barkwell exaggerated the truth of the matter. In actual fact, the federal government had voiced optimism that it would be willing to *match* local funding up to that amount - but only on the proviso that the City invested its share of the money. In other words, if the City expended half a million dollars on the Project, then the federal government would donate an equal amount.

In the event, the City of Hamilton never invested *any* money in the Project. Consequently, no funds were forthcoming from the federal government. The newly named Project died aborning through lack of local support, if indeed it had not been aborted or, perhaps, never conceived.

The Dirt Digger

During the winter there was a convention in New York that was attended by archaeologists, politicians, and maritime attorneys from both the United States and Canada. One attendee was Ole Varmer, the NOAA attorney who represented

THE TRIALS OF POSTPONEMENT

the government for two of the four trials that resulted from my suit to procure public access to the *Monitor*. He prevailed in two of the trials, but the court's opinion was overruled by Congressional action. Public access was thereby assured.

Another attendee was Peter Barkwell. Barkwell had thoroughly investigated my background, so he knew all about the *Monitor* case. He asked Varmer, "What kind of dirt can you give me on Gentile?" This knavish device was in keeping with his attempt to besmirch my character instead of arguing his case on points of law.

Varmer replied, "I don't have any dirt on Gentile. In fact, I think you should let him dive the wrecks."

Varmer later related this conversation to Hess, who related it to me and Yormak. I was gleeful but astonished at his pronouncement. After all, he had been my stern adversary, and had had to suffer the ignominy of prevailing in two trials, only to have the final ruling overturned in my favor. Despite our adversarial positions, he - along with other newcomers to the ranks of NOAA - had slowly come to realize that public access was not only a fitting civil right, but was ultimately beneficial to both the public and the *Monitor*.

The resultant publicity elevated the *Monitor's* image in the public consciousness. This heightened awareness was partly responsible for encouraging Congress to allocate large-scale funding for continued studies of the wreck, as well as for several highly publicized recovery efforts. Over the course of several years, Navy divers recovered the propeller, the turret, and the engine. Funding was also allocated for long-term preservation, custodianship, and display.

I was gratified by Varmer's change of heart and his defense of the righteous stance.

I was appalled that Barkwell stooped to such a low and unethical posture.

More Depositions Scheduled

Two more days of depositions were scheduled for March 25 and 26, 1999. The City of Hamilton again produced Peter Waddell. His deposition was supposed to have been taken place after mine, but because of Lyon's feigned illness and subsequent day-long questioning there had been no time. Englebert was being recalled for re-direct by Lyon. She desperately needed to do some damage control on the facts that Yormak managed to wrangle out of Englebert. Her cross examination should have taken place after Yormak completed his questioning, but because of Englebert's frustrating delaying tactics, there had been no time.

For personal reasons, Yormak was unable to appear for Englebert's deposition until 11 o'clock in the morning. He notified Barkwell and Lyon to that effect. When he arrived at 11:13, he was informed that everyone had left at 11 o'clock, despite his instructions to remain for his appearance.

Weeks later, Lyon suggested that Englebert's cross examination be completed in Ottawa. This location would require Yormak to travel by air or train, thus incurring the additional expenses of travel and lodging.

The trial date was set for May 31, 1999: only two months away.

Undertakings, or Undertakers?

An "undertaking" is a promise that one attorney makes to another to produce documents. Barkwell and Lyon made a number of undertakings during my deposition and the depositions of Havelka and Englebert. These undertakings were necessitated by the fact that (in my case) issues arose which referred to documents that opposing counsel had neglected to furnish, and because (in the cases of Havelka and Englebert) questions went unanswered due to their avowed lack of knowledge. In the latter instance, Yormak asked Barkwell and Lyon to produce documents that would either substantiate the testimony or supplant it.

Professional courtesy demands that undertakings be undertaken in a timely manner. Neither Barkwell nor Lyon acted professionally or courteously. Yormak's reminders and Barkwell's and Lyon's bad-faith promises created a long paper trail that decimated a number of Canadian forests. No one wants to admit damaging evidence, but in a courtroom setting, full disclosure is the only way in which justice can be served.

While I had nothing to hide, opposing counsel opposed full disclosure because it was detrimental to their case. They adopted a steadfast policy of refusing to honor their undertakings. Barkwell had also promised Yormak that he could visit the *Hamilton/Scourge* "lab": a repository at which the City stored documents relating to the wrecks.

The only legal recourse that Yormak had to obtain these documents and force a visit to the lab was to file a motion and explain to the judge that, not only were opposing counsels failing to honor their promises, but they were withholding important information that was pertinent to the case. Opposing counsels would argue that the documents should not be produced. The judge would then order the production of the documents.

There was no penalty for refusal, and therefore no incentive to produce. As a result, opposing counsels continued to withhold the documents. Yormak filed another motion, and another, and another . . .

These machinations were occurring in the background while the rest of the case was proceeding, and generated additional work for Yormak. He was a sole practitioner, while the City and the Province had unlimited resources (both physically and monetarily) to plead their objections. They had nothing to lose and everything to gain by this process. At the very least, part of their strategy was to wear me down financially, for every time Yormak had to appear in court, it cost me money.

In the end, we never received most of the documents. I wonder what was so damaging about them.

The Money Drain

Hess had yet to put up his share of the costs. I will still paying all the bills. So far I had laid out more than $14,000, with no end in sight.

Since I was maintaining a negative cash flow, outside funding became paramount. I knew from my experience with the *Monitor* case that obtaining donations was a fruitless and frustrating exercise in futility. But until Hess repaid me for the half that I had loaned on his account, I had no way to cover the ever-growing costs other than to borrow more money. But I was getting too far into the red, and was fast approaching my credit limit.

According to Yormak, the first four depositions alone cost $2,700. I had to send him additional money as soon as I returned from Toronto. Again, Hess pleaded poverty.

Yormak substantiated his bill by claiming that the court recorder had to be paid her daily salary, and that extra money was needed to purchase written transcripts. It seemed to me that $2,700 was an exorbitantly high cost for four days work and the printing of the transcripts from her computer.

It was - but I did not know it then.

The truth was finally disclosed in April, when Yormak submitted a Summary of Fees. He claimed to have expended $33,720.00 in my behalf. This amount included actual expenses, plus an hourly charge of $200 for every hour or portion thereof that he claimed to have worked on the case.

I was dumbfounded. Hess had led me to believe that Yormak was working pro bono. Now it seemed that he had been charging $200 an hour all along. That was why the court recorder and transcript cost was so high. The bill was not based upon how much the services *cost*, but how much Yormak *charged*!

I called Yormak right away. As was his practice, his secretary fielded the call and refused to put me through to him. Nor did Yormak return my call. I had to call Hess to act as an intermediary, because Yormak would take Hess's calls. Hess spoke with Yormak, then arranged a three-way conference call.

A heated discussion ensued. Yormak insisted that he had never agreed to accept the case pro bono. Hess argued counterpoint. I was caught in the middle because I had only Hess's word to contradict Yormak's declaration. After long negotiations, Yormak agreed to become one of a triumvirate in support of the case: as if he, Hess, and I were equal partners and financial backers. By this means he suggested that his hourly charge would be split into thirds, and that he would donate his third of his fee. In effect, he was willing to reduce his hourly charge to two thirds of his "usual" rate, to $133 per hour.

This reduction did not include expenses that were actually incurred. Yormak claimed reimbursement in the amount of $1,514.62 for lodging, and $322.65 for travel expenses, among other distributions.

I wanted to know why Hess was not helping in the legal work in order to reduce Yormak's hourly charges. Hess claimed that he did not know Canadian legal formality, did not have access to Canadian case law, and was not in a position to write any of the briefs or motions. In fact, he had so far done not a lick of legal work on the case.

Hess's major contribution was in writing letters to hopeful supporters and begging for donations, in order to make up for his lack of contribution. In other words, he was trying to get other people to pay his portion of the legal expenses. I was still the sole supporter. What irked me as much as his lack of pecuniary assistance was that he was promoting himself as a financial supporter of the litigation - taking credit for Yormak's legal work and for my monetary expenditures.

Mission Statement

I spoke with several of my Canadian friends about asking for donations from local divers. Some of them suggested their willingness to donate small sums of money to the cause, because all of them would be affected by the precedent-setting outcome. Admittedly, though, they were more interested in changing the Province's position with respect to shipwrecks and archaeology than they were in obtaining access to the *Hamilton* and *Scourge*.

Susan Yankoo thought that I could best achieve my goal by issuing a Mission Statement: a document that expressed the background and objectives of the litigation for those who were unfamiliar with the case. I thought this was a good idea.

While drafting the Statement, I kept in mind the likelihood that the opposition would obtain a copy through its spy network, and attempt to use it against me. By its general circulation, the Mission Document could be construed as a public document that was admissible in court. Therefore, I appended the objectives with facts that were intended to make the Statement potentially disadvantageous to opposition counsels - their gains might be more than offset by their losses. I constructed the Mission Statement so that it fit on a single sheet of paper:

Mission Statement

This statement is intended to clarify the concurrent goals with respect to my suit against the City of Hamilton. The primary purposes of this suit are as follows:

• To gain lawful access to the underwater shipwreck sites *Hamilton* and *Scourge* for the purpose of recreational diving.
• To ensure future access to the *Hamilton* and *Scourge* for the purpose of recreational diving.
• To refute the claim made by Ontario Ministry's archaeology license bureau that a license is required to search for lost shipwrecks.
• To refute the claim made by Ontario Ministry's archaeology license bureau that a license is required to conduct recreational dives on shipwreck sites, when the avowed purpose of the dive is recreational and not archaeological.
• To refute the contention made by Ontario Ministry's archaeology license bureau that it is vested with the authority to confiscate the personal possessions of those who conduct non-archaeological activities on shipwreck sites, on the premise that the archaeology license bureau has misinterpreted its authority, if any authority exists at all.
• To refute the claim made by Ontario Ministry's archaeology license bureau that it has the authority to arrest, or to cause to be arrested, those who conduct non-archaeological activities on shipwreck sites, on the premise that the archaeology license bureau has misinterpreted its authority, if it has any authority at all.
• Also being considered is an attack against the Province's

foundation to enforce anything archaeological (The Heritage Act) by asking the Court to strike down the entire legislation on the grounds of vagueness and uncertainty.

The Province of Ontario Ministry's archaeology license bureau has intervened in this case on the side of the City of Hamilton, both of whose goal is to prevent recreational diver access to the *Hamilton* and *Scourge*, with the additional goal of the Province to affirm and establish its sole authority to determine which activities constitute archaeology and are therefore licensable and fall under its control.

One of the main thrusts of the defense prosecuted by the City and the Province appears to be to impugn my character - as if my character were at issue instead of recreational access to the *Hamilton* and *Scourge*, and instead of abuses of the authority vested in the archaeology license bureau.

For example, Peter Barkwell, representing the City of Hamilton, tried to besmirch my reputation by calling Ole Varmer, the NOAA attorney who opposed me at the *Monitor* hearings, and asking, "What kind of dirt can you give me on Gentile?"

At my deposition, Anita Lyon, representing the Province of Ontario, made continual accusations against my integrity, in part by insinuating that my purpose in wanting to dive the *Hamilton* and *Scourge* was not recreational but commercial. She badgered me constantly about the purity and sincerity of my intent.

My position is that the actions of the City and the Province are discriminatory, that the City has violated its public trust with respect to the *Hamilton* and *Scourge*, and that the Province's interpretation of the authority vested in the archaeology license bureau is not only overbroad, but self-serving, arbitrary, and capricious.

As I expected, opposition counsel obtained a copy - I suspect, by having someone pose as an interested party on the side of recreational diving. Lyon introduced the document into evidence despite Barkwell's provocative protests. Barkwell was absolutely incensed by the fact that his perfidy and lack of professional conduct would be brought to the attention of the court, and that it would become public knowledge. He tried to have the document dismissed, but Lyon would not hear of it.

Dribbles and Drabs
I sent copies of my Mission Statement to interested parties, and asked them to distribute the Statement as they saw fit. Response was lackluster. Susan Yankoo and George Wheeler donated money to the cause, and collected some donations from fellow Canadians. Rather than have them send the money to me so that I could send it to Yormak, I asked them to keep their own account. Otherwise, the money would have had to be exchanged to American dollars and

then re-exchanged to Canadian dollars, incurring a two-time loss in the double process.

Money dribbled in slowly, and never in amounts more than a few dollars. Some people called or sent queries and asked how they could help the cause. When I replied, "Send money," I never heard from them again. Either they lacked sincerity, or they were shilling for the City of Hamilton or the Archaeological Licence Bureau.

Long-time correspondent, researcher, and shipwreck salvor Howard Tower wrote, "I'll help you out as best I can. We're getting too old for this. I wish the younger generation would breed a few fighters." I disagreed with his sentiments about age, but his second allegation conveyed too much of a tinge of truth.

Several divers were willing to make small donations if they were promised a spot on the boat in return. I made my point clear to one respondent: "Understand that I am not selling spots on the dive, if a recreational trip should ever eventuate. I don't even know if you are a diver. But to be clear, divers will be selected by their technical diving experience and expertise, and by having a recent history of diving to equivalent depths. It would be unconscionable for me to offer the reward of a dive to someone who put up money for the cause, if that person were not qualified to conduct the dive safely."

Hess steadfastly refused to cough up his full share of the cost. He did, however, forward to Yormak a check for $2,800. Some of this money he had collected from other donors, and some was his own contribution. I never ascertained the actual breakdown. This was enough to persuade Yormak to continue litigation.

Not until a year later did I learn that Yormak also received more than a thousand dollars that Yankoo and Wheeler collected, but I never learned precisely how much, and I never received an accounting of how that money was spent. It simply vanished into Yormak's endless coffer.

Justice is available only to those who can afford to pay for it.

Never-ending Delay

The City and the Ministry had already conspired to postpone the trial date in order to miss the 1998 diving season. Now they were conspiring to make me miss the 1999 season. As Yormak so succinctly phrased the situation, in the absence of firm legal grounds, the primary strategy of the opposition was "to delay, obstruct and complicate the litigation thereby driving the expenses skyrocketing beyond any reasonable expectation in the hope, we presume, that you will forego the balance of these proceedings and abandon your application.

"While I do appreciate your full support to date it is obvious that for this matter to continue other support must be forthcoming in the immediate future."

I replied on April 17: "Peter Hess said that he would call you to discuss his financial participation. He told me that a settlement is pending on a case that he is handling, after which he will seek to match my investment in this cause. (He has been telling me this now for several months.) He said also that he was going to seek outside support. For now, he will send an amount that should see us through the next phase, particularly in light of the cost reduction stipulated in the following paragraph.

"Per your letter of April 8, 1999 to Anita Lyon, I hereby specifically deny the continuance of Englebert's deposition. I do this not because of the cost it would incur, but because I agree (as does Peter) with your initial assessment that we have more to lose than we have to gain by continuing his deposition. We have been given an advantage, and I see no reason to throw it away."

Englebert never got to say any damaging last words.

I also advised Yormak not to worry about losing the 1999 summer diving season as a result of the opposition's procrastination. "The dive can easily be conducted in October or November."

Background Support

Scott McWilliam sent a memo to Peter Hess (who, despite his lack of legal and financial support, was trying to win the case through correspondence). McWilliam wrote:

"As I mentioned in the past one of the unusual things our friend Peter Englebert had to predict was that 'hell would freeze over before Gary got to dive those wrecks.' On a separate matter Mr. Englebert has captured my attention. At this time I have sufficient material to demonstrate, in my view, that Mr. Englebert has repeatedly acted extra-legislatively in his efforts to impose his view of submerged cultural resource management in Ontario. Also, that Mr. Englebert is not particularly credible and that Mr. Englebert has repeatedly acted in Bad Faith in his dealings with Mr. Gentile and others. Should an opportunity become available to assist your client (?) I would make myself available."

His allegations were worth noting. McWilliam was formerly employed as a police officer in Thunder Bay, Ontario. In addition to his other duties, he did police diving during his five years of service. Afterward, McWilliam worked as a commercial diver. He was a qualified hyperbaric technician. He held a Bachelor of Arts degree in history and anthropology, and he had an Honors degree in anthropology specializing in archaeology and marine archaeology.

Yormak obtained additional support from Larry Murphy: a respected expert who reputation weighed mightily in the underwater archaeological community. Murphy's credentials were even better than Englebert's, in that he had actually worked in the field full time for twenty years, rather than simply issuing licenses. He was a member of the prestigious Submerged Cultural Resources Unit (known as the SCRU Team), which conducted surveys around the world under the auspices of the U.S. National Park Service. Murphy agreed to either testify in my behalf or to write an affidavit in support of my case, in contradiction to Englebert's felonious allegations that - among other items - photography and searching for shipwrecks constituted archaeology. He was a staunch supporter of human rights and public access to shipwrecks. His association with the NPS would carry weight in Canadian court.

McWilliam had worked occasionally with the SCRU Team between 1980 and 1985, during the Team's assessment of shipwrecks in Isle Royale National Park.

On the Legal Front

Yormak's research unearthed Canadian Supreme Court decisions which prohibited a city from "attempting to legislate or exert authority beyond its geographical borders." He also "uncovered cases where conflicts with the federal law disallows entry into the field altogether."

The implications were twofold: The City of Hamilton had no legal authority to keep people from visiting the *Hamilton* and *Scourge*; or, alternatively, the City itself might be enjoined from visiting the sites. This double-edged legal sword could conceivably cause the City to back down from its prosecution of the case. Englebert and the Archaeological Licence Bureau were another matter entirely.

Oh, Say Can You See . . .

The opposition's delaying tactics worked to our advantage.

One point that the opposition kept making was that visibility on the sites was limited to three feet - this despite the fact that Margaret Rule noted ten feet or better. I knew differently. I had been diving in the Great Lakes for more than a decade, and during that time I had seen visibility improve significantly in all the lower lakes in which zebra mussels proliferated.

Whereas the visibility in Lake Erie, for example, was commonly three feet or less in the 1980's, now it was often seventy-five feet, and sometimes exceeded one hundred feet. Lake Ontario was no exception. Visibility in Lake Ontario has always been good, now it was great! I noted this in my correspondence with the City, but City minions did not want to hear it. They were comfortable with poor visibility because it enhanced their chances of denying access.

We needed corroboration that could be submitted to the court. Any number of local divers was willing to testify in my behalf, but visual proof would be more effective. Enter Mark Oliphant.

Oliphant was unwilling to donate any money to the cause, but he claimed to be presently "involved" in procuring permission to dive on the *Hamilton* and *Scourge*. He even claimed to have an attorney by the name of Rob Mark'Antonio who was working out the details. I called the attorney, but he refused to take my call. I left a message with his receptionist that my business dealt with the case of the *Hamilton* and *Scourge*. Mark'Antonio never returned my call. I figured that Oliphant's "involvement" was either a smokescreen or wishful thinking.

Oliphant also claimed to have information about a Canadian company by the name of Aquatic Sciences, which was going to conduct a commercial survey of the wrecks during the summer of 1999. If this survey rumor was true, it was a closely guarded secret. The City had not divulged any documents in that regard. Yormak questioned Barkwell about it, but he disavowed all knowledge of any negotiations to conduct a commercial survey.

Furthermore, Oliphant claimed to have access to a submersible that could be used to descend to the bottom of Lake Ontario to make a videographic record of visibility. Whatever the truth of his other allegations, a visibility test in the vicinity of the wreck sites could prove invaluable. I implored him to proceed with the test at once.

THE TRIALS OF POSTPONEMENT   117

Yormak prepared a motion to supplement the evidence with the videotaped results.

Oliphant did not produce the submersible as promised. After months of excuses and delays, he dived on scuba in Lake Ontario to a depth of 150 feet, about 8 miles from the wreck sites. Visibility was thirty feet. Zebra mussels were present in great numbers on the bottom. This already well-documented information was not helpful. Exit Oliphant.

Exerting Some Mussel

Englebert contended that zebra mussels could not exist below 180 feet, and that therefore the *Hamilton* and *Scourge* were in no danger of becoming encrusted with the glue and the weight of their shells. I knew otherwise and I set out to prove it. I dived on the wreck of the *Roy A. Jodrey*, which lay in the Thousand Islands area of the St. Lawrence River, between the State of New York and the Province of Ontario.

At 240 feet, the zebra mussels clustered in such incredible thickness that I could not distinguish wreck from rock. No line of demarcation was visible between the steel plates and the granite boulders on which the hull rested. If zebra mussels were that prevalent at 240 feet - 60 feet deeper than Englebert swore in his affidavit - another 40 to 50 feet would make little difference.

My photographs confirmed the truth of the matter: zebra mussels not only lived at that depth, but thrived there. The river bed was choked with the shells of mussels that had died. I scraped some mussels off the boulders that lay on the river bed, and estimated the thickness of encrustation to be in the range of three to four inches.

If this had been the *Hamilton* or *Scourge*, the wooden hulls would have been totally obscured by the concentration of shells, and the weight of all those mussels - some thousands of pounds - would have caused major damage: especially in light of the City's contention that the wrecks were fragile.

I swore an affidavit about the proliferation of zebra mussels at depth.

I wrote to Yormak, "My greatest fear now is that the wrecks may be largely or completely encrusted. Perhaps the opposition will try to have a law passed in that regard, and have the police arrest any violating mussels. That would appear to be their mindset."

More Money Demands

The trail was more than a year behind schedule, and so far no date had been set. Perhaps September . . .

In July 1999, Yormak again pleaded for more money. I was on an expedition to the *Andrea Doria*, so Hess had to handle the discussion. Yormak complained (again) that he had yet to receive Hess's matching funds. He claimed that his own "fees" (read "hourly charges") had "dramatically escalated. . . . In addition, unfortunately through no fault of either of you a bookkeeping error occurred in my office some months ago with funds received from you whereby it was deposited in the wrong account. This has to be rectified immediately according to our own rules in this province."

He wanted $3,500 immediately.

Hess replied: "My impression is that if there was $3500 paid you and placed in the wrong account, how can we be held financially accountable for the consequences. . . . I am tapped out for funding the H & S litigation for a while at least. I will continue to try to develop new sources."

I had to put up the money which Yormak had misallocated, and which Hess was still unwilling to pay.

Fund Raising

On the *Doria* expedition I met Michael Kane, a West Coast technical diver and the owner of a company which managed the business of entertainers by arranging concerts, and by collecting and distributing the money that was generated by ticket sales. I gave him a copy of my Mission Statement, and explained my need for obtaining funding for the suit. He said that he would like to help, and he did. He thought that one way for me to generate funds was to sell more books. He bought a large assortment for his personal collection, and promised to take orders from California divers. He did as he promised, selling several hundreds of dollars worth of books, the proceeds of which I could use to offset my outstanding and still growing debt.

Kane also donated $1,000 free and clear. That made him the second largest contributor to the case. (I did not count Yormak's "fee reduction," which in my mind was equivalent to a phony sale price that was compared to an inflated retail price.) Furthermore, Kane pledged matching funds up to $5,000 to be paid after he received settlement in a civil suit in which he was involved.

I was so astonished by Kane's prompt action that I sent him immediate thanks: "You sure jump into matters with both feet! Your personality is a welcome relief to me after dealing with so many people whose convictions are imaginary or who tell a great story but never follow it up with action. . . . . You and I are very much alike. . . . Money certainly does not make the man - although it can lead him to emotional ruin if he lets it go to his head. Money is to be used, not abused. That's why I have always been willing to spend mine on just causes which I initiated. You can't take it with you, but you can use it to leave the world just a little bit better."

Later in the letter I shared my mixed feelings and state of mind about Yormak's handling of the case as well as his mishandling of my money. "I thought of having donations sent directly to the Canadian attorney, but finally decided that it was not a good idea - I'm afraid that such funds would seem to him like a gift and I would not receive proper accounting. Don't get me wrong. I have great faith in Steve Yormak - he is doing an incredible job, he has a strong handle on the law, he has enthusiasm and a sharp legal mind, and is dedicated to the case (if not necessarily to the cause). But he has been a bit of a spendthrift - as many lawyers are wont to be when they are spending a client's money. I think it becomes a habit - a perk that they take advantage of when corporate funds seem unending. For example, when we went to Toronto to give my deposition, he

THE TRIALS OF POSTPONEMENT 119

stayed in the city's most expensive hotel. I spent the first night sleeping on the floor of the bus station, then for the next night I stayed in the cheapest dive I could find. Now I make him justify each expenditure before I approve it. I just don't want money filling a bottomless maw.

Immediate Needs

Yormak pleaded that he was in desperate need of money. He claimed that by week's end he would have insufficient funds to pay his staff. I was bewildered by this announcement. He employed only one person: a secretary. If he charged at the rate of $200 per hour, I could not understand why he did not pay his secretary's weekly wages with the $8,000 that must have been generated by the previous week's charges to other clients. Why did he always have to pick on me for money, when the *Hamilton/Scourge* case represented only a fraction of his legal time?

Another bone of contention was timing. Whenever Yormak requested money - which he never did directly but by going through Hess - he wanted it delivered on the very next morning by Federal Express. This demand incurred the additional expense of international overnight delivery by air. He did not care because he was not paying the bill. I protested, suggesting that whenever he saw the need for money arising, he should contact me several days *before* the actual need arose. Then I could post the checks via ordinary mail. That was not good enough for him. When he wanted money, he wanted it *now*.

I called him - it was after five o'clock on Friday afternoon. For the very first time since this long case began, he accepted my call. I asked him why he did not get the needed payment from Hess. He said that Hess was still pleading bankruptcy. The case could not proceed unless he received an interim payment. "Could not" meant that he "would not" do any more work unless he was paid in advance.

I told him that I was departing on a trip early in the morning, and that I still had suitcases to pack, but I promised to send more money. He said, "Courier a check to me right away."

It was too late to send a check via Federal Express. And besides, I had lost patience with his insistent tardy demands. I put a check in an envelope and dropped it in the mail box the following morning on my way to the airport.

History was made again on Monday. Yormak actually broke down and personally called my house to complain that he had not received my check - the first call that he had ever placed to me. I do not know why he bothered. I had clearly informed him that I would be away for two weeks. He left another message on my answering machine on Tuesday, and yet another on Wednesday. Naturally, I did not learn of his calls until my return. He did not call on Thursday because he received my check in the mail. The delivery cost me sixty cents instead of twelve dollars.

Expression of Interest

My lawsuit was having an affect in bureaucratic circles if not on public awareness. After nearly two decades of inactivity, the City of Hamilton had finally been goaded hard enough to give the appearance of taking action. Facing the possibility that the *Hamilton* and *Scourge* might become open to public access, the City Council wrote what it termed an "Expression of Interest."

This 24-page document was a diarrhea of words but a constipation of ideas. It merely rephrased and reiterated language from previously written guidelines. The Expression of Interest was replete with highfalutin academic catchphrases that were designed to impress the pedantry. "Ghost Ships Millennium Project Module Strategy" reminded me of a book I had read about monotremes and marsupials, in which the author kept noting that animals in captivity exhibited a "stereotypic locomotive pattern." Near the end of the book I finally deduced that this meant "pacing." By the same token, a "manually operated, single-throw, cease-flow alternating electricity disconnect device" is still a light switch. A rose by any other name . . .

The sole purpose of the Expression was to get someone or some company to pay for the Project - and to pay honorariums to the City bureaucrats who held the puppet strings of authority. Members of the Steering Committee and the Technical Study Team were given as the primary recipients, as well as members of the City Council. It has long been known that the first job of a bureaucrat was to justify its existence.

The Expression glorified the achievements of the photographic documentation of the three previous expeditions (Jacques Cousteau, National Geographic, and Woods Hole), but neglected to mention that the City had not bothered to procure any of the film, video, or photographs of the latter.

Commercialization was stressed as the major motivation for the Project, which could "enhance the tourism potential locally and become an economic generator. . . . Interest in the Project can capitalize on the new trends of cultural and eco-tourism, which should ensure sustainable tourism development."

The impetus for the Expression of Interest was clearly given: "Given advances in diving technology, the City must act before technical and sport divers compromise or destroy the archaeological potential of the site or the 'as found' condition for mapping purposes." The City was still promoting the absurd presumption that "diving" and "sightseeing" were destructive activities, equivalent to "dynamiting."

Fancy phrases may look good on paper, but to explore a shipwreck, affirmative action takes place under water. The Expression of Interest drowned in its own rhetoric, and ran aground.

Motionless

The year was nearing its end, and still the trial had not been placed on the docket. This did not mean that the case was not proceeding. On more than one occasion Yormak appeared in court in order to force the production of documents from opposing counsels. He wrote briefs in support of his motions to produce. The City filed motions that the case be dropped because of the inability to adhere to the original court ordered time lines. This was absurd, as the City was the culprit responsible for dragging out the case. But that was how Barkwell and Lyon were playing the game.

Yormak informed me that the motions would not even be heard until January 2000. The date was soon changed to February.

He turned up the heat by submitting an amended application which attacked the constitutionality of Ontario Heritage Act. This caused a anticipated furor from the City and the Province.

Reneging on his Word

I was in debt to my eyeballs. Printing costs were due for my next book, I had taxes to pay, and other financial obligations to satisfy. My overdraft protection was tapped out. I could not borrow any more money without taking a second mortgage on my house. I appealed to Hess to repay the money that I had borrowed on his account.

He claimed to have paid Yormak approximately $5,000 for the case. Even if this was true, it was not all his own money, but was partially money that he had collected from other donors. How much of that $5,000 was his personal money I never ascertained. But even taking the entire $5,000 into account, he still lacked $6,000 for matching the amount that I had already contributed. I demanded that he pay up immediately. Not only was I borrowing money for him in my name, but I was paying the interest on his loan. I wanted him to borrow his own money, in his own name.

Hess refused to pay me a dime. "You never loaned me any money; you paid more than half of Steve's fees, but I never received a cent of this and I, too, have made substantial payments to him. Moreover, I have donated thousands of hours of my own legal expertise. . . . I have always been concerned with Steve's continuous stream of bills with no end in sight. . . . So I am reluctant to keep sending $1-2 K at a time in response to the latest litigation crisis in your case."

My ire was up and my patience was at an end. "I am disappointed that you now refer to the *Hamilton/Scourge* litigation as 'my' case. It began as 'our' case. You and I shook hands on the deal and agreed to split the costs of litigation. The way I loaned you money was by putting up your share of these costs when you declined to do so. . . . I expected - and still expect - you to live up to your obligation to pay half the expenses. To date I have put up $17,000 of my own money - in cash, not in hypothetical billing hours.

"As far as Steve's continuous stream of bills, remember that you selected him. I went along on your recommendation.

"I have not kept a count of the hours I have put into this case, but I am fairly certain that I have put in more time on it than you have. Or to paraphrase your own wording, I have donated many hours of my time and expertise without ever being paid anything. That, if you recall, is what we agreed to do. How you arrived at the figure of 'thousands of hours' is beyond me. Each 1,000 hours equates to 25 weeks or 6 months of continuous work. Pluralizing 'thousand' equals more than a year."

I asked Yormak how many words Hess had contributed to writing the numerous briefs, motions, and affidavits. He replied, "None." Hess had done no legal work whatsoever - not even research. All he had done was to write long-winded, self-promotional letters in which he begged for donations to make up for the money that he should have paid out of his own pocket.

The worst was yet to come.

Shot from Behind

Years before, Hess had proposed a book about the deadly war that "archs" and "bocrats" were waging against successful treasure salvors, and which ultimately resulted in the passage of the Abandoned Shipwreck Act. He wanted to call the book *The Treasure Wars*. Initially, Hess did not want to write the book. He wanted me to write it. But he wanted his name on the byline as co-author because he intended to furnish the legal documents on which the book would be based.

I demurred. I did not want to spend half a year in writing a book whose publication was doubtful. I suggested that he write the book himself. Hess contended that he was too busy in his legal practice to take the time away from his case load to write a book. Furthermore, his name was unknown in the publishing industry. In addition to wanting me to do the actual work of writing, he needed my name in order to sell the project to a publisher. I did not like the idea of doing all the work while receiving only half the royalties.

Hess then suggested that we write the book as a team. I would write the historical narrative, and he would insert the legal interpretations that would stitch the narrative chapters together. I still did not think that the book would sell, and I was unwilling to write the book on pure speculation. But I agreed to write my portion if he found a publishing house that accepted the proposal.

My promised commitment enabled him to exploit my name and reputation as he circulated the proposal throughout the publishing industry. This arrangement was a match made in Heaven: my professional writing background wedded to his natural talent and vast experience in self-promotion. Hess circulated the proposal with my name as the lead author. Credibility to our credentials of authorship was bolstered not only by the many books that I had already written, but also by the fact that I had published a lengthy article entitled *Shipwreck Legislation: Legality vs. Morality* in *The Freeman: Ideas on Liberty* - a monthly magazine that was dedicated to the concept of democracy and individual freedom.

Eventually, Hess informed me that he was negotiating with a publisher which professed a profound interest in the book. The publisher was considering an advance in the neighborhood of $500,000! For this amount of money, Hess was willing to take six months off his practice, and to subcontract his case load to other attorneys.

Unfortunately for me, after using my reputation to secure the deal, Hess now wanted to cut me completely out of the project, so he could keep the half a million for himself.

In the event, the deal was never consummated. The book is yet unwritten.

Chapter 8
The Bill 13 Caper

Sneak Attack

The Province retaliated against Yormak's offensive on the Ontario Heritage Act by submitting a new Act known as Bill 13: "An Act to preserve Ontario's marine heritage and promote tourism by protecting heritage wrecks and artifacts." In Canada, 1999 was a year that would go down in infamy.

Local divers quickly dubbed the Act as Englebert's Wish List, because it granted him autonomous authority and control over every shipwreck in his phantom domain. If Englebert did not draft the bill personally, he certainly must have had a strong hand in framing the language and specifying the attributes. This designer bill proposed to put truth to the lies that Englebert had been spreading for years about his divine rights and powers of arrest.

Toby Barrett, the Member of Parliament who proposed the bill, said that it had been suggested to him by Jim Murphy. Coincidentally, Murphy was the SOS member who accompanied Englebert to the Port Dover marina when the latter accused the Wachters and Soules of removing artifacts from Canadian shipwrecks, and of committing other illegal activities for which he could have them arrested and their boat seized. (See Chapter 3.) Could there have been some collusion? We will never know.

The Wish List

Bill 13, 1999

Her Majesty, by and with the advice and consent of the Legislative Assembly of the Province of Ontario, enacts as follows:

Purpose

1. The purpose of this Act is to enhance the protection and preservation of Ontario's marine heritage resources and to promote responsible exploration of marine heritage sites.

Definitions

2. In this Act, "heritage wreck" means the abandoned remains of a vessel, aircraft or any other prescribed object that is fully or partially submerged in waters on Crown land in Ontario and has been so submerged for a period of time [unspecified] prescribed by regulation; "marine heritage site" means the site of a heritage wreck and its associated debris area and the parts of the lake or river bed that are under them and includes any other parts of the lake or river bed that have been modified as a result of the sinking of the wreck, or as a result of subsequent sedimentary processes; "Minister" means the member of the Executive Council to whom the administration of this Act is assigned by the Lieutenant Governor in Council; "prescribed" means prescribed by the regulations made under this Act;

"protected artifact" means an object in a marine heritage site that was part of a vessel or aircraft that is a heritage wreck or that was in or on the vessel or aircraft before it sank.

Ownership

3. The Crown in right of Ontario owns every heritage wreck and protected artifact.

Prohibitions

4. (1) No person shall engage in any of the following activities unless the person is specifically authorized to do so by the terms of a licence issued under Part VI of the Ontario Heritage Act:

1. Enter a heritage wreck, or cause an object to enter a heritage wreck.

2. Move part of a heritage wreck.

3. Remove silt or other naturally occurring substances in a marine heritage site.

4. Remove a protected artifact from a marine heritage site.

5. Damage a heritage wreck or a protected artifact.

6. Take any other action that alters or adversely affects, or is likely to alter or adversely affect a marine heritage site, a heritage wreck or a protected artifact.

7. Any other activity specified in regulation.

Exception

(2) Subsection (1) does not apply at such marine heritage sites as may be prescribed but only with respect to such activities at those sites as may be prescribed.

Seizure of property

(3) A person having the power and authority of a member of the Ontario Provincial Police Force may seize a vessel or equipment which the person believes is being used or has been used to contravene this Act.

Record of wreck sites

5. The Minister shall publish, in a manner prescribed by regulation, a record of marine heritage sites known to the Minister.

Discovery of evidence

6. A person who finds physical evidence that a site is likely a marine heritage site which is not listed in a record published under section 5,

(a) shall not do anything that may alter or adversely affect the site; and

(b) shall notify the Minister of the nature and location of the evidence and the site as soon as possible.

Offence

7. (1) Every person who contravenes subsection 4 (1) or does not comply with section 6, and every director or officer of a corporation who knowingly concurs in the contravention or failure to comply, is guilty of an offence and on conviction is liable,

(a) if the person is an individual, to a fine of not more than $50,000 or to imprisonment for a term of not more than one year, or to both; or

(b) if the person is a corporation, to a fine of not more than $250,000.

Forfeiture

2) The court may also order that any vessel or equipment used in the commission of the offence be forfeited to the Crown in right of Ontario.

Factors

(3) The court may take into account the following factors in deciding upon a penalty under subsections (1) and (2):

1. The degree of damage to a heritage wreck or protected artifact, if any, caused by the person.

2. Whether the person acted for profit.

3. Whether the person has previously been found guilty of an offence under this Act or the regulations.

4. Such other factors as the court may consider appropriate.

Regulations

8. The Lieutenant Governor in Council may make regulations in respect of such matters as are referred to in this Act as being prescribed.

Crown prerogative

9. This Act shall not be construed to derogate from any Crown prerogative.

Commencement

10. This Act comes into force on the day it receives Royal Assent.

Short title

11. The short title of this Act is the Ontario Marine Heritage Act, 1999.

EXPLANATORY NOTE

The Bill creates a new Act, the Ontario Marine Heritage Act, 1999. Under the new Act, the Crown is the owner of every abandoned wreck sunk in waters on Crown land in Ontario that has been submerged for more than a prescribed period of time [again, unspecified]. These wrecks are called "heritage wrecks" in the Act. The new Act defines "marine heritage site" and prohibits anyone who does not have a licence under the Ontario Heritage Act from entering a heritage wreck or damaging or removing a heritage wreck or a protected artifact. The new Act creates an obligation to notify the Minister of evidence of a marine heritage site. The Minister must publish a record of marine heritage sites known to the Minister.

First Glance

The title of the bill - and by inference, all it contained - was stupid from the standpoint of the English language. According to the dictionary, "marine" is defined as "of or pertaining to the sea;" the word has nothing to do with rivers, bays, or fresh water lakes. Therefore, in accordance with definition, the bill applied only to those shipwrecks which lay in the ocean within Ontario's territorial limit.

The Province of Ontario is bounded on the east and west by the land of adjacent Provinces. Its southern boundary is drawn through four of the five Great Lakes. Its northern frontier borders Hudson Bay and James Bay. Nowhere does Ontario touch upon an ocean or marine environment (although the northern bays connect to the ocean on the same level. By stretching the definition, shipwrecks in the northern bays could conceivably fall under the sovereignty of the bill.)

The word that should have been was "maritime," not "marine." The dictionary meaning of maritime is, "Of or concerned with shipping or navigation."

Be that as it may, the intent of the bill's framers was clear: to assume supreme control over all shipwrecks that lay on Ontario's submerged bottomlands. This shipwreck appropriation bill went far beyond proprietorship of the *Hamilton* and *Scourge*.

Yormak's sharp legal mind immediately perceived two major flaws in the bill. Its general coverage was overbroad in that the proposed Provincial authority conflicted with and attempted to supersede Federal prerogative, which even then was being revamped as federal Bill C-35. Shipwrecks in Canadian territorial waters were already protected by the Canada Shipping Act. Yormak was way ahead of the opposition's attorneys in this regard. For months, through his contacts in the Federal government, he had been feeling out the Federal position with respect to the access to the *Hamilton* and *Scourge*. He wrote, "The feds may now consider coming into the fray now that the Province has made it clear that they think this is their jurisdiction while the feds feel it is theirs. And it may be just the case the feds may want to get involved in (*Hamilton/Scourge*) as the test case they were waiting for."

Yormak was hoping to convince the Federal government to intervene on our behalf. He cautioned that dealing with the Federal government might be a two-edged sword. Always looking at the positive side of human affairs, I was quick to point out, "One of the main problems we face now is not necessarily with the . . . Act, but with the attitude of those (or he) who administer it. A benevolent administrator would not take the hard stance which the current, totalitarian administrator(s) has taken. Thus, joining forces with the feds is not the same as jumping from the frying pan into the fire - because there might not be any fire."

In addition to the above, the bill's specific coverage conflicted with the rights of the City of Hamilton to exercise its authority over the *Hamilton* and *Scourge* as remote property. Bill 13 essentially subsumed all submerged property rights, even including Yormak's hypothetical rowboat. Without a specified age limit, any vessel that sank or any personal item that was dropped in Provincial waters became the property of the Province.

Yormak noted that under the provisions of the bill, "a LICENSE will be required of EVERYONE, individual and otherwise for EVERY dive on every occasion. . . . ADDITIONALLY it will now be a CRIMINAL OFFENSE to dive punishable up to $50,000 per individual ($250,000 for corporate) - AND (this is the unbelievable part) if you do not REPORT a wreck (yes, any wreck) this is also a criminal offense under the ACT - AND yes, they've finally said it - the Province of Ontario from here on in will officially be the OWNER of all wrecks." (Yormak's capitals.)

Imagine that: failing to report a newly located wreck would become a capital offense that was punishable by incarceration. I could not help but think of Big Brother in George Orwell's classic book of totalitarianism, *1984*. This bill went far beyond the fundamental issue of public access. Not only was it vague, overpowerful, and devoid of a system of checks and balances, but it relied upon regulations that had yet to be written, such as the age of a wreck to qualify for heritage "protection."

The silt removal prohibition was right out of Englebert's affidavit and deposition. Such a restriction could be employed to forbid diver access simply because of finwash.

Parliamentary Procedure

Bill 13 was introduced not quite in accordance with Parliamentary procedure. Under Canadian law, any proposed bill must be posted for public review, with sufficient time given to allow affected citizens to voice their concerns. Convenient public hearings must be held so that citizens could speak directly with their Members of Parliament. In order to be fair to its constituency, the Canadian government should have advertised the bill and disclosed copies to the people who were most affected by it - Canadian divers.

Instead, Barrett introduced the bill with no fanfare and with only minimal advanced notice. If he could put up the bill for vote before any divers learned about it, he could avoid the mandate to schedule public forums for discussion, and avoid unfavorable feedback until after the foul deed was an accomplished fact. Normally this sneak attack works because few average citizens pay attention to the ongoing affairs of government - they expect their MP's to keep them informed of current events. But in this case, a casual article in a local newspaper alerted local divers that they were about to be blindsided.

The Marshall Plan

Bill 13 would have had a fair chance of passing five years earlier. But modern communication systems enabled people to exchange opinions and information with little cost or effort. The mechanism that contributed the most to the bill's dissemination was the Internet. E-mails shot around the World Wide Web at lightninglike speed - quite literally, as lightning propagates at the speed of free electrons, the same as in telephone wires. In the mid-1990's, one question that was often asked was, "Do you have an e-mail address?" The Internet revolution erupted with such exponential acceleration that practically overnight the question was changed to, "What is your e-mail address?" The assumption was that everybody had one.

Previously, I tried to convince people that the *Hamilton/Scourge* situation was equivalent to a neighbor's burning house. It made sense to help the neighbor extinguish the blaze before the flames leaped across the yard and put your own house on fire. Most people took the attitude that the wind was blowing in the other direction, so why bother? "It doesn't affect me." Bill 13 changed the direction of the wind.

The two people most responsible for exploiting the Internet as a communication device were Ian and Barbara Marshall, residents of Stevensville, Ontario. Stevensville was located on the Canadian side of Niagara Falls, near St. Catherines - ironically, almost the closest point of land to the *Hamilton* and *Scourge*. Ian was a technical diving instructor, Barbara was the president of the Niagara Divers Association. Ian and Barb "marshaled" their efforts by conducting an e-mail blitz. They sent an e-mail in protest of the bill to every MPP in the Province. They e-mailed information about the bill to more than one *thousand* Ontario divers, dive shops, dive clubs, and charter boat operators.

This was no little task. But they did not stop there. They expressed their views to their fellow club members. The Niagara Divers Association voted unanimously to support opposition to the bill.

Dialogue, not Soliloquy

Divers were outraged. Bill 13 stirred up the proverbial hornet's nest. Thanks to the Marshalls' quick and relentless efforts, the Ontario wreck-diving community was galvanized into action. In December 1999, the Marshalls organized a special meeting in order to brainstorm ideas for lobbying against the unpopular Englebert Bill (as some pundits called it), and to discuss ways and means to thwart its passage.

Yormak wanted to get into the act. He solicited their business not only as an additional source of revenue, but as potential supporters for my suit against the City of Hamilton.

Yormak opined that the *Hamilton/Scourge* suit and his amended application had triggered the proposed legislation. I asked him not to make this fact known to the diving community, as it might prove counterproductive and have harmful side effects for the cause. I did not want to anger divers into misplacing their aggression. They needed to stay focused on the real culprit. Nor did I accept responsibility for Englebert's political manipulations.

Rhetoric ran rampant. But this time divers did more than complain. They hired Yormak to represent their interests, and they started a letter-writing campaign that was unprecedented in Canadian diving history.

The Marshalls created a Bill 13 website. The website provided information about the bill's dire implications. The website provided links to all the Members of Parliament. The website contained a form letter that could be printed and photocopied for people who did not have Internet access. This letter could be signed and sent to MPP's as it was written, or it could be altered if the sender wanted to add his or her own personal views.

Other clubs joined in the collaborative effort to oppose the bill. Funds were raised. Another six hundred e-mails were sent to divers, dive shops, dive clubs, and charter boat operators in the U.S. Americans did not possess any constitutional right to vote against the bill, but they could provide moral and financial support - which they did.

The Professional Association of Dive Instructors threw its not inconsiderable weight on the side of divers in opposition to the bill. PADI's official corporate mission statement reads, "We are committed to the protection of underwater cultural heritage for the future of divers and non-divers alike."

A large number of Great Lakes wreck-divers - both Canadian and American - belonged to Save Ontario Shipwrecks. Most members were incensed by the fact that the bill had been proposed by an SOS member. They felt that they had been sold down the river (or down the lake) by a fellow member. Individual members objected to the bill - so many, in fact, that SOS adopted an official posture in opposition to the bill. Jim Murphy became persona non grata.

The Marshalls instigated an awareness campaign that stimulated the news media. Press releases were circulated. Newspapers and dive magazines aired misgivings about the bill.

Barrett was shocked at the violent diatribe that "his" bill fomented among the citizenry. If he had been led to believe that the passage of the bill would be uncontested, he was strongly disabused of the notion. He went on the defensive by suggesting modifications to the bill. Divers - perhaps the most ardent group of preservationists in the country - were neither appeased nor mollified by his continually changing stance that sought to win their support or to appease their dissent.

Shipwrecks 2000

The Niagara Divers Association organized an annual conference that was attended by more than five hundred divers from around the continent. Ian Marshall asked me to speak at Shipwrecks 2000 - not only to give a slide presentation, but to talk with attendees about the *Hamilton* and *Scourge*, and the ramifications of Bill 13.

I was already negotiating with another conference holder for the same weekend in March. After conferring with Ian, however, I realized that more was at stake than simply entertaining an audience. I also discovered that my fight against the City of Hamilton was more widely known among divers than I had imagined. A silent and hitherto unknown (to me) minority was rooting for my victory because of the precedent that it would establish for diver access to shipwrecks in Canada. Ian thought that my appearance could help the cause.

I agreed to attend. When I informed Steve Yormak about my participation in the event, he thought that it would be a good venue for him to make a formal presentation about Bill 13.

The conference was paying my expenses as well as a stipend. I volunteered to stay at the Marshall's house instead of a motel. This not only saved money for the Niagara Divers Association, but it offered a homey atmosphere in which I could get to know my Canadian hosts a little better.

Friday afternoon before the conference, Ian and Barbara met me at the airport in Buffalo, New York. They drove me across the border to their home in Stevensville. Yormak drove from his home in London (100 miles to the west) the following morning. He brought all his case files with him - three milk crates filled with miscellaneous papers. We spent most of the day in discussion. I took the opportunity to familiarize myself with aspects of the case which Yormak had been handling on his own: motions and countermotions, more motions and countermotions, appearances in court in support of his motions to produce documents, and so on.

I was awed and impressed by the amount of work that he had put into the case. I did not see Hess's signature on any of the documents. This led me to ask how much of the paperwork had been generated by Hess. Yormak said, "None." He was working with Hess for the benefit of ProSEA. When they were together at ProSEA meetings, they discussed the *Hamilton/Scourge* case, but that was as much input as Hess had given. This occasional verbal exchange constituted Hess's "thousands of hours" of "legal expertise" - about the laws of a country of which he professed to be ignorant.

This led Yormak to lament about his need for more money. He understood my desperate financial straits. He acknowledged Hess's endless quest to find donors to make up for his lack of financial support. But Hess was a fellow attorney with whom he was working on this other matter, so Yormak extended unprejudiced professional courtesy.

On the stage that afternoon, I gave a slide presentation and made a short pitch about divers' right. I did not mention the *Hamilton* and *Scourge* publicly, because of the likelihood that the City and the Province had shills in the audience. I let Yormak talk about the legal aspects of Bill 13. Afterward, in private, I talked with quite a few people about the *Hamilton* and *Scourge*. One of these - who figured prominently in forthcoming events - was Nick Drakich, owner of Kingston Diving Centre.

The conference generated a great deal of sympathy and not a little money to continue lobbying for the cause. The auditorium, the vendor's room, even the hallways, resonated with discontent over Bill 13. These divers were facing the loss of their favorite avocation - all because of the self-deification of a single individual.

In addition to the money collected to fight Bill 13, Ian and Barbara dug into their coffers to add a couple of hundred dollars to my own personal fund, to defray my continuing and escalating costs of litigation.

That evening, Yormak whisked me away before the post-conference dinner, and drove me to a restaurant in Hamilton (30 miles to the west), where we met Ed Burtt. Burtt was a successful treasure salvor and the owner of a long-standing commercial diving outfit. He was currently involved in salvaging treasure wrecks off Cuba. In inland home waters, Burtt had discovered a wreck that he believed was the *Speedy* - an 80-foot schooner that sank in 1798. He wanted to salvage the wreck. He had been trying to get permission since 1989.

Provincial archaeologists did not know the location of the site; they were therefore unable to confirm that the wreck was in fact the *Speedy*. Nonetheless, Burtt was experiencing the same obstructionist tactics with the Province that I was having. The Archaeological Licence Bureau refused to grant him a license to even explore the site, much less engage in total hull salvage. He wanted to retain Yormak to initiate a suit against the Province of Ontario over the *Speedy*.

He offered to give Yormak a check for $5,000 on the spot, with more to follow. Yormak wanted $10,000 before he would even consider filing the suit. In a businesslike manner they discussed the legalities involved. Since the same issues were at stake, the same Ministry was involved, and much of the groundwork had already been laid in the *Hamilton/Scourge* suit, Yormak proposed piggybacking Burtt's suit onto mine. There was no need to do the same work twice. Yormak suggested that some of Burtt's money be used for both his suit and mine. Winning my suit would ensure the winning of his. It made sense, and Burtt agreed.

But Yormak still wanted $10,000 up front. Burtt said that he would think about it.

Burtt donated money to fight Bill 13. He also gave money directly to Yormak for the *Hamilton/Scourge* case (although I never ascertained how much). Burtt and I spoke later by telephone, but by that time Yormak was asking for so much money that all negotiations for financial support fell by the wayside. (The money issue will be examined in more detail in the following chapter.)

Book Suggestion

During the return ride to the Marshalls' house, Yormak waxed long about the time being ripe to seek coverage in the press. I was against it, but deferred to his judgment. He saw press coverage as a precursor to a book that he wanted me to write, in the vein of my book about the *Monitor*. On this point I was emphatic: I never had any intentions of writing a book about the *Hamilton* and *Scourge*, and I harbored no such intentions at that time.

I wrote the *Monitor* book because I thought it would make a difference in the world of contemporary politics, while warning the diving community of the dire consequences of apathy. The book was important as a monograph about the abuse of bureaucratic authority in a supposed democratic society, and would provide future historians with an example of bureaucracy gone wild and the follow-up whitewash. But the book did not achieve the purpose for which I had written it. *Ironclad Legacy* did not sell as well as my other, less influential books. The message to me was clear: the public at large did not care about injustice or the constant erosion of freedom unless they were directly affected by the outcome of events.

Because of my passionate personal involvement in the case, the writing of the book was an intense emotional drain that I never wanted to re-experience.

Amendments to the Commandments

Resistance to Bill 13 was phenomenal - as Barrett soon discovered to his chagrin. He was forced to backpedal by deleting or revising some of the bill's excessively strict provisions. He hoped to make the bill acceptable to the diving public by making concessions.

For example, he deleted the section that dealt with the removal of silt. The original provision was Englebert's ace in the hole, because it could be used to justify the arbitrary denial of permission to dive on any shipwreck in the Province. Also deleted was the provision that prohibited wreck penetration ("Enter a heritage wreck, or cause an object to enter a heritage wreck.").

As Ian and Barb Marshall noted, "In our opinion, this still leaves a completely unsatisfactory piece of legislation. . . . Unknown regulations are still to be written under section '8'." (In the U.S. Army, Section 8 is a discharge from service due to mental instability.)

Most important of all, "Someone still has the power to decide which wrecks are diveable and which are closed." No emphasis was placed on that "someone," but everyone in the diving community knew to whom it referred.

Meetings were planned among divers throughout the year. Their goal was "to guarantee public access to wreck sites while affording protection to our marine heritage."

Ian Marshall wrote a lengthy memo in which he enumerated fourteen points of contention. He noted that the Ontario Heritage Act had been used (or abused) to restrict diving "at numerous Ontario sites." He noted, "There are strong ties between SOS Port Dover and the Marine Archaeologist for the Province."

He noted that the government had recently banned the sinking of ships as artificial reefs, because as owners of the vessels, the government might be held liable for any injuries or fatalities that occurred on government property. *"If the Province is now refusing to allow the sinking of shipwrecks because of possible liability, one can only imagine what they will do, if they obtain outright ownership of all shipwrecks."* (Marshall's italics.) Provincial ownership was another Englebert ace in the hole.

Fully half of Ian's points - seven in all - mentioned me by name with allusion to the *Hamilton/Scourge* case. For example, "Bill 13 addresses Gary Gentile's Mission Statement almost point for point."

In summation, Ian noted, "Whether you believe in Gary's fight or not, the outcome of his battle will affect your ability to dive in Ontario waters and the rules and restriction that will be put on you."

Power Mongering

The diving season waxed and waned in controversy. Hardly a diver was not appalled by the sinister implications of the bill. Tens of thousands of words were written by divers in derision of the bill. Some were vigorous, some were eloquent, all were defamatory.

Canadian bureaucrat Bob Carey compared the proposed legislation to submerged cultural heritage protection that was overseen by the State of Michigan. Michigan resident and diver Dave Trotter - who had located more lost shipwrecks in the Great Lakes than any other person in the world - was incensed by the comparison. In his denunciation of the bill, he emphasized, "Michigan legislation preserved the shipwrecks for divers while 'GUARANTEEING THE RIGHT OF RECREATIONAL DIVERS EXPLORATION OF SHIPWRECK SITES.' " (Trotter's capitals.)

As Trotter so rightly noted, "THE SHIPWRECKS WERE FOUND BY DIVERS FOR THE ENJOYMENT OF DIVERS . . . not so some damn bureaucrat or control freak could make the ultimate 'power grab' by controlling access. I have watched with absolute amazement the rollover to the GESTAPO approach by control freaks wanting to restrict the right of access by divers to enjoy the shipwrecks of the Great Lakes. I thought NAZI Germany died in 1945 . . . such is not the case. No doubt the Archeologists (AKA-ArcheNAZIS) are in this behind the scenes. . . .

"IF YOU CARE ABOUT YOUR FREEDOM TO ENJOY THE GREAT LAKES, THEN IT IS IMPORTANT TO DRIVE THE STAKE INTO THE HEART OF BUREAUCRATIC VAMPIRES (THESE VAMPIRES ARE THE MOST DANGEROUS OF ALL AS THEY SUCK THE LIFE OUT OF OUR FREEDOMS)."

Despite the evident overzealousness of Trotter's memo, truer words were never written. His sentiments echoed throughout the wreck-diving communities of two great nations which shared a common resource that was divided by an artificial barrier drawn on a political map of the continent. I think he spoke truest when he wrote, Canadian bureaucrats "place more value on the misguided view that an old rotting hull lying on the lake floor is more valuable and important for mankind than the basic right of FREEDOM."

Trotter tempered his outspoken rhetoric by quoting U.S. President Herbert Hoover: "No one with a day's experience in government fails to realize that in all bureaucracies there are three implacable spirits - self-perpetuation, expansion and the incessant demand for more power. . . . They drive always to extension of power by interpretation of authority, and by more and more legislation."

I cannot help but add another quote from Trotter - one which established the fact of relative values. "I have seen one case where a local diver made a bad judgment call and took home a small 'goodie' from a local wreck, and ended up in jail with a huge fine. The local drug dealer received far less for peddling drugs than the diver. The diver's personal home life and job was nearly destroyed because of the excessive action taken to quote 'make him an example.' All this for what was no more than a piece of junk. Where was the logic for the penalty to match the size of the crime?"

Perhaps Trotter did not say it all, but he certainly said it best - and loudest. Many other concerned citizens - of both countries - jumped into the fracas with righteous indignation.

To his grief, Barrett quickly learned that the issues at stake were extraordinarily controversial. The diving community soon disabused him of any belief that passage of the bill would be a pushover. He learned, too, that not only did the bill affect American wreck-divers as much as Canadian, but it adversely affected Canadian tourism by essentially eliminating American spending in Canadian waters. He had concentrated so hard on ramming the bill down the throats of the Canadian public, that he had not considered the deleterious consequences on the economy. Nor did he pause to ponder the incredible injustice of ignoring the rights of millions of citizens in order to vest omnipotence in "one guy and a secretary in one office." (See Tom Legate's reference below.)

First Reading

Parliamentary procedure provides for two readings of a bill before it can be voted on for passage. Barrett placed the bill on the docket seemingly at the last minute, apparently in an attempt to catch the dive community off guard. But too many people were keeping their eyes on current events. Five individuals scurried out of their way to attend the extemporaneous first reading, which was held on October 4, 2000.

Espousing divers' rights were Bob Cronkwright (representing the American Canadian Underwater Certifications), Nick Drakich (owner of the Kingston Diving Centre), Randy Giles (representing the Professional Association of Diving Instructors), Tim Legate (representing Save Ontario Shipwrecks), and Brian Taylor (owner of Diver City Dive Charters). Each had only days to prepare a presentation, but all spoke firmly and eloquently in opposition to the bill.

Giles quoted a guideline from the Abandoned Shipwreck Act (of the U.S.), which was hashed out in Congress for six years - against tremendous opposition - before it was passed through malicious subterfuge: "Guarantee recreational exploration of publicly owned shipwreck sites. At a minimum, any person should be able to freely and without a license or permit dive on, inspect, study, explore, photograph, measure, record, fish at, or otherwise use and enjoy publicly owned shipwrecks (including historic shipwrecks and shipwrecks whose historical significance has not yet been evaluated) when the use or activity does not involve disturbing or removing parts or portions of the shipwreck or its immediate environment." (For all the sordid details of the passage of the ASA, see Book Two of this author's *The Lusitania Controversies*.)

Such a guideline was reasonable and was written for the good of the public for whom the wrecks were being preserved. Under the present circumstances it would make Englebert impotent.

Giles: "Their second guideline is to establish lists of shipwrecks having recreational value. Their third point is to facilitate public access to shipwrecks. Their fourth point is to consult with interest groups prior to imposing any restrictions on access. Their fifth point is to regulate access at few, if any, shipwrecks."

None of these points would have found favor with Englebert and his ideal of despotic control. All these democratic points were absolutely anti-authoritarian.

The point that was reiterated by all opposition citizens was that of public access.

Not all the MP's in attendance were in favor of the bill. One noted "the importance of wreck conservation to the tourism industry, particularly in the small communities that dot the Great Lakes on the Canadian side. Lodging, campgrounds, restaurants, dive shops, charter operators and marinas can all benefit from the increased popularity of sport diving." Overly restrictive legislation that precluded diver access could conceivably destroy lakeside tourism.

Also, "Imagine if you will the reaction of our citizens if vandals were allowed free access to a cemetery anywhere across this province to desecrate graves that marked the final resting place of loved ones. We would be outraged. I would challenge anyone to explain to me why shipwrecks should be considered any differently."

I must plead ignorance about the conduct of Canadian citizens in Canadian cemeteries, but in the United States, cemeteries are open to the public so that friends and family members can visit the graves of their loved ones. Anyone may visit a cemetery for any reason. In national cemeteries such as Arlington, visits by tourists are encouraged. To my knowledge, vandalism and desecration have never been problems in the United States.

Another MP noted, "It's incumbent upon the Minister to publish a list of these archaeological sites. My biggest concern on publishing this list is that it's going to lead to piracy. There are going to be individuals out there who aren't going to respect this act. On a six-month basis, they're going to contact the Minister's office and say, 'I'm curious to see all the latest shipwrecks that have been found,' and they're going to use the information that a true diver or archaeologist has done to register that site to go out early in the morning or late at night with lights and they're going to pilfer and pirate those wrecks. Those artifacts are going to be lost."

Yet another MP believed that divers were diving on the *Hamilton* and *Scourge* "on a regular basis and are stealing the skeletal remains of the crew."

These MP's were worse than misinformed - they harbored notions and fancies that displayed an amazing lack of sophistication for supposedly educated representatives of the people. I applaud their opposition to the bill, but I wish their opposition had been based on reason rather than on ignorance and juvenile beliefs.

The most absurd digression of all was committed by MPP Kormos. Consider this repartee: "I am disgusted by this chamber this morning. I find this chamber repugnant. I find it hard to have any respect for anything that this institution should be standing for. Only a week ago this government stood up, and only by virtue of compulsion, apologized to the women who were victimized, abused, raped - "

Acting Speaker: "Speak to the bill, please."

Kormos: " - assaulted on a daily basis over the course of decades while they were wards of the state, and today this chamber says no - "

Acting Speaker: "The member will know he should speak to the bill."

Kormos: "Thanks you, Speaker. This chamber now says no to a campaign against violence towards women. You disgust me. . . . "

And so on, and so on. The assembly eventually got back to discussing Bill 13.

Many members of SOS (Save Our Shipwrecks) were incensed when they learned that the bill had been suggested by one of their members who might have been in cahoots with Peter Englebert. Dissension raged among the ranks of the constituency: Jim Murphy's views did not represent the views of the majority of the members. Tom Legate represented SOS at the first reading with a more enlightened attitude that better matched the persuasion of the members.

Legate tempered his opposition to the bill by first noting that certain shipwrecks were overdived, that some were fragile, and that a few needed protection from divers of lesser experience and should be visited only by those possessing superior skill. He mentioned two wrecks by name: "Wrecks such as *Hamilton* and

Scourge have absolutely no value if nobody ever looks at them or goes down and does the archaeology. Those things have been known for 25 or 30 years; nothing has been done."

While Legate stressed the need for preservation in its purest form, he stipulated, "Does this mean that SOS wants to legislate divers off wrecks? Not in any way, shape, or form. This is who we are. We love to dive on shipwrecks. We're there because we want to be." He made the valid point that any attempt at preservation "has to be with the goodwill of the dive community." Access was paramount.

He hit the nail on the head when he said, "The Province's total dedication to Ontario's marine heritage at this point is one guy and a secretary in one office. Give me a break."

Second Reading

Only one week passed between readings. But during those seven days, leaders in the wreck-diving community were able to garner their objections and make a greater showing in opposition to the bill. Among those who presented their views on October 11 were several who had great relevance to the subject matter of the present volume: Ian and Barb Marshall, Scott McWilliam, David Mekker, and Steve Yormak.

Mekker was in charge of organizing Shipwreck 2000, the annual divers' conference. He noted a couple of items that were obvious to everyone except Barrett: "Wreck diving and protecting marine heritage are not mutually exclusive. The whole issue of maintaining a list of accessible wrecks is unworkable. This will keep the law-abiding citizens away while providing others with a quick list of sites that are rich for the picking and looting. If we require a list, it should be by exception only. Many questions regarding the formation of a list remain unanswered, such as: Who creates the list? How are wrecks added or removed from the list? What determines whether a wreck should have restricted access? Does the list procedure have provisions for an appeal process? Some have suggested that we should restrict access to certain wrecks until the money is available to do a full archaeological study. How practical is it to expect that this will ever happen?"

"Time is also of the essence. Since the zebra mussels invaded in late 1989, wrecks are being covered with these crustaceans. Over time, with the added weight of the mussels, many wrecks have fallen and will fall apart. We should allow the diving community to learn about and document as much as possible of our wrecks and not wait for government funding that is unlikely to ever come. . .

"Any plan to limit access to a wreck must include a way for groups to visit a wreck for non-research purposes. This would even include wrecks such as the *Hamilton* and *Scourge* and could be accomplished through some sort of notification procedure."

McWilliam remarked: "If you read the Ontario Heritage Act, you will find that the word "shipwreck"or "wreck" does not appear anywhere in the act. This is not because they did not realize that shipwrecks were important archaeological entities when that act was penned in 1995 but because there exists a specific legal problem associated with shipwrecks. Unlike Mr. Barrett's office, whose researchers drafted the first incarnation of Bill 13 in 11 days, there was a little bit more time spent looking into the Ontario Heritage Act. Essentially the problem with shipwrecks is that the British North America Act, 1867, the powers of Parliament, section 91, subsection (10), Navigation and Shipping, clearly places all things to do with shipping in the domain of the federal government.

"The Canada Shipping Act uses the word "wreck," or a derivative thereof, 205 times. In part VI, 'Wrecks, Salvage and Investigations into Shipping Casualties' of the Canada Shipping Act deals specifically with shipwrecks and clearly defines them as the domain of the federal government and defines the role of the research of the wreck."

McWilliam pulled no punches. "I find section 6(b) of Mr. Barrett's bill particularly offensive. This is essentially a state-sanctioned appropriation of intellectual property. . . .

Speaking of the almighty, "What we have are people who are involved in the Ministry of Citizenship, Culture and Recreation. We have one provincial underwater archaeologist who had a vision, who had a dream. There's a vague line under the Ontario Heritage Act that requires the province to acquire new archaeological sites, and with this mandate he went forward, regardless of the law, to try to get this." Unfortunately for the public, the vision and dream in citation were more like those of Adolph Hitler than those of Martin Luther King.

Talking about nepotism, "Ontario has been shelling out approximately $26,000 a year to save Ontario's shipwrecks. . . . Strings were pulled; calls were made. Jim Murphy has been mentioned in the House by Mr. Barrett. Jim Murphy received $20,000 from the government of Ontario to go out and look for shipwrecks. You were also sent a copy of my brief in December. It outlines how that was a misexpenditure. They plagiarized. They represented other people's data as their own. . . . Nobody is prepared to admit that there's any kind of wrongdoing involved here.

On home base, "Litigation is now pending in the City of Hamilton involving a US diver who would like to go diving on the *Hamilton* and *Scourge* shipwrecks. He has applied for archaeological licences for, I believe, three or four years. He has been denied. The only reason anyone can be denied an archaeological licence is competence. Under the act, he is competent. There is no legal mechanism, as I understand it, to prohibit diving on the *Hamilton* and *Scourge*. Subsequently, the ministry phoned their fan club at SOS, Port Dover, wrote a letter to Mr. Barrett, said they could have Bill 13 brought in and it would intercede and change the law prior to this matter going to court.

"I have never seen more obsessed or more manipulative people than the Ministry of Citizenship, Culture and Recreation. They were sanctioned from the bench by Judge Lissaman during the *Atlantic* trial, they have been sanctioned by the Ontario Human Rights Commission, and I now believe they have perjured themselves in the *Hamilton* and *Scourge* matter. . . . In the archaeological community I met with friends of mine who are archaeologists in Quebec City, the

Society for Historical Archaeology, and we talked about Peter [Englebert]. As far as we know, Peter pretty much snapped around 1987. He was so alone and so stuffed away in his little world in Ottawa, nobody in the ministry even noticed."

McWilliam stated that after lodging his complaint, Barrett sent him a letter in which he wrote sarcastically, "Thank you for the mutiny."

Barrett objected, stating that the same letter was sent to a number of people. "I don't think that was in the letter."

McWilliam: "Mr. Barrett is lying."

The Chair produced a copy of the letter and thought that the word under discussion looked like "meeting," not "mutiny."

Yormak was more restrained. He explained that he was a founding director of an international organization called ProSEA (Professional Shipwreck Explorers Association). "We have representation in Paris under UNESCO for exactly this issue, which is underwater cultural heritage." The United Nations Educational, Scientific, and Cultural Organization was at that time attempting to pass global legislation that would ban *all* treasure salvage anywhere in the world!

He expounded about conflicts with the Canada Shipping Act, then offered this objection. "Your Ontario Heritage Act is an archaeological act. To get a licence, you have to be an archaeologist. I can't get it, I can assure you. I could be retired at 65 and apply 100 times and I will not get an archaeological licence under the Ontario Heritage Act. That's what you're proposing your licensing system be."

On management: "Who's making these decisions? You wonder, why is it always archaeologists making these public access decisions? There's a very simple reason for it. Fifteen or 20 years ago when all this came to the forefront it was a very unpopular type of issue. No one wanted it. So who did it fall to? The archaeologists. That's why you hear archaeologists are the ones who give you your opinions today.

"I have a friend, Ken Vrana, who's a management expert, a Michigan State PhD. He is very big on what the federal people in the United States are doing, that this is a management issue, not an archaeological issue. Archaeology should be one of many aspects. Tourism is another aspect; access to the diving community is another aspect; charter. There should be a manager who decides this, not an archaeologist. I find no fault with archaeologists. What is it they do? It's like saying to a lawyer, "Don't give me a lawyer's answer." Of course we'll give you a lawyer's answer. Ask an archaeologist and what answer are you going to get? You're going to get an archaeological answer. That's not what we should do, and we're at fault if we give them that authority. . . .

"Are there precedents for it? Yes, there are, plenty of them, all over the world. Tobermory is Parks Canada. They have allowed diving on wrecks. . . . There's a Mr. [Larry] Murphy, who some of the people behind me are well familiar with, a very high-ranking US parks official, who has said, "You know what's wrong with what you're doing up in Canada? You're not dealing with it as a management problem." What you should be doing is, if there's a risk, and we all recognize that we don't want to damage our own history, then deal with it. Don't

THE BILL 13 CAPER 139

prohibit it, deal with it. So you have licences that are not archaeological licences; they're user permits perhaps. There's an enforcement procedure. There's a way of overseeing it. There are many different approaches that could be done, and Bill 13 contemplates none of this. It's prohibitory in nature."

Barb Marshall was eloquent. After reiterating the major shortcomings of the bill, she addressed the issue of archaeological licenses. "The licence quoted in the bill is not an acceptable form of admission to a wreck site. As one who holds one of these licences, I can attest that it is a licence to conduct an archaeological survey, an extremely involved process. The requirements to obtain a licence include participation in a survey course, a detailed application and specific reporting, recording and documentation. This licence is issued to only one individual for a site, with option to renew for an additional year. This is the same licence referred to in Bill 13 and is not readily available to divers. . . .

"No wreck site should be closed to the diving public. Public access must be guaranteed to all wrecks in Ontario waters. We are not asking for no rules to govern these sites. What we are asking for is legislation which does not restrict access, but which will allow for penalties for removal of artifacts and willful, intentional or frivolous damage to our wrecks and wreck sites. Put in place an effective law which would do this.

"Bill 13 cannot be salvaged. The damage has been done and diver attitudes firmly entrenched. Bill 13 is now synonymous with the stripping away of divers' rights and freedoms. To be effective, marine heritage legislation must receive the buy-in of all stakeholders, and divers have the most at stake. I urge you to work with all stakeholders to come up with an effective and simple bill to accomplish this. The participation of the dive clubs, training agencies, shops, operators and organizations such as SOS, Preserve Our Wrecks Kingston, and the OUC [Ontario Underwater Council] is vital."

Ian Marshall began his presentation by stating, "My wife is a hard act to follow." His other points were equally as valid. He took exception to Barrett's interpretation, "Most dive sites would be exempt from restrictions, especially if they have been stripped clean." Ian equated this vanity to an advertising slogan, "Come to beautiful Kingston. Although we have historic forts, buildings and museums, we are going to let you take a tour of the local landfill site instead. . . . Allowing divers to dive on a bunch of old boards is not going to promote tourism in any way. . . . Restricting them in any way would kill the sport and related business in the province. . . . The *Munson* . . . is one of the most visited shipwrecks in the province. Is this one of the shipwrecks that's going to be restricted [because it is covered with artifacts]?"

Ian noted that in British Columbia, "wrecks over two years of age are considered protected - not owned, just protected."

And, "Mr. Barrett has stated numerous times that the removal of silt was meant to cover such things as dredging and not a diver's stray fin kick, yet in the current ongoing litigation between Gary Gentile and the province, that is exactly what the underwater archeologist for the province is claiming. Likewise, the term "to enter a heritage wreck" is being interpreted into "to enter the area of" which, depending on the day, seems to be anywhere from 100 meters to a mile away. . .

"Above all, access to the shipwrecks must be guaranteed. What good is there to have a heritage site if the people of Ontario can't see it? I'd just like to leave you with this question or thought. Can you imagine being a land tourist out in front of Fort George in Niagara-on-the-Lake? After listening to the tour guide describing the fort, the history and importance, he ends his talk with this comment: "Unfortunately, this has been declared an Ontario heritage site so we cannot allow you inside. If you would like to see what the inside is like, please take the ferry across to Fort Niagara on the US side."

Julian Colman made some interesting comparisons. He thought that Bill 13 "put a legal fence around all dive sites and let the public through the gate one at a time, after an arduous application process. And it's proposed that a bureaucrat both build the gates and keep the keys, without direction from or accountability to stakeholders. The province's marine archaeologist is on record that in his opinion divers disturb wrecks by their very presence.

"By the way, my wife, who is not a diver, observed, 'Why would they want to keep divers away from wrecks? The only people who can see and enjoy these wrecks are divers. Isn't that strange?'"

It is interesting to note that not a single presenter favored the bill. In response to this unanimity of adverse opinion, MPP Marchese stated, "Since the flurry of letters we got, we realize that the problem is bigger than I obviously anticipated, and now we've got a problem in terms of how to address the issues that all of you seem to be raising with marine heritage. I'm interested in doing that; obviously we're all interested in doing that. How we do that before we proceed toward passing the bill is, I hope, something we can manage, but I'm not sure how we're going to do it."

End of a Nightmare

Barrett deleted the ownership provision of the bill, but would not add any provision to guarantee public access. The bowdlerized bill was unacceptable to the dive community. Further debate was useless.

Barrett was finally forced to admit - in writing - that "a consensus must come from the marine heritage/dive community." The current session of the Parliament was "prorogued" (discontinued) without achieving passage of the bill. "As a result, bills not yet passed - including Bill 13 - are terminated."

Chapter 9
Money, Money, Money

The China Syndrome
I hit upon another idea for raising money. I had been recovering artifacts from the *Andrea Doria* for fifteen years: plates, cups, saucers, glassware, and the like. I displayed one of each item in my home, and sometimes I displayed a selection of items at public functions. I was always looking for items and designs that I did not have in my collection. In the course of recovery I accumulated a number of duplicates.

Every so often I received queries from people who wished to purchase a souvenir from the *Andrea Doria*. Occasionally I sold one of my duplicates. I had never publicized the items for sale; rather, collectors sought me out and tracked me down. My increasing need for funding the case gave me pause to think about the untapped market potential of *Doria* china and glassware. If collectors were willing to go to such lengths to obtain a souvenir, why not advertise the duplicates on my website, and enable other collectors to find me? Not only would the sale of china generate some income that I could dedicate to the *Hamilton/Scourge* cause, but it would gladden the collectors of ocean liner memorabilia to own a piece of the *Andrea Doria*.

I compiled an inventory of duplicate items. I wrote a promotional piece for the website. I photographed representative items, and scanned the images so they could be displayed on the website. I established prices for each item according to scarcity and condition. I was in business!

I asked potential buyers to request a copy of my duplicate inventory list.

This advertising ploy generated a great deal of interest, but few actual sales.

Neither Gold nor Silver, but Irony
I kept insisting that Hess contribute his share of the costs. He had yet to come even close to matching the amount that I had invested. Had he kept his word, the case could have proceeded without the constant bickering over money. Instead, Hess kept trying to raise money from other sources in order to make up for his deficit.

Hess kept pleading with Mike Kane to send the $5,000 that he had pledged. But Kane had made his pledge on a contingency: that he could not make the bestowal until his own lawsuit was settled, after he collected the money that was awarded to him by the court. The loser in his case refused to pay.

In the American civil court system, the court has no power to force an unsuccessful litigant to pay. All the court did was to rule against a litigant. It was up to the winner to collect. This can be a costly and lengthy process, and Kane's loser was trying to make the process as costly and lengthy as possible. Kane was forced to pay his attorney extra money to apply alternative collection methods, or to negotiate a settlement amount that was smaller than the amount that was awarded by the court.

Hess overlooked the irony in the situation. He bemoaned the fact that Kane was not living up to his pledge, while Hess himself was guilty of the same breach of promise. The difference was that Hess had not based his promise on any contingencies.

I wrote to Hess: "It is ironic that you castigated Mike Kane for not keeping his recent promise to provide some additional financial support, when you will not keep your own promise of support. Furthermore, you have misinterpreted his pledge. He never stated that he would donate $5,000 to the cause. He stated that he would match funds pledged by other divers, to a limit of $5,000. So far he has received pledges of only $200.

"One who has failed in his own obligations should not be so eager to criticize others for failing in obligations which they did not even make."

Reality Check

When Yormak submitted his next bill, Hess informed me that he was not going to pay his fifty percent share, that he was withdrawing entirely from the case, and that he had no intention of repaying the money that I had borrowed on his account. I was shocked by his pronouncement. I expressed my evident dissatisfaction in the following letter:

"This is a reality check.

"It grieves me to have to write this letter but I must put things in perspective because you seem to have lost sight of the facts.

"When you and I entered into an agreement to litigate the case of the *Hamilton* and *Scourge*, we agreed to split the costs of litigation evenly. Recently, you let me put up your share of the costs because you pleaded a shortage of funds. I put up your share fully expecting you to reimburse me in a reasonable time. Several months later, when I needed money to pay for the printing of my next book, you refused to honor your pledge. Instead, you left me holding the bag - your bag. You would have let the case drop rather than inconvenience yourself by putting up your share of the cost. Several months later, when I asked again - because another printing bill came due - you left me holding the bag once again.

"The agreement we made is binding upon you, both legally and morally. As an officer of the court, you know this better than most. Should there be any doubt, you can ask Steve Yormak. He is fully aware of our agreement and will testify to that effect if called upon to do so.

"So far, my financial input exceeds yours by $12,000. Stated another way, I have put up $6,000 of your portion of the pledge. We can resume an equal footing if you return the $6,000 that I lent to you for the portion of the costs, which you were unable or unwilling to meet at the time. Now, to my horror, you have stated expressly that you have no intention of keeping your pledge, or of returning my money. This attitude is not only morally irresponsible, it is legal indefensible.

MONEY, MONEY, MONEY 143

"I cannot afford to be your bank. If you do not have the money to keep up with your legal obligations, borrow the money from a lending institution - the way I did when I acceded to your excessive demands during the litigation of the *Monitor* case. When you let the expenses for that case get out of hand, I borrowed money from the bank in order to pay the costs of litigation. I expect you to do the same in the present and analogous situation.

"I am insulted by your statement that your time is worth more than mine. There is a great disparity between what you wish your time were worth, and its actual value. I have put far more time and effort into this case than you have: I exchanged numerous correspondence with City and Provincial representatives, I wrote and submitted permit applications, and I did all the preparation work that preceded taking the case to court. You wrote nothing: no letters, no briefs, no correspondence. Any energy you have expended to seek alternative sponsorship has been done with the intention of finding someone to put up your share. Your idle chats with Steve Yormak do not constitute legal consultation because you know nothing about Canadian law and therefore have nothing to offer by way of expertise.

"A person's word is his honor. You have a legal and moral obligation to return the money that I put up on your behalf, and to continue to match my funding.

"A person's character is determined by his actions, not by his broken promises.

Post Script

The $6,000 figure that I quoted above was based only upon Hess's say-so that he had donated some $5,000 to the cause. I received no itemized list of his disbursements, no proof of actual payment, no accounting from Yormak as to amounts that he received, and no way to ascertain how much of the money that Hess sent to Yormak was Hess's, and how much constituted money that he received from other donors.

Furthermore, Hess declared that some of the funding that he had provided was in the form of services exchanged, or expenses that he covered. My follow-up letter explained the situation:

"I neglected to mention some inconsistencies in your attitude toward failing to uphold your legal and moral obligations with respect to financing the *Hamilton/Scourge* litigation. You claim to have rendered financial aid to Steve Yormak by letting him share your hotel room during the pursuit of other cases. While this may have saved him money, it did not cost you any money out of your own pocket. Worse yet, your hotel expenses were defrayed by your clients in those other cases, so that you did not even pay for the room in the first place. This is a clear case of legal double dipping."

I added, "You once advised me (in the *Monitor*) case to use every bit of ammunition one could obtain, no matter how costly, in order to prevail. Now, with respect to expenditures that have been incurred in the instant case, you refuse to heed your own advice, and you balk at every expense. Perhaps you have gotten used to spending clients' money profligately, but do not like it when your own money is spent in a way which, from your perspective in the instant case, appears wasteful.

"Your change of attitude has disappointed me greatly. Now perhaps you understand that fighting for a cause when you pay for the fight is much different from being paid to fight."

Win, or Lose Twice

In November 1999, I received a disturbing e-mail from Yormak. The City of Hamilton was bringing a motion for "security costs." Under Canadian law, a defendant may plead that a suit filed against him has so little merit that, in the likely event that the plaintiff will fail to prove his case, the plaintiff must pay all the defendant's legal costs. The purpose of the law was to discourage frivolous suits, but like many well-intentioned laws, it was often abused.

Barkwell's abuse was twofold. First, the time to bring a motion for security costs was at the initiation of the suit, not two years later, and after all other postponements and subterfuges had been exhausted. (Both Barkwell and Lyon had yet to produce the documents which they had promised during the depositions. Worse, both continued to file countermotions to Yormak's motions to produce, in order to prevent those documents from being introduced as evidence in court.) Second, it took a long stretch of the imagination to claim that my case was without merit, and that there was little or no likelihood that I would not prevail. The evidence against the defendant was so overwhelming that, even without the additional productions, Yormak could prove the City's skullduggery (to say nothing of the wholesale falsehoods, deceptions, and perfidy of the intervener.)

In a case between Canadian citizens, companies, or corporate or governmental entities, the plaintiff is not required to post a bond if his assets exceed the estimated cost of the defendant's litigation. Should the plaintiff fail to prove his case, the court can and will seize his assets: savings accounts, stocks and bonds, real estate, even his personal property. Thus a Canadian citizen might lose his home and everything he owns if his suit is unsuccessful, in order to reimburse the defendant for his legal fees. (The intervener had no such recourse because it was not a defendant in the case, but entered voluntarily.)

The Canadian court had no jurisdiction over me as a U.S. citizen. Therefore, Barkwell demanded that I post cash in the amount of $22,000. Barkwell's estimate of the City's projected *total* cost of litigation was equivalent to the amount that I had already expended (including donations), not counting the fact that Yormak demanded more money before he would agree to proceed.

Yormak wrote, "Of course, this is a ploy by the City to get rid of the application. The court will look at firstly the merits of the proceeding and likely success, the financial position of the party (you) and the overall justice."

I asked Yormak why Barkwell had not invoked this gimmick earlier. His reply: "Because he's stupid."

MONEY, MONEY, MONEY

The Ebbing Cash Flow

I was cash poor. I had assets like most people: stocks and bonds, real estate, and personal possessions. I lived in my house and I lived on the dividends of my stocks and bonds, but mostly I lived on a disability pension from the Veterans Administration. Everything I owned was tied up in real estate investments, securities, and books that I sold through my publishing business. If I sold my house I would have nowhere to live. If I sold my stocks and bonds, I would not have enough supplemental income to support myself. Income from the business I pumped back into the business, to publish my next book. I had to make investments in order to guarantee future income for retirement purposes. The publishing business was my retirement fund.

Worse, I had borrowed so much money to pay for the costs of litigation that I was dangerously close to the limit that was allowed by the value of my securities. My account executive warned me that should a drop in the stock market occur, my securities might no longer cover the amount of my rising debt, in which case the sale of my securities would be forced in order to conform to the regulations of the Securities and Exchange Commission. A drop of only a few hundred dollars in the value of my securities would see my ruin.

I had a negative balance in my bank account. Every time I paid a utility bill, I did so on borrowed money. I was in desperate financial straits, and my publishing business was not generating enough income to meet Yormak's constant demands.

I explained my position to Hess. I was still paying interest on money that I had borrowed for his share of the legal fees and expenses. Hess turned a deaf ear.

Security Costs Rebuttal

Yormak researched the law on security costs. The law clearly stipulated that the clause was not to be employed as an afterthought, but that a defendant had to enter the plea at the beginning of the case. Yormak found numerous precedents in which tardy pleas for security costs had been denied. A six-month delay in entering a plea for security costs was the longest that had ever been granted, and that one was granted only because of special circumstances that did not apply to the present case.

Yormak submitted this evidence to the court. Yormak also wrote an affidavit for me to sign. The affidavit pleaded the justice of the cause for the benefit of the public: "My application is one of significant merit, a case wherein I am in effect representing the public interest in maintaining access to our own heritage and history." In other words, I had nothing to gain personally by the outcome of the trial.

Yormak also mentioned the obvious: "The City of Hamilton has delayed the entire length of these proceedings, waiting almost two years to bring this motion for security of costs despite the fact that all facts presented now were known to them almost two years ago when the Application was brought."

Yormak furthermore took the opportunity to bring to the court's attention that the City's denial was knowingly based upon false information, to wit: "They have relied upon the premise that because of lack of visibility . . . no dive can be done safely. This is based on 10 year old observations prior to the lakes being cleaned up by zebra muscle activity. . . . They are aware that visibility is now dramatically different and improved. It is now well known by divers and other experts that visibility in the *Hamilton* and *Scourge* area no longer presents a difficulty. . . . With visibility no longer a factor, no dive presents any threat or risk of damage to the sites."

With respect to the intervener, Yormak noted, "The Province has taken the extreme and untenable position that a diver who just looks at or views a wreck site is committing an act of archaeology and so they say, must apply for an archaeological license pursuant to the Ontario Heritage Act. If this were the case this would be absurd enough, but it has been demonstrated that Provincial officials are not consistent and in fact, despite their evidence under oath otherwise have granted in effect recreational permission to dive archaeological sites, (See McWilliam affidavit and *Gunilda*) without a licence."

Emphasizing Provincial absurdity, he wrote, "Mr. Englebert in his cross-examination, admitted that even the finder of an underwater abandoned coke bottle may be subject to fines according to a technical interpretation of the Act."

Finally, "Given my own financial circumstances and the obvious merit of this Application it would not be in the best interests of justice to grant the City's motion for security for costs, particularly given the City's delay and the fact that this Application is more in the nature of an Application made on behalf of the public for public access to its own history."

Precedent and Poverty Notwithstanding

Never in the annals of Canadian law had a judge ordered the posting of security costs after a case had been proceeding for six months. Thus Judge J. Crane set a precedent and made history when he sided with the City of Hamilton nearly two years after the onset of the case, and after attorneys for the defendant had abused the law in order to stall the case by constant delaying tactics and by failing to provide documents that the defendant was legally obliged to provide.

The judge wrote, "The applicant has elected to remain silent as to his full income and as to his net worth." The reader might ask: How did the judge arrive at such a conclusion?

The answer is: Through the chicanery of the City.

In the City's endless quest to find scandal and depravity in my character, its attorneys continued to investigate my personal life. They knew that I had a website. They must have kept tabs on the website's updates - perhaps looking for mention of the *Hamilton* and *Scourge*. I made no such mention, but the City discovered that I commenced to sell china from the *Andrea Doria*.

When potential buyers queried me about purchasing china, I sent them my entire inventory list of duplicate artifacts, along with the prices that I had assigned to individual items.

The City obtained a shill to pose as a buyer. Under false pretenses, this shill requested a copy of my inventory list, which he then gave to the City's attorneys. They added the items, multiplied the total by the suggested price per item, and

MONEY, MONEY, MONEY

obtained a product in excess of $35,000. The City claimed that I had hidden these assets from the eyes of the court.

Had the City sent a shill to my house to appraise my furniture, it would have been disappointed - most of my furniture I obtained years ago by "trash picking." I had assets in the form of scuba and camera gear, a vehicle, kitchen appliances, and so on. It seemed to me that in Canada, a person must put everything he owns on the line in order to pursue the cause of justice.

Judge Crane: "I am not satisfied that the applicant has demonstrated his impecuniousity."

If the judge only knew the truth of my financial situation, he might have been more sympathetic. My total personal annual income was $14,000. The federal government considered such earnings to be below the poverty level. After allowable deductions, my taxable income was so small that I did not even have to pay federal income tax. One year the Internal Revenue Service sent me a rebate of several hundred dollars, despite the fact that the tax due shown on my tax return was zero! The government paid *me* instead of the other way around!

Despite my placement among American wage earners, I did not feel poor. I simply lived within my means.

Unfortunately for the City, Judge Crane also wrote, "I find that the claim does have merit. . . . The application does raise issues important to the public interest and justice is served that these allegations be determined by the court."

Crane also noted the City's evident delay. "I consider this time factor, that had the motion for security for costs be made following the delivery of the application record, the applicant would then have had the opportunity to elect either to proceed with the action or withdraw before potential liability for substantial costs would have been incurred."

Weighing these deliberations, Crane rendered the opinion "that the applicant pay into court the sum of $7,500." He gave me thirty days to comply. Otherwise, "The City of Hamilton, may move, without notice for dismissal of the application."

When Yormak informed Hess of the judge's ruling on security costs, Hess whined, "He can't do that." Yormak assured Hess that the judge had indeed "done that." Hess continued to whine, "He can't do that."

The judge did do that, and he was unlikely to back down as a result of Hess's whimpering.

Either I put up the money, or I would lose the case by default.

The Philosopher's Stone

I may have possessed china that was arbitrarily valued at $35,000, but converting that china into gold or silver was another matter. In the year since I had commenced to advertise the sale of china on my website, I had sold about one thousand dollar's worth. All that money had been eaten up voraciously by Yormak, with the speed of a great white shark devouring a morsel. I still have most of that china today.

My idea to generate revenue for the case by selling *Doria* china resulted in a net loss of some $6,500.

Then I had another brilliant idea. Since the City claimed that my *Doria* china was so valuable, why not post $7,500 worth of china as collateral for the bond? In the event that I did not prevail in my suit, the City of Hamilton could sell the china for what it claimed the china was worth.

Yormak liked the idea, and he submitted it as an alternative to posting cash.

The City declined to accept this reasonable proposition. Such a scenario did not serve the City's true and villainous purpose, which was to make the cost of continuing litigation prohibitively expensive. The City's attorneys knew as well as I that the china was basically a non-negotiable asset that could not be readily converted to cash.

Windfall: Gone with the Wind

Mike Kane was still wrapped up in expensive litigation, but a healthy donation came from an unexpected source. My long-time dive buddy and soul mate, Pete Manchee, sent me a check for $1,000. This made his contribution equal to that of Kane, tying for second place in support of the case (apart from Hess's questionable contributions, bartered services, thousands of hours of legal advice, and donations that he collected from unnamed donors).

Manchee's money was gone in a flash. According to Yormak, it merely paid for his defense of the City's request for security costs. Yormak now wanted another $8,500.

A few dollars dribbled in, but these were mere drops in the bucket. Pete Trembath contributed $250. Dave Trotter contributed $100. Trotter wrote, "If we could get 300-400 divers to contribute a like amount, I am sure it would reduce your financial burden. Hopefully, others will see the value in providing financial support." Trotter's money was welcome but his sentiments proved to be will-of-the-wisps.

Several people contacted me, wanting to know what they could do to help the cause. As usual, when I replied, "Send money," I never heard from them again. I needed cold hard cash, not cheers from a feckless sideline. Most people wanted to know, "What's in it for me?"

I wrote to Hess, "I will handle the bond issue. You must immediately send Steve a check in the amount of $8,500." I added, "Send it tomorrow via FedEx so he can receive it by Tuesday." Whenever a client was paying the bill, Hess, as Yormak, resented the employment of ordinary mail service when expensive courier service would suffice. Hess neither sent the money nor condescended to reply.

Hess once again seethed with molten irony when he wrote to Yormak about Kane's contingency pledge, "As we have seen, talk is cheap."

I tried to contact Kane for part of the money. "If there is any way possible for you to furnish the $5,000 which you suggested donating to the cause, I will make good the remaining $3,500."

Kane did not reply to my e-mail, he did not accept or return my phone calls. I never heard from him again. I do not even know if he is still alive.

Policy of Attrition

Since the City lost its deterrent in the amount of $22,000, the City moved the have my application summarily dismissed. This forced Yormak to file a counter-motion - which took legal time and cost more money because Yormak was charging by the hour, and Hess was not doing any of the work.

The City's plan was obvious: instead of trying the case on its merits, it was hoping to run me out of money. Even if the City could not win the case, the power hungry bureaucrats might gain the satisfaction of causing my bankruptcy.

Judge Crane expanded on his previous opinion: "I am of the view that there is sufficient merit in the argument of the applicant on the merits that this application should not be quashed on the present motion. In my view, the substance of the motion to quash is also the argument of the Attorney General as respondent on the hearing of the application on its merits. Further, I am of the view that the issues raised in this application and by the Attorney General in its response to it are of sufficient importance that the matter be heard by a full panel of the Divisional Court."

The End is Near

My contemporary correspondence delineated my woes and my troubled state of mind. To Yormak (on March 30, 2000): "I have made preliminary contacts with several lending institutions, and plan to visit two banks today in order to learn more about procuring a loan in order to back the $7,500 bond. One thing I've learned already - loans are not made on the spur of the moment. There are forms to fill out, qualifications to be checked, and so on. This procedure takes several weeks. . . .

"If we can overcome this obstacle, I still need to know this: Will the bond buy some time in order for me to secure additional funding? In other words, once the bond is in place, do we then have time to relax the pace of the proceedings until I can either borrow more money or find alternative financial backing? Then, if further funding is not forthcoming, can I call it quits and recover the bond (and my debt)?

"It seems a shame to throw away all the money that has already been spent, and to squander all your effort, hard work, and hard-earned victories - especially when we seem to be so close to prevailing on the merits - but I must ask myself whether the case is worth going into debt for, or going bankrupt over, or giving up everything I have worked my entire life for. If I secure a second loan - or extend the first one - I am then faced with making payments and paying interest: an additional drain on my limited income. On the other hand, can I continue to throw away money on a case which no one but me wants to pursue? I can no longer count on Peter Hess to fulfill his obligations. Mike Kane's commitment is insufficient. The diving community is financially apathetic. And you want a guaranteed income. Perhaps I should let the next generation try to regain the freedom that the current generation is not willing to fight for. (Sorry for waxing philosophical.)

"I do not see any rich benefactors in the wings. Nevertheless, I want to proceed with this case. I am even willing to borrow money in order to do so. But how much can I afford to lose? Perhaps I should just call it quits and go on with my life. That would certainly be easy to do. I can't recoup my losses (I never expected to), but at least if I call it quits now I will incur no future debts. I don't need more money to live on - my income is adequate because my needs are simple. But it will be difficult to survive on less.

"If my sentiments appear wishy-washy, it is because the scales of justice are unbalanced by tempestuous seas and tough decisions: idealism versus pragmatism. Perhaps I should view this case not as a war, but as a battle within a larger conflict. Then I could retreat from this battle honorably, and fight another one later when the odds are more in my favor. But to lose the ground we have already taken would be a waste."

I had some major decisions to make - and some soul searching to do - by April 22.

Extension Granted - For One Month

I wrote to Yormak on April 9, "The opposition is using my collection of *Andrea Doria* artifacts as the basis for supporting its defense. If I could sell that entire collection tomorrow, I would spend every penny of the money the collection generated in support of this cause. However, lending institutions do not consider the collection to be an asset to back a loan. If the court is going to consider the collection as an asset for the purpose of supporting the defense, then I need time to reduce that asset to a negotiable form. In that regard, it would be appropriate for the court to grant an open-ended continuance - one which will allow me to continue the case after I have converted the collection to cash. This may take several months.

"I am surprised at the opposition's attitude. I would think that an officer of the court would want to confirm the government's legal position once and for all, to try this case on its merits in order to establish that legal position firmly. Else the issues will only have to be tried again at some future date. I thought the purpose of a government's defense was to test the fairness and validity of its position.

"There is no way that I can meet the April deadline."

My philosophical waxing notwithstanding, I continued working toward obtaining not only the bond, but the money necessary for future funding of the case.

With my promise in this regard, Yormak managed to obtain an extension for placement of the bond. "We now have until May 22 to have everything in place to comply with the court order. It is obvious there will be no further court extensions." Once again he demanded $8,500 to continue the case beyond the bond issue. "I can tell you I have continued to attempt to have Peter [Hess] contribute with no success. He has told me he had tried to raise the security costs through another client to no avail."

He mentioned "the 1/3 reduction of my fees which I have offered as my part to the cause." I do not think he intended sarcasm when he wrote, "I hope and trust that this battle does not continue just on the basis of you and I supporting the cause for the many."

A Masked Man, or a Loan Arranger?

I opened an account at a local bank. Into that account I transferred money for the bond from another account in which I had a line of credit on which I could borrow (using my securities as collateral).

I soon learned that it was not sufficient for me to have the money in a separate account in order to satisfy the Canadian court's demand. The money had to be "irrevocable": that is, placed in an account to which I did not have access, and from which the money could be paid automatically to the court on the court's demand.

Furthermore, the bond constituted only "up front" money. In the event that I lost the case, the City could file suit against me in U.S. court to obtain the rest of the money that the City claimed to have expended in its defense. The City could then force the sale of my securities or foreclose on my house, in order to obtain the full $22,000 which it claimed its defense would cost.

I investigated the possibility of obtaining a second mortgage from the local bank. The bank was happy to oblige me - *but*, significant fees were charged to process the paperwork, obtain an appraisal, acquire title clearance, and a host of other details: several thousand dollars in all. Instead, I found it more favorable to obtain a revolving line of credit from my brokerage firm, to which I was already indebted because of the money that I had borrowed by using my securities as collateral. My brokerage firm was willing to lend me an additional $50,000 by using my real estate as collateral. And no up-front fees were required to procure the loan. They wanted my continuing business and interest payments.

This amount would provide a temporary solution to all the debts that I had incurred in the prosecution of the case, the money that I had borrowed to make up for Hess's refusal to contribute his portion, the outstanding bill for printing costs, and the deficit in my savings and checking account. By consolidating my loans, I needed $36,000 - and that was just to break even!

That left $14,000 for future investments. The bond was $7,500, and Yormak still wanted $8,500 - which he now claimed was for *past* fees and expenditures. Already I was $2,000 short, and this did not leave any excess to pay for Yormak's *future* fees and expenditures - or for the City's litigation costs should the court rule against me.

There was another part of the equation that I had to take into account. The interest on $36,000 was nearly $200 per month, or almost $2,400 per year. Lately, growing interest fees had been gradually reducing my ability to live on my fixed income, which meant that I had to borrow more money to pay the increasing interest charges. If I paid the interest out of book sales from my publishing business - which heretofore had been self-sustaining - then I would have no money to print my next book, which would adversely affect the viability of the business by reducing its future earning power.

On the other hand, now that I no longer had loans against my securities, I was free to sell them in order to pay the monthly interest. But that would reduce my income, because I would lose the dividends that those stock and bonds were paying. Alternatively, I could sell my house for its market value instead of using it as collateral for a loan. Then I would have to move into a small apartment. When I looked into rental rates, I learned that living in an apartment would cost more than owning a home.

No matter how I viewed the situation, it was a downward spiral into bankruptcy. The only way I could win my suit against the City of Hamilton was by giving everything I owned except my first-born child to Steve Yormak. This I was unwilling to do. I told him so.

After much soul searching and great trepidation, I dropped the case in order to get on with my life. Justice would have to be put into abeyance.

Slow Death

After Hess abandoned me to my fate, I never wanted to have anything more to do with him. In fact, I have neither spoken with him nor exchanged any communication with him since the last plea that I quoted above. I do know, however, that he is still alive. He has yet to reimburse me for the money that I borrowed for him - and for which I am still paying interest.

Yormak alerted him about my secession from the case. Hopefully, he wrote, "If the security for costs issue is resolved our next legal move is to complete the outstanding motions (undertakings, refusals, attend at City lab archives) and bring a motion to introduce the recent sworn affidavits in support of our application (McWilliam, L. Murphy). Our Record will then be filed along with our Factum, and the other sides' Factums filed, and finally a hearing date scheduled before the 3-judge Divisional Court."

Hess commented, "There is no way I will allow the *Hamilton* and *Scourge* matter to just die." He did not mean to imply that he would meet his funding obligations. His plan was to use money in his escrow account in place of a bond. He did not intend to open a separate and irrevocable account, but to hold funds in the name of the court until the time that the money could be released.

The money in this escrow account did not belong the Hess. It was money that belonged to clients who were awaiting its disbursement. In other words, he wanted to post his clients' money in place of a bond - another case of legal double dipping. He went so far as to write an affidavit to that effect, giving his word that he would disburse the money to the court as soon as he received a court order to do so.

As we have seen, the value of Hess's word was contestable. Yormak "discarded Peter Hess' affidavit as all but useless."

Once again he bemoaned his belief that Kane was "a lot of talk and no action." Hess realized the irony of his statement, and followed it with, "Perhaps this is what Gary thinks of me as well, so be it."

Yormak informed Hess that he had to "send me the funds . . . with instructions to place it in a trust account to be disbursed upon the order of the Ontario court."

Hess did not want to part with either his own money or that of his clients. He wanted to hold it in his escrow account and be able to use it. Hess wrote, "Requiring security at this late stage in the litigation is unprecedented."

Hess: "This case must be seen through to its conclusion. If we cannot proceed due to the cost of legal fees, I intend to fully explore any means possible to be permitted to represent Gary for the final stages of the case now pending. You have indicated that you would facilitate this if it became necessary, which, unfortunately, is probably where we are right now."

Yormak replied, "If you . . . wish to appoint yourself counsel here in Canada I can assist you, although given the lateness of the date I have some serious reservations in that regard. I say this to you with sincerity since you do not seem to accept my advising you as to the procedures here. I cannot keep repeating the same things over and over."

Despite his admonition to the contrary, Hess effectively let the matter die by failing to take appropriate affirmative action. In the vernacular of the peasantry, he liked to talk the talk but not walk the walk.

Work Ethic

Although Yormak sustained his efforts to raise money, he refused to do any more legal work beyond emplacing the bond if the funding should ever materialize. He viewed the bond as a respite, during which more time was available to obtain additional funding. In other words, he was willing to let the matter die unless he got paid. One might view this attitude as a form of blackmail. But let us put it into perspective.

During my occupation as an electrician, I sometimes worked on private homes that were being renovated by their owners. I did these "side jobs" on weekends. The homeowner furnished the materials, and paid me at the end of each day for the number of hours I worked. If an owner had told me that he was temporarily short of funds, and asked me to buy the materials and complete the job upon his promise of later payment, I doubt that I would have agreed.

Despite the satisfaction that I derived from doing craftsmanlike work, and seeing a job through to its functional completion, I had a mortgage to pay and a family to support. I had nothing vested in another homeowner's house, and nothing to gain by completing the job for the simple sake of completion. I would more than likely have spent my weekends working for one who could afford to pay on time.

To an attorney, a client's case was a job - and little more. Win or lose, he had nothing to gain by the outcome. Most attorneys try to do the best job they can. But an attorney is also running a business. The primary criterion of any business is to earn a profit. If one client runs out of money, an attorney is not legally obligated to keep working for him. There are other clients who are willing to pay for his services.

The Bond Issue, or 007 with a License to Kill?

Barkwell submitted a motion to dismiss my application if I did not post the bond as directed by the court. He scheduled an appearance before the judge for the end of the day on which the bond was due. If the bond was not posted on time, the City of Hamilton would automatically win the case by default - and a horrible precedent would be set: one that would be difficult if not impossible to overcome in the future.

In essence, every unsubstantiated point that the City had made would become law - and without any determination from the court as to the legality of those points. The City would have carte blanche: not the keys to the City but the keys to the *Hamilton* and *Scourge*. Forever.

It looked as if I had let an evil genie out of the lamp to plague mankind.

P.A.D.I. to the Rescue

After Nick Drakich and I spoke at Shipwrecks 2000, he assumed the chore of calling divers, dive shop owners, charter boat operators, and so on, in an attempt to obtain funding for the cause. Along with Ian and Barb Marshall, he helped to raise the awareness level of Canadian divers about Bill 13. But he had not been able to obtain any funding that was earmarked for the *Hamilton/Scourge* case. Like Hess, local divers considered that to be "my" case, not theirs. Few of them saw it as part of the process of erosion of human rights and public access.

Time was running out. I called Drakich to explain the situation with regard to security costs - the hurdle that was balking me from continuing the race. If I leaped that hurdle, there would be a respite before the case came to trial. The respite would afford more time in which to obtain additional funding.

Drakich did not waste any time. He called John Kronen, one of his contacts at PADI. Kronen told him that PADI supported public access to all dive sites around the world, and might be willing to post the bond. (The reader will recall that PADI representative Randy Giles spoke at one of the Bill 13 hearings in opposition to the bill.) Drakich called me to relay the news.

I was astounded. If PADI was serious, I told Drakich, it was imperative that one of their duly authorized representatives call Yormak the moment the corporate decision was confirmed.

Yormak did not learn of PADI's affirmative decision until the afternoon of the last day on which the bond was due. He was sitting at his desk when he received the call. He immediately dropped whatever he was doing, grabbed the necessary paperwork (which he had already prepared), and jumped into his car to make the 100 mile drive from his office in London to the courthouse in Toronto.

The hearing was already in progress when Yormak ran breathlessly into the courtroom. The time was less than half an hour before closing. Barkwell was making his final remarks to the judge. Yormak submitted his paperwork with the announcement that I had secured the money for the bond, and that he would see to it that an irrevocable account was opened with the court designated as the holder.

I wish I could have seen the look on Barkwell's face. He was about to win the case uncontested. Then, with unearned victory within his grasp, Yormak knocked the wind out of his blustering sails.

PADI had saved the day. Now the way was open to go to trial. I asked Yormak how much he would charge to represent me at the trial (which he estimated would take one or two days). He wanted $5,000.

Resuscitation

With the posting of the bond, Yormak also submitted a wealth of additional information that contradicted the allegations of the City and the Province, particularly with respect to water clarity. The primary source of this information was a 27-page sworn affidavit of Scott McWilliam.

McWilliam: "There has been a profound change, an improvement, in underwater visibility in the region since 1990. Visibility has continued to improve and is now the best that it has ever been in my lifetime. In this part of Lake Ontario, there has been a 75% improvement in visibility since 1990. This change has been so dramatic that . . . any opinion or statement of fact on visibility or water clarity in the area . . . based on observations made prior to 1995, should be totally disregarded as irrelevant."

More condemning, "At a Save Ontario Shipwrecks general meeting in 1997 I discussed the change in Zebra mussels with Peter Englebert who stated that the change in water clarity was phenomenal in the lower lakes. A substantial body of research has been conducted on Zebra and Quagga mussels in the lower lakes and the change in water clarity that is well known to all divers in the area. I am puzzled as to why anyone with any understanding of diving conditions in the lower lakes would enter these papers based on such old data and suggest that it represents current lake conditions."

As an archaeologist, "In my opinion, diving operations can be safely conducted on either site safely and with no danger of damaging the site. . . .

"In terms of a diver disturbing the silt there is little difference between a diver disturbing the silt or a fish." As I had done during my deposition, McWilliam described the different kinds of kick, including the frog kick, and explained how it prevented the disturbance of silt.

"It has been suggested that the *Hamilton* and *Scourge* have large deposition (debris) fields around the hull of the wrecks. This is also incorrect. The *Hamilton* and *Scourge* were very small ships by today's standards; one under fifty feet long, the other approximately seventy five feet. Small ships, as a rule, leave small depositional patterns. By reference to Havelka's affidavit which describes the sinking event both ships were becalmed, that is to say they were not under way. They were dead in the water when the squall hit. A ship that sinks while underway will have a large depositional field as opposed to one that is not moving. As it moves and sinks the flotsam and jetsam are spread out along the surface of the water and across the bottom. In this case the ships experienced what is known, in sailing terns, as 'knock down.' The squall hit them broadside filling their sails and pushing them over, this was facilitated by the ship's cannons and armaments that had been added to the vessels when pressed into war service, this changed their centre of gravity. Water came over the side; they lose buoyancy, they started to right themselves but could not be effectively pumped out and sank quickly. The deposition field would be highly localized.

"There has been considerable discussion on the remarkable degree of preservation of the *Hamilton* and *Scourge* sites. There is nothing remarkable about the degree of preservation of these sites. They are extremely typical of ships of this age in this environment."

McWilliam minced no words when he stated, "In reviewing Mr. Englebert's cross examination I note at best inaccuracies to suit his views, and at worst falsehoods."

Perhaps his most telling testimony had to do with licensing procedures of the Archaeological Licence Bureau. With respect to recreational diving on the *Gunilda*, he attached a 1992 letter from Lisa Beram (Ministry Archaeological Advisor) in which she wrote, "No licence is required so long as I was not proposing to do archaeological field work."

He attached a 1998 letter from Bernice Field, and which was copied "to others including Mr. Englebert," in which he proposed conducting recreational dives on the *Gunilda*. "He is well aware that I was allowed to dive this site purely for recreational purposes."

In contradiction, "Mr. Murdock's views are based on outdated research and poor diving technique. Mr. Englebert has complete control over which underwater archaeological site licences are granted. In my view his decisions are capricious and arbitrary and they are clearly not based on any archaeological concern."

Finally, "Mr. Gentile is not a sport diver but an experienced technical diver. This, in my view, would be analogous to comparing a pedestrian to an Olympic athlete."

The Kicked Dog Barks Back

Yormak may have thought that Barkwell was stupid, but he was getting smarter. After all, by conspiring with Lyon, he had managed to stall the case for two whole years. Now he filed a motion in which he objected to the legality of an outside party (PADI) to post the bond!

Such a notion was the height of absurdity. Nonetheless, any motion, no matter how ridiculous, had to be heard in court. Yormak was forced to respond by defending the motion. This required time to conduct legal research, and to prepare an appropriate defense. He wrote an affidavit which he faxed to me for immediate endorsement. I signed the affidavit in the presence of a notary, then faxed it back to him - all within the hour.

Yormak called certain facts to the attention of the judge: "The City of Hamilton, Respondent, relied upon certain items I retrieved from the shipwreck *Andrea Doria* and which I have listed for sale which fact the City relied upon to demonstrate that I had assets upon which they based their Application for security for costs. However, the City refused to accept these same items as security for costs which they had previously relied upon.

"I attempted to negotiate loans to provide the funds for security for costs but was unable to proceed based upon my own financial situation and fixed income.

. . .

"I am aware that this Application and the issue of public access to historical shipwrecks has received some publicity, particularly in the diving community. I am informed by my solicitor Steven R. Yormak and so verily believe that he received inquiries as to the status of these proceedings, and informed these parties that given the fact that I could not provide the security for costs that the Application would be dismissed. I am further informed that individuals residing in Ontario who have a connection to the diving industry took it upon themselves to attempt to raise funds which resulted in P.A.D.I. providing the security for costs.

"P.A.D.I. was not involved in this litigation previously. I am informed by Mr. Yormak and do verily believe that P.A.D.I. has decided to assist to protect the interests of the public knowing that I could not provide the funds for security for costs. P.A.D.I. is assisting in the public interest, and specifically for its diving membership who comprise P.A.D.I. and to whom P.A.D.I. is accountable, some of [whose] interests may be adversely affected should the Application and the issues of law not succeed."

Barkwell's motion was overruled.

The Last Minute Syndrome

I could never understand by lawyers waited until the last minute to file a motion or brief. When I worked with Hess on the *Monitor* case he was forever missing deadlines. I had known him to work overnight on a brief that was due the following morning. He then faxed one copy and sent another by Federal Express. He bent the rules so hard that once, when a brief was due by closing time on Friday, he wrote it over the weekend and faxed it to the court on Monday morning, justifying his action by claiming that the judge would not see it until Monday anyway. He was a staunch supporter of fax machines and Federal Express.

My 2000 summer schedule was hectic to say the least. I wrote to Yormak, "I have extensive travel obligation during the next several months. Please do not count on faxing documents to me on the day on which they are due in court, expecting that I am sitting in my study with nothing else to do but to dash out to the notary and fax the documents back to you that same afternoon. I cannot guarantee to be available for such last-minute notice. If the continuance of the case hinges on such close timing, we will be hard-pressed to have our eventual day in court. Please anticipate these situations by at least two and a half weeks, so there will be sufficient time for me to sign these documents during my brief and infrequent intervals at home, and get them notarized."

Still Shilling?

I received a number of e-mails from strangers who professed to have an interest in the case. I cannot state categorically that I doubted their words or sincerity, but considering the City's history of underhanded tactics, I was a little gun shy.

I prepared a script that I habitually employed as a reply: "Before I can answer your questions, I need to know if you are working with either the City of

Hamilton or the Province of Ontario in any capacity whatsoever with respect to the *Hamilton/Scourge* case, or in any other case, or if you intend to impart any information to anyone associated with those entities."

Call me paranoid, but I found it astonishing how many people never wrote again.

Mussel Mass

Despite Englebert's official protestations that zebra mussels did not present a problem, the *Washington Post* ran an article that added weight to McWilliam's sworn comments. The article noted that water clarity in western Lake Erie "has increased by 77 percent."

That was the good news. The bad news was that, according to Brendon Baillod (director of the Great Lakes Shipwreck Research Foundation, which was based in Milwaukee, Wisconsin), "We can't even see the form of the wrecks. They're ruining some of the most historic and best-preserved wrecks in the world."

Arthur Cohn, executive director of the Lake Champlain Maritime Museum, in New York, presented evidence that "the iron spikes that hold the hulls of Revolutionary War ships together are disintegrating because of the massive colonies of zebra mussels that cover the vessels." Zebra mussels were creating an environment in which sulfur-reducing bacteria "flourish and cause a breakdown of iron."

Cohn: "Zebra mussels are here to stay, and they will probably encrust all of the hundreds of ships in Champlain and the thousands in the Great Lakes and St. Lawrence Seaway. So, we better get out and locate and document these wrecks while we can."

Baillod noted that zebra mussels "remove pieces of whatever they are attached to, and the effect is gradual disintegration."

For the purposes of the court case, municipal and provincial authorities did not want to accept the validity of scientific studies that did not support their case.

See is Believing - for Some

On October 1, 2000, Ian Marshall and Ed Burtt conducted a water clarity study in the vicinity of the *Hamilton* and *Scourge*. Marshall employed a drop video camera, Burtt deployed a remotely operated vehicle on which a video camera was mounted. They reached the test location on Marshall's boat.

During preliminary discussions, I had suggested that Marshall remove all electronic navigation and locating equipment from the boat, and to rely on a compass heading and timed run to reach a depth that was equivalent to that of the *Hamilton* and *Scourge*. That way, if the never-present Coast Guard or marine police accosted them, Marshall and Burtt could not be accused of trespassing on the sites.

Marshall motored away from shore to a point which was shown on the charts as 250 feet. By the time they got their equipment ready, the wind had blown the boat to where the depth was 260 feet. Marshall measured the depth by lowering a depth gauge to the bottom. Marshall then rigged a weighted drop line to which six lights were secured at eight-foot intervals. A video camera pointing downward was secured to the line eight feet above the highest light. One depth gauge was mounted with the camera, another with the lowest light on the line.

Marshall: "The water was so clear that even the 10 watt bulb mounted 8 feet away, overpowered the camera and blocked out everything below. On our second attempt, we removed the top four low powered lights. Again, we could only see the one light 40 feet below. On our third attempt, we used only the bottom light and although the battery was entering a discharge state and the bulb was already yellowing before we lowered it, you could still see it 48 feet below the camera at a depth of 261 feet."

The distance between the camera and the light was measured by subtracting the depth of the camera from the depth of the light. Burtt deployed the ROV, but because of the speed at which the boat was moving (it was not anchored, but adrift), he was unable to catch up to the light line and videotape the bulb laterally. Nonetheless, visibility in excess of fifty feet was duly recorded on videotape.

Marshall sent copies of the tape to me and to Yormak, for introduction to the court as evidence to substantiate his sworn affidavit.

The proof is in the pudding, as they say. Marshall's videotaped proof of water clarity, plus my photographic proof of zebra mussel infestation at depth, constituted incontrovertible proof of the true conditions on the bottom of Lake Ontario.

DEMA Declines

PADI's donation gained a last minute reprieve, zebra mussel awareness was in the ascendancy, and water clarity was improving on a daily basis. The opposition's strategy of wrongful procrastination had provided time in which to obtain more explosive ammunition to refute the lies of municipal and provincial witnesses. But the cost had been great in terms of money to pay for the time to write motions and countermotions.

I had not exaggerated my financial situation to the court. I was in debt over my head and was dangerously close to insolvency - or at least, close to the point at which my assets would have to be sold in order to pay the interest on my loans, the sale of which would further reduce my income, and so on, and so on. Yet I was hopeful that my future earnings would increase because of the wise investments I had made. In the mean time I had to maintain my status quo, in order to protect and save those investments that took me a lifetime to accumulate, in order to realize a long-term gain.

Nick Drakich developed another plan to obtain funding for Bill 13 and the *Hamilton/Scourge* case. He approached the Dive Equipment Manufacturer's Association. As the name implies, DEMA's membership consisted of practically every manufacturer that made or sold scuba gear. DEMA held an annual convention at which manufacturers, wholesalers, retailers, repair businesses, dive shops, charter boat operators, travel agents, service providers, and promoters displayed their wares and advertised their services. An area the size of a football field was required to contain all the booths. Attendance approximated 5,000 people.

Drakich reasoned - and explained to the DEMA board of directors - that equipment sales in Canada would plummet dramatically should the opposition gain a foothold in barring public access to shipwrecks. The City's attitude toward the *Hamilton* and *Scourge* represented the foot in the door on which the Province could take hold. He asked DEMA to take a lead role in the funding and lobbying efforts for both Bill 13 and the *Hamilton/Scourge* case.

DEMA declined to provide any funding. The most they would do was e-mail their members, asking them to make donations to the twin causes. This kind of support was not without value. DEMA was a widely recognized name in the dive industry. The Association's endorsement could add credibility to what was, in the wide world of diving and the grand scheme of business, strictly a small-scale local event.

It was a fantastic idea - that went practically nowhere. Not even Canadian manufacturers, retailers, and dive shops lent their support.

Gary Kulisek, a representative of the National Association of Underwater Instructors (NAUI), maintained a website which sent synopses of current events to over 3,000 subscribers. He wrote a paragraph about the cause, and included a link to my e-mail address. He received a handful of replies, but no money. I received a few e-mails asking for elaboration but, again, no money.

The only equipment manufacturer that offered backing was Scubapro, which generously donated $1,000 directly to Yormak. Eventually, I received private subscriptions of $150 each from Dave Alderson and Dave Sawchuck. Much later I received $1,000 from my long-time dive buddy Mike Caudle, a Nova Scotia diver who bestowed the largest share, and who encouraged his friends in Halifax to add to the pot.

These funds were enough to staunch the flow of blood sufficiently to satisfy Yormak's insatiable demands.

Last Ditch Effort

Drakich's father was ill. In addition to Drakich's dive shop, Drakich now had to operate his father's business. He had no time to continue his lobbying efforts. The only positive response he received through DEMA came from Ocean Management Systems. Drakich suggested that I call OMS to ask for support.

John Griffiths, the owner of OMS, was a long-time friend. We had participated in a number of dive trips throughout the years, including several to the *Andrea Doria*. I had field tested items of the OMS line of technical equipment. Because of our longstanding friendship, I felt uncomfortable about asking Griffiths for a donation. I did not want to put him in an awkward position in which he might feel obligated to me because of our close relationship. I did not think that would be fair to him.

As his swansong to the cause, Drakich called Griffiths in my behalf and explained the situation. Griffiths made a proposition: he would give me a place at his booth at DEMA from which to solicit funding, and he would let me share a hotel room with one of his representatives. In the event, he paid for my meals as well. My only investment, other than my time, was the purchase of a plane ticket to New Orleans, Louisiana, where DEMA was holding its next convention.

Ocean Management Systems

I had never before attended a DEMA convention. Griffiths introduced me to Mark Reeves, the OMS rep from Scotland with whom I was rooming. Reeves owned a dive shop and a charter boat operation in Scapa Flow. He and I got along so well that he invited me to stay with him and dive on the German High Seas Fleet that was scuttled after World War One. Coincidentally, the following year I was invited to speak at a diving conference in Glasgow. I extended my stay and spent two weeks diving with Reeves, not only in Scapa Flow but in the Orkneys. (While I was there I also climbed Ben Nevis, the high mountain in the British Isles.)

The OMS "booth" was actually a large floor space about thirty feet square. The full line of OMS products was on display, and various reps were there to demonstrate equipment. Griffiths obtained a lectern which we located at one corner of his assigned area. I brought copies of my Mission Statement for handouts. I spoke with hundreds of people.

The convention was like a reunion. I saw friends and acquaintances whom I had not seen in more years than I cared to remember. I met numerous people who had read my books and who wanted to chat. I spoke at length about Bill 13, the *Hamilton* and *Scourge*, and the ominous portents for wreck-diving in general. Most people were interested in my travails. When they left my lectern, invariably they said, "Good luck with your fight."

Steve Yormak was manning a booth for ProSEA. He gave me some of his handouts (against the UNESCO convention) and I gave him some of mine. He suggested that I send to his booth anyone who wanted clarification about the legal implications of Bill 13 and the *Hamilton* and *Scourge*. He would be happy to talk with them.

I thought this was a pretty good gig for him. Three days work plus a day or two of chargeable travel time amounted to quite a few thousand dollars (at $200 per hour). He told me that he was not getting paid.

I had a truly wonderful time during the days at DEMA and the evenings in New Orleans. But I did not raise a dollar for the cause. Of all the people who said that they would get in touch again after the convention, I heard from only two - and neither one donated any money.

Out-of-the-Blue Pay Raise

The case was still plagued with the lack of funding. PADI gave another thousand dollars to Yormak, but he claimed that the full amount was consumed by his cost to photocopy documents to bring PADI up to date on the proceedings. According to my calculations, one thousand dollars was equivalent to 20,000 pages at a nickel a page (the going rate at Kinko's).

Yormak circulated an update to PADI, DEMA, and others who professed an interest in the case. He closed his letter with this sentence: "I am prepared to continue to contribute 1/3 pro bono discount to my fees (usual hourly rate of $300)." He had previously stated that his usual fee was $200 per hour (and I did not believe him even then). This closing gambit sounded like a "sale" scam to me: the claim that the retail price was higher than it actually was, in order to make the slashed-down ticket price appear to be "reduced."

That being as it may, Yormak still demanded an immediate infusion of funds in the amount of $5,000 before he would consider taking the case to trial.

City Cost Overruns

After Barkwell lost his bid to have PADI's donation declared invalid, the City began urging for an immediate trial date. This was ironic in that for two years the City had been intentionally dragging its feet by keeping the hearing off the docket. Yormak asked for a postponement. But now that the City was made eminently aware of my inability to continue funding the case on my own, it wanted to rush the case to court before I obtained additional outside funding.

However, this new rush policy had barely gotten underway when the City began to whistle a different tune. Suddenly there was silence from the City solicitors. No longer did they complain about Yormak's request for postponement.

Not only did I not have the funding to continue the case, neither did the City of Hamilton.

The standing political party got ousted in the elections. The incumbent mayor was aghast at how many of the taxpayers' dollars had been wasted in defense of a case as moronic as keeping people away from their cultural heritage.

The legal strategy of the City solicitors had backfired, and the tables were now turned by wiser heads. In their attempt to run me out of money, City solicitors had been so profligate in their spending of time and money that the comptrollers balked at the extravagant expenditures. The City auditor recommended that the City drop the case. Imagine that: an impecunious individual had run an incorporated City out of money!

Shot Again from Behind

It now appeared that if I forced the trial, not only would the City not object, it might not even mount a defense. I might win the case by default!

Even if I did not prevail at the hearing because of some minor technicality, Yormak had word from his contacts in the federal government that it would side with me on appeal - intervening on my behalf the way the Province of Ontario had intervened on behalf of the City of Hamilton. The federal government viewed the extension of the Ontario Heritage Act into the underwater realm as a conflict with the Canada Shipping Act. Federal legislation superseded provincial legislation. The newly proposed federal Bill C-35 guaranteed public access.

The time to strike was now!

In one fell swoop I could prove by means of both logic and law that the City did not have the authority to prevent divers from looking at their cultural heritage; I could establish for the record that the Archaeological Licence Bureau did not have the powers of enforcement or arrest; I could prove that individuals within the City and the Province had committed perjury, and had conspired to obstruct justice; I could set a precedent in Canada for the guarantee of public access to

MONEY, MONEY, MONEY 163

shipwrecks; and I could prevent for all time the recurrence of Bill 13 or its clone.

This was a heaven-sent opportunity to balance the implacable scales of justice. This was worth running the risk of eventual bankruptcy. No matter what it cost - increased debt or sale of assets - I was now willing to front the money.

I told Yormak that I would immediately send him a check in the amount of $5,000.

Yormak now wanted $25,000!

Afterword

I once told Yormak that I had no intentions of writing a book about this case. I meant what I said when I said it. The City of Hamilton and the Archaeological Licence Bureau will ignore this book the way that NOAA ignored my book about the *Monitor*. Despite the fact that my suit against the City is now part of the history of the *Hamilton* and *Scourge*, City officials and Provincial administrators will treat the case as if it never existed - the way NOAA has neglected to acknowledge my suit in any public pronouncement or brochure.

Nor do I expect the public at large or the diving community in general to appreciate relevant current events. As I stated in the Foreword, I wrote this book not for the present generation but for the next. I cannot predict the prevalence of democracy in the future. I *hope* that the erosion of human rights will hit rock bottom, then swing back toward the unfettered freedom on which democratic principles are based.

Law is supposed to reflect the morality of the society which fostered the legislation. All too often, the reality is different from the theory. Special interest groups lobby for laws that promote their special interests at the expense of the interests of the larger public. This can result in the passage of unjust laws that favor a minority while disfavoring the majority. Then again, well-intentioned laws may be abused by bureaucrats and individuals in authority who are protected by the legal framework.

A municipality can lawfully deny entry to a public building under certain circumstances. But it does not have the constitutional right to prevent close approach to public property. The City of Hamilton has an obligation to the citizenry to be accountable for its actions and for the actions of its administrators. Neither the City, nor the Province, nor paid archaeologists have a monopoly on cultural heritage.

A quarter of a century has passed since the U.S. Navy transferred title of the *Hamilton* and *Scourge* to the Royal Ontario Museum, which then transferred title to the City of Hamilton.

What affirmative action has the City taken with regard to raising or studying the *Hamilton* and *Scourge*? Absolutely none. The highly touted Feasibility Study was never conducted. No one has even seen the wrecks for fourteen years.

Spurred by my observations of the accumulation of zebra mussels on shipwrecks in the Great Lakes - which was documented by photographic evidence and which was bolstered by contemporary newspaper articles - the City of Hamilton bleated about conducting a drop-video survey of the *Hamilton* and *Scourge* in order to ascertain the density of encrustation. The City commenced negotiations with a commercial outfit to do the job.

Ironically, Englebert would not grant an archaeological license to conduct the study. In effect, he prohibited the City from looking at its own property! As

AFTERWORD

Yormak stated, at least he was consistent. Or perhaps he thought that if he issued the license, I could use it as ammunition in the furtherance of my case.

The City of Hamilton has become quiescent about the case - perhaps out of fear that I will bring it to trial and win, thus embarrassing the "bocrats" who fought so hard against public access. In my opinion, if the City of Hamilton had any faith in the legality of its position, it would have forced the issue by bringing the case to trial. It never would have embarked upon a strategy of character assassination and cost inflation in order to avoid a legal ruling.

The case was never closed. It still resides in limbo - as do the *Hamilton* and *Scourge*. The two wrecks represent a heritage that has been stolen from the people by the bureaucratic lust for control and manipulation. The "bocrats" gain has been the people's loss.

The present generation slept through this important object lesson. Hopefully, the next generation will wake up to the travesty that has occurred, and will possess the will, the determination, and the money to correct the errors of the past, and to recover the heritage that was stolen from their antecedents.

Time will tell.

Author's Biography

Of the thousands of decompression dives that Gary has made, over 180 of them were on the Grand Dame of the Sea: the *Andrea Doria*. He was the first scuba diver to enter the First Class Dining Room, from which he recovered many examples of elegant china. He also recovered and restored hundreds of items of jewelry and souvenirs from the Gift Shop, located at a depth of 220 feet. More important, he discovered and recovered a number of ceramic panels that once adorned the walls of the First Class Bar. These colorful panels were the work of famed Italian artist Romano Rui.

In the early 1990's, Gary was instrumental in merging mixed-gas diving technology with wreck-diving. His dive to the German battleship *Ostfriesland*, at a depth of 380 feet, triggered an unprecedented expansion in the exploration of deep-water shipwrecks, and the advent of helium mixes as a breathing medium. He wrote the first book on technical diving. In 1994, he participated in a mixed-gas diving expedition to the *Lusitania*, which lies at a depth of 300 feet.

Gary has specialized in wreck-diving and shipwreck research, concentrating his efforts on wrecks along the eastern seaboard, from Newfoundland to Key West, and in the Great Lakes. He has compiled an extensive library of books, photographs, drawings, plans, and original source materials on ships and shipwrecks. He has conducted surveys on numerous wrecks, some of which have been drawn in the form of large-sized prints that are suitable for framing. He has either discovered or been the first to dive on scores of previously unknown shipwrecks.

Over the years he has rescued from the ravages of the sea many thousands of shipwreck artifacts, making him a leading authority in recovery techniques. He has gone to great lengths to preserve and restore these relics from the deep, and to display them to thousands of interested people, divers and nondivers alike. Throughout the years, these artifacts have been displayed at various museums, symposiums, and club-oriented exhibitions.

Gary has written scores of magazine articles, and has published more than three thousand photographs in books, periodicals, newspapers, brochures, advertisements, corporate reports, museum displays, postcards, film, and television. He lectures extensively on underwater topics, and conducts seminars on advanced wreck-diving techniques, high-tech diving equipment, and wreck photography.

He is the author of fifty-two books: primarily novels of science fiction and adventure, and nonfiction volumes on wreck-diving and on nautical and shipwreck history. The Popular Dive Guide Series will eventually cover every major shipwreck along the east coast of the United States.

There is also another side of Gary's life: that of an outdoor adventurer. In this guise he has climbed rock and mountains, backpacked through country high and low, bivouacked in the snow, and paddled his canoe through rapids and down

AUTHOR'S BIOGRAPHY

untamed wilderness rivers - often for weeks at a time. His longest trip lasted a month, when he and five companions paddled 380 miles down the George River in Labrador. For three weeks straight they did not encounter another human being, or see signs of civilization. Gary embraces total self-sufficiency in the wilderness.

He has captured on film all of these wonderful outdoor adventures, as well as the splendor of nature's colorful scenery. He has given slide presentations to dive clubs, hiking clubs, canoe clubs, elder hostels, church groups, cub scouts, power squadrons, Naval associations, Civil War societies, Masonic lodges, Mensa, corporate functions, scientific organizations, and many, many other groups too numerous to mention.

In 1989, after a five-year battle with the National Oceanic and Atmospheric Administration, Gary won a suit which forced the hostile government agency to issue him a permit to dive the USS *Monitor*, a protected National Marine Sanctuary. Media attention that was focused on Gary's triumphant victory resulted in nationwide coverage of his 1990 photographic expedition to the Civil War ironclad. Gary continues to fight for the right of access to all shipwreck sites.

For a list of available titles, visit Gary's website at
http://www.ggentile.com

www.ingramcontent.com/pod-product-compliance
Lightning Source LLC
Chambersburg PA
CBHW031147160426
43193CB00008B/282